VICTORIAN BIRMINGHAM

The Making of
VICTORIAN BIRMINGHAM

Victor Skipp

Published by the author
from 5 Clay Lane, Yardley, Birmingham B26 1DU.

To my Father
— one of the last surviving Victorians.

First published 1983

© 1983 Victor H. T. Skipp

Filmset by
Ventset Limited, 59-61 Summer Lane, Birmingham B19 3TH.
Printed by
The Studio Press (Birmingham) Limited, Lower Tower Street,
Birmingham B19 3NE.

British Library Cataloguing in Publication Data

Skipp, Victor
    The making of Victorian Birmingham.
    1. Birmingham (West Midlands, England) — History
    I. Title
    942.4′96081   DA690.B6

ISBN 0-9506998-2-9
ISBN 0-9506998-3-7 Pbk

Contents

Slum property, 1876.

The Grim Realities

During the nineteenth century Britain was being transformed— almost out of recognition—by three great inter-related developments. Its population was increasing rapidly, it was becoming more and more industrialized, and there was a massive growth of industrial towns and cities.

With Leeds, Manchester, Liverpool and Glasgow, Birmingham was in the very top flight of the upstart provincial centres. In 1837, the year of the Queen's accession, it contained about 170,000 people. By her death in 1901 its population had risen threefold, to 522,204; and both its industrial capacity and geographical extent had expanded more than proportionately.

Such rampant demographic, economic and territorial growth brought many difficulties and problems. The older parts of the town, most of which were already descending into slumdom, soon became quite impossibly congested, delapidated and unhealthy. Meanwhile, as if by magic—and a magic which was arguably of the black variety—new districts of factories, workshops and houses were springing up on every side, with scarcely a hint of public control or planning.

In fact, no one was—or perhaps could have been—in control of such a spontaneous, tear-away process. More people meant more children to nurture, more workers to employ, more families to house, more corpses to bury. As numbers soared ever growing quantities of provisions had to be brought into the markets and shops of the town; and, in the absence of a piped sewerage system, ever growing quantities of nightsoil had to be—quite literally—carted out of it. Smoke and soot from the constantly mounting number of factory chimneys and domestic hearths increasingly blackened the air and poisoned the atmosphere. Less noticeably, but more inimically, because of the high population density and primitive sanitation, many of the thousands of wells from which inhabitants drew their water became increasingly polluted. The extent of Birmingham's public health problem can be gauged from the fact that even as late as the 1870s its average death rate—at 25.2 per 1,000—was 50% higher than in nearby rural villages; and for some of its central wards the discrepancy was well over 100%.

Almost as challenging as the town's physical difficulties was its need to supply basic public, social and community services. Law and order had to be preserved; and year by year, increasing institutional accommodation was necessary, not only for convicted criminals, but for the care of the sick, the blind, the deaf, the insane, the orphaned and the destitute. Inevitably, the provision of such facilities lagged far behind requirements. In a still predominantly illiterate society, so did the provision of schools—not to mention Utopian-seeming amenities like public libraries, public baths, recreation grounds and parks.

It is worth bearing in mind, too, that in struggling to cope with the consequences of over-rapid urban growth, the inhabitants of nineteenth-century Manchester, Glasgow or Birmingham had no possibility of learning from history, or even from the experience of other countries. On the contrary, with Britain way out in front of the rest of the world both in terms of industrial and urban development, these sensationally mushrooming towns were, in effect, themselves pioneering a radically new way of life. Devoid of experience or example, limited in technical know-how, with a tradition of local government mainly derived from the manor and parish, with no precedents for raising large sums of public money, it is only in retrospect that their eventual success can be taken for granted. Add to all this an underlying contemporary philosophy which exalted the wisdom, not of planning, but of 'leaving things alone', or *laissez-faire,* and it is hardly surprising that the world's first great industrial cities should have passed through a long period of administrative disorganization, social *malaise,* and of intense human wretchedness and suffering. As a recently published general survey, *The Victorian City,* says:

> The new industrial cities and towns into which . . . people poured were as unprepared to receive them as they were unprepared to live in an urban environment. By the 1840s it was evident that the consequences of this migration were nothing short of catastrophic. Lack of proper housing, overcrowding, inadequate environmental sanitation, polluted water supplies, and malnutrition combined to make the life of the city dweller . . . and that of his family, hard, desperate and hazardous to health and life.

Yet the same work elsewhere points out that:

> . . . if the distinctive achievement of Britain in the latter part of the eighteenth century was to inaugurate the Industrial Revolution, her no less remarkable feat in the first half of the nineteenth-century was to accomplish the first urban transformation.

By means of parliamentary legislation, the repeated reorganization of local government, herculean feats of civil engineering, countless philanthropic enterprises, and a great deal of Victorian paternalism, hyperbole and earnestness, well before the end of Queen Victoria's reign, modern city life had been made reasonably tolerable, at any rate for the vast majority of people concerned.

In fact, living and working conditions were never so bad in Birmingham as in most other large industrial centres. This is not to say that at one stage they were not bad enough. In his poem *Birmingham,* published in 1852, Harry Howells Horton, after evoking the 'life of drudgery and pain' which was the lot of many local artisans, factory girls and labouring children, concluded disgustedly:

> Talk not to me of negro slaves who bleed,
> That tyrant man on luxuries may feed —
> A far worse penalty than whips and chains,
> 'Mid all our broad enlightenment obtains

And Horton justified these words in a note by claiming:

> . . . I will undertake to draw a picture of the evils of our *own* social system,

The Queen Victoria statue, Victoria Square. The original, marble figure was unveiled in 1901. This is a bronze copy, erected fifty years later.

Left and Below: The Council House (1874-9), and the Town Hall (1832-61), both seen from Colmore Row. Right: The General Post Office (1891).

quite as repugnant to humanity (to say nothing of religion) as that of Mrs. Stowe, and without exaggerating one whit more. But the fact is, we are so familiar with the inherent evils of our own system that we have become blind to them.

Yet ultimately Birmingham overcame its nineteenth-century traumas to such an extent that, having long been known as 'the great toyshop of Europe', by 1890 an American observer could describe it as 'the best governed city in the world'. And indeed, bearing in mind the shining achievements of the Chamberlain epoch, Birmingham can perhaps justifiably claim that in the end it played as significant a part in the history of 'the first urban transformation' as in the Industrial Revolution itself.

Victorian Archaeology

'Birmingham', declared a Victorian Society pamphlet in 1965, 'is very largely a nineteenth-century city and, however fast the pace of redevelopment, it will remain so, just as York is a medieval city and Bath a Georgian city'. It follows from this that the face of the town as it is today still represents an extremely useful and precious resource for the study of its Victorian history.

Naturally, site-by-site demolition and rebuilding have been going on steadily ever since the great Queen left us. Nevertheless, the bulk of the high Victorian city survived right down to the gargantuan redevelopment programme which ran through from the 1950s to the 1970s. And even this evidential Armageddon was not quite so destructive as some have been inclined to suppose.

Despite the surrounding multi-storey glass and concrete, Victoria Square is still living up to its name, with the marvellously sited statue of the Queen herself, the Parthenon-like Town Hall, the vast Italianate Council House and the recently reprieved 'New General Post Office' of 1891. Else-

where it is difficult to miss St. Chad's Roman Catholic Cathedral, the Grand Hotel and fine Victorian banks of Colmore Row; or, at the top end of Chamberlain's still just about recognizable Corporation Street, the red-brick and terracotta Victoria Law Courts. Indeed, many late nineteenth-century civic, institutional and commercial buildings are to be found within the central business area, which is now — roughly speaking — encircled by the Inner Ring Road.

Outside this district, the making of the five 'new towns' of Newtown, Nechells Green, Highgate, Lee Bank and Ladywood, together with subsequent redevelopment, has resulted in the cutting of great swathes and divots out of the Birmingham Chamberlain knew. In such 'comprehensively' redeveloped areas a mid-nineteenth-century church is sometimes the only obvious relic of the Victorian era — like the red-brick St. Matthew's at Nechells Green (Duddeston), which, consecrated in 1840, was the first of five churches erected by the Birmingham Church Building Society. But in between these cleared and now tower-block dominated stretches, substantial segments of essentially pre-1870 townscape remain available for exploration. Among these are the select residential suburb of Edgbaston, the famous 'Hockley Square Mile' or Jewellery Quarter, and the rather less well known 'low town' district which is to be found in the maze of narrow streets on either side of Digbeth and Deritend.

In this last area, despite considerable piecemeal renewal, there is much that is relevant to the industrial archaeology of the emerging Victorian city. At the top of Cheapside, for instance, the fieldworker will come across the attractive white stucco façade of the 'Cheapside Works'. In *Kelly's Post Office Directory* of 1874 this property is described as 'the brassfoundry and gasfitting establishment of J. and W. Breeden and Booth'. Today the name on the facade is S. Booth & Co. Ltd., and the trade has changed only marginally to that of 'plumbers and brassfounders'. Next door is a twentieth-century industrial premises. Yet here too, there is an element of continuity. For the

Augustus Pugin's St. Chad's Roman Catholic Cathedral (1839-41), photographed from St. Chad's Circus.

Left: The Victoria Law Courts (1887-91), Corporation Street. Below: St. Matthew's Church, Duddeston (1839-40), from Nechells Parkway.

1874 directory attributes this site to 'Nichols, Joseph & Son, wire workers, weavers, etc.' And, sure enough, the blue and white sign boards across the front of the works today read 'Joseph Nichols & Son Ltd., Established 1841/Wire Goods, Domestic & Industrial/Woven Wire for all trades/Welded Mesh'.

But in the light of what has been said earlier, it would be a pity to concentrate just on the industrial archaeology of Victorian Birmingham. For industrial archaeology—however interesting and popular—is concerned with only one aspect of the massive changes in the western way of life which Britain was prospecting during the eighteenth- and nineteenth-centuries. And indeed, when one stops to think about it, this is an odd academic specialism anyway. Virtually every other branch of archaeology — Prehistoric, Roman, Medieval, etc. — is concerned, not with one aspect of a given culture or period, but with the whole spectrum of its physical remains, and the whole living reality which lies beyond them. Perhaps by now then, we should be concerned, not merely with industrial archaeology, or even industrial archaeology plus urban archaeology, but rather with 'modern' — or in this case 'Victorian'—archaeology, as an integrated totality.

Had people been alert to this more comprehensive approach thirty years ago — when the term 'industrial archaeology' was first seizing the popular imagination — perhaps this would have ensured the preservation of typical blocks of back-to-back and courtyard houses for a surely not disinterested posterity. Or, mindful of the enormous contribution made by the cart-horse to Victorian Birmingham, that a few of the 'granite cattle troughs' once found along every road could still be seen *in situ*. But until we start appreciating the distinctive features of our nineteenth-century townscapes to the same extent as the 'monuments' of industrial archaeology, such educationally valuable and evocative remains will continue to disappear without trace.

Happily, there is still much that is worthy of attention.

Below: J. & W. Breeden & Booth's Cheapside Works. Right: Joseph Nichols & Son Ltd., Cheapside.

Staying in the same 'low town' area, take for example the block of properties at present occupied by Cranes Screw in Floodgate Street. On investigation these turn out to include the purpose-built premises which the Birmingham Medical Mission opened in 1879; together with the chapel-like Birmingham Free Christian Society Sunday School, which was erected in 1865.

Left: The Birmingham Medical Mission (1879), Floodgate Street. Above: The Birmingham Free Christian Society Sunday School (1865), at the junction of Lower Fazeley Street and Floodgate Street.

In 1855, at a time when it is thought that two-thirds of the people of Birmingham were abstaining from public worship, John Cale Miller, Rector of St Martin's, declared that the Church had to see its 'work among her HOME HEATHEN as truly missionary as is work in her outposts in the Punjaub or amid the Dyaks of Borneo'. It must have been against this kind of background — plus the appalling health hazards of this already run-down district — that the Floodgate Street Mission was founded for the 'provision of medical attendance for the sick poor, combined with the reading of the Gospel and other measures calculated to improve the spiritual, physical and social condition of the poor'.

Arguably, the Free Christian Society Sunday School is of even greater interest. For such a building reminds us that the transition from a predominantly rural to a predominantly urban society was also the transition from a predominantly illiterate to a predominantly literate one. And moreover, that down to the Forster Education Act of 1870, and indeed for long after, Sunday schools were in the forefront of the long hard struggle to bring a modicum of elementary education to the children, and also to the by-passed adults, of Victorian Birmingham.

Quite close to these once significant, but now forgotten, Victorian institutions, in the neck of Heath Mill Lane, where it runs into Deritend, there is another superficially puzzling Victorian Gothic building. Now used by Keystone Trading

Right: The Deritend Free Library and News Rooms (1866), Heath Mill Lane.

Co., since its red-brick façade presents a row of stone-dressed Decorated windows to the main street, one's first thoughts are ecclesiastical. But reference to the 1874 directory — or to the 25 inch Ordnance Survey map of the 1880s, for that matter — soon shows that this was once a 'Birmingham Free Library and News Rooms (branch)'.

In fact, this Deritend Library was the first specially designed branch library to be built in Birmingham, being opened on 26 October 1866, or on the same day as the original Central Reference Library. In inaugurating the latter, George Dawson, the foremost 'prophet' of Birmingham's renowned 'Civic Gospel', declared:

> . . . that a great town is a solemn organism through which should flow, and in which should be shaped, all the highest, loftiest, and truest ends of man's intellectual and moral nature. I wish, then, for you, Mr. Mayor, and for myself, that, in years to come, when we are in some respects forgotten, still now and then, in this room, the curious questions may be asked: Who was Mayor on that famous day? Who said grace before that famous banquet? Who returned thanks for that gracious meal? Who gathered these books together?

The ill-fated Central Library in which those words were uttered was burned to the ground in January 1879. So this Deritend building is the oldest surviving public library in Britain's second largest city.

Surely a plaque ought to be placed on its walls without delay. And — at least among those who believe that books and education are important — this attractive little building ought to be regarded as every bit as precious and worthy of conservation as any steam locomotive, canal bridge or pumping station.

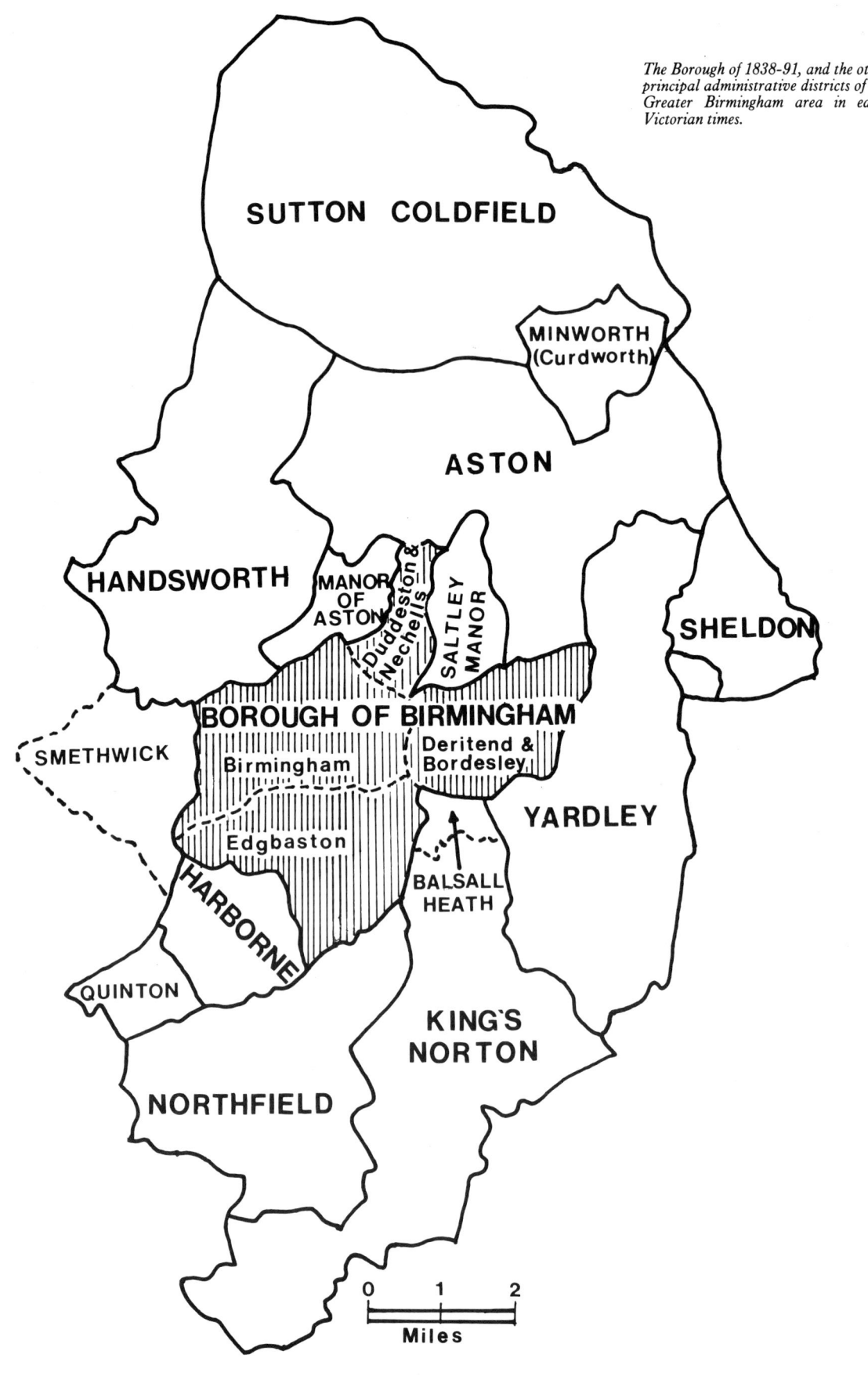

The Borough of 1838-91, and the other principal administrative districts of the Greater Birmingham area in early Victorian times.

SUTTON COLDFIELD

MINWORTH
(Curdworth)

ASTON

HANDSWORTH

MANOR OF ASTON

Duddeston & Nechells

SALTLEY MANOR

SHELDON

BOROUGH OF BIRMINGHAM

SMETHWICK

Birmingham

Deritend & Bordesley

Edgbaston

YARDLEY

HARBORNE

BALSALL HEATH

QUINTON

KING'S NORTON

NORTHFIELD

0   1   2
Miles

Thomas Attwood and the Political Foundations

The 1830s laid the foundations of Victorian Birmingham in much more than the straight-forward chronological sense. In 1832, after itself playing a major part in the protracted Reform Bill campaign, the town at last had conferred upon it the status of a parliamentary borough, with the right to elect two M.Ps. Six years later, in 1838, Birmingham obtained the charter of incorporation which made it a municipal borough.

Like much else that happened in this exceptionally formative decade, these developments were more significant for what they promised than for what they immediately achieved. The 1838 Act brought a considerable territorial expansion. Apart from Birmingham itself, the boundaries of the municipal borough, which corresponded with those of the parliamentary constituency, were drawn to include the whole of Edgbaston, together with the Deritend, Bordesley, Duddeston and Nechells districts of the parish of Aston. As such, the 1838 municipality had a circumference of 21 miles, contained 100 miles of streets, plus 40 miles of suburban roads, and covered 8,420 acres. However, with a £10 rental qualification, only about 7,000 of the 170,000 people living within this area qualified for the parliamentary franchise; and under 6,000 were entitled to vote as 'burgesses' in the early municipal elections. Nor was it until 1851 that the powers of the three separate Street Commissions — of Birmingham, of Deritend and Bordesley, and of Duddeston-cum-Nechells — together with those of several lesser administrative bodies, were finally handed over to the Borough Council, so that Birmingham became a municipal corporation in authority as well as in name.

Yet, apart from the parliamentary acts and their long-term consequences, the 1830s were politically significant in several less obvious but no less fundamental ways. It was during this decade that the Radical-Liberal power-base which was to dominate the local political scene for the bulk of the Victorian era was firmly established. This was the time, too, when a town that had for long been of considerable economic significance to the nation at large also acquired major political significance. And finally, it was the time when the distinctive character both of Victorian Birmingham's Liberalism and of its national influence were largely determined. All these developments were by-products of the local agitation for parliamentary and municipal reform, and must be mainly credited to that extraordinary man, Thomas Attwood, and to that extraordinary historical phenomenon, the Birmingham Political Union. Henry Horton wrote of Attwood:

> Before his time, Birmingham was celebrated only for its mechanical ingenuity and its manufacturing industry . . . The time had arrived,

The statue of Thomas Attwood (1783-1856). This originally stood at the head of Stephenson Place (see view of New Street, page 185) but is now at Larches Green, Sparkbrook. However, Attwood is such a major figure in Birmingham's political history that the monument ought really to be restored to a central position.

however, when it was to occupy a position in the political history of the country. The task of rousing its spirit . . . was reserved for Thomas Attwood, and those able coadjutors whom he had succeeded in drawing around him.

At first sight it seems strange that, less than forty years after the town had witnessed the Tory-inspired, anti-radical Priestley Riots of 1791, tens of thousands of pro-radical townsfolk should be streaming to the gala-like Political Union meetings on Newhall Hill; and hardly less strange that Thomas Attwood, who was by that time the universally acknowledged leader of the local radical cause, should have been a High Tory banker.

Without doubt, the main reason for this transformation in public opinion was the long period of high food prices and languishing trade, which, with only brief intermissions, stretched right through from 1795 to 1830 and beyond. Such conditions, together with the failure of successive governments to ameliorate them, gradually convinced many working and middle class people of the absolute necessity for parliamentary reform.

The process seems to have begun in earnest during the economic crisis of 1812, when hundreds of workers supported an employers' campaign—led by Thomas Attwood—against the government's Orders in Council, which were then having such devastating local effects on profits, wages and employment.

At this stage, however, Birmingham businessmen were mainly preoccupied with economic self-help: regularly lobbying the county M.Ps., pursuing their campaign against the Orders to a successful conclusion, and in 1813 establishing the Birmingham Chamber of Commerce to represent the 'manufacturers and commerce of Birmingham' against 'shipping, colonial and other great and powerful interests'.

Among local artisans, by contrast, the unrelenting economic hardships led to the foundation of the Birmingham Hampden Club in 1816. The leading light in this organization was George Edmonds, the son of a local Baptist minister. In 1817 he presided over the first known radical demonstration to be held on Newhall Hill, which is reputed to have attracted between 10,000 and 20,000 people. Due no doubt to the government's repressive measures, the Hampden Club held its last recorded meeting in the following year. However, working class radicals remained active in the town, circulating political tracts, forming other short-lived associations, and even holding further mass demonstrations as and when opportunity offered. Edmonds, like several of his fellows, was eventually sent to Warwick gaol for 'seditious conspiracy'. But on his release early in 1823 an enthusiastic crowd gathered in the Bull Ring to welcome him home.

Meanwhile, increasingly frustrated by the government's indifference to high wheat prices and flagging trade, the

George Edmonds, from a drawing published in R. K. Dent's Old and New Birmingham (1880).

Thomas Attwood, from a portrait by G. Sharples.

middle classes of the town were also beginning to produce their radical activists. By the mid-1820s Joseph Parkes, the leader of a group of Whig businessmen and lawyers known as 'The Cabal', was openly arguing not only for the enfranchisement of the new industrial towns but for a widespread extension of the suffrage, and even the secret ballot.

The Tory radical group which followed Attwood came round more gradually to the idea of parliamentary reform. In fact Attwood, who hailed from Shropshire and was a partner in Spooner and Attwood's Bank, opened the messianic side of his career as an economic, rather than a political, reformer. He believed that the post-war slump was the result of misguided government policies. What was needed, according to him, was the introduction of 'inconvertible paper-money' — or paper notes which would not be exchangeable for gold. Then, instead of pursuing the sterile doctrine of *laissez-faire,* the government ought to 'manage' the economy, using the issue of currency to stimulate productive expenditure during periods of recession, and in this way actively fostering the return of better times.

Attwood's missionary zeal for what we would today call Keynesian ideas soon converted many of his fellow townsmen. By 1829, however, when the economic plight of the town became particularly critical, he had totally despaired of converting the Duke of Wellington's Tory government. And it was at this point that he turned to parliamentary reform — not for its own sake, but because he now saw it as an unavoidable interim step in the furtherance of his economic gospel.

At a public meeting in May 1829 Attwood stunned the town by declaring that he had become 'a Radical Reformer'. Never a man for doing things by halves, before the end of the year, he and his supporters had evolved a detailed plan for establishing a 'Birmingham Political Union', which was specifically intended to provide leadership to the rest of the country.

Parliamentary reform was to be the main aim of this movement. But just as significant — both in the short and the long term — were the two fundamental principles of action through which Attwood hoped to achieve it. Firstly, he insisted that the 'distant oligarchs' must be compelled to reform Parliament, not by force, or even the threat of force, but peacefully, by what he called 'moral action'. Secondly, his Unions were to be 'unions' in the profoundest sense of the term. For what Attwood sought was a 'union between the lower and middle classes' — or in other words, a union of the great mass of the British people. Such a bringing together of classes, he realized, must first be accomplished in Birmingham itself, where some sense of mutal interest between master and man already existed. But he believed that it would then spread throughout the whole country, by the sheer force of

Birmingham's moral example.

In one way this concept of the union of classes was highly conservative and traditional. The politics of pre-industrial England had never been dominated by 'the horizontal solidarities of class'. What had mattered in the past had been 'the permanent vertical links' which bound the masters and dependents of various localities, industries and professions into like-minded 'interest groups'. So from this viewpoint, Attwood's approach may be seen simply as an attempt to prolong the 'interest' politics of pre-industrial England into the new industrial epoch. On the other hand, the idea of an interest group which would embrace the whole nation — or at least the whole nation, except for the landed aristocracy who then monopolized power — was as revolutionary as anything to be found in Marx. And almost as far-fetched perhaps — particularly in the repressive political atmosphere of the time — was the idea of forcing the ruling *élite* to make concessions by peaceable 'moral action'.

A public meeting to inaugurate the Birmingham Political Union was held at Beardsworth's Repository in Cheapside on 25 January 1830, when a gathering of perhaps 10,000 carried the motion in favour of going ahead by a majority of 20 to 1. Although the paid-up membership grew comparatively slowly, from that moment onwards, there was never the slightest doubt regarding the popular appeal of the parent union. Similar bodies were quickly founded in nearby towns, particularly in those of the Black Country, the area whose economic well-being — or lack of it — was so intimately bound up with that of Birmingham itself. Further afield the response was more hesitant and patchy. But by November 1831 the national tally of Political Unions had risen to at least 100.

Even in Birmingham, Attwood's 'union of classes' had its limitations. For Horton, 'the secret of his success lay in his power to inspire love and devotion . . . he had only to identify himself with any movement, in order to entitle it to respect, and seal it with a species of authority'. Nevertheless, although Attwood readily secured the support of Edmonds and other moderate radicals, the more extreme artisans remained suspicious of his intentions. So initially did many members of his own class. Most of his radical Tory followers were small manufacturers and other lower middle class people, who were particularly affected by the harsh economic conditions. Wealthy businessmen, by contrast, were invariably of regular Tory or Whig persuasion, and as such — like Attwood's Tory banking partner, Richard Spooner — did their best to avoid involvement. In the early days, the same even applied to the Whig radical group under the leadership of Joseph Parkes and William Redfern.

The governing body, or Council, of the Birmingham Union came out firmly in favour of 'such reform . . . as may

Looking down Newhall Hill today, with the town centre beyond – note the new Birmingham Repertory Theatre on the skyline. The 'semi-circle of wagons' must have been drawn up somewhere near the T-junction with Parade.

The 'Great Gathering of the Unions' on Newhall Hill, 7 May 1832. The porticoed building at the top of Newhall Hill is Mount Zion Chapel, while the spire of St. Paul's Church can be seen to the right.

ensure a real and effectual representation of the lower and middle classes of the people'. The measure which the Whigs introduced early in 1831 fell far short of this. But at least it offered to extend the franchise to the middle classes, and would for the first time give Birmingham and other big urban centres a voice at Westminster. It was therefore decided to work 'for the Bill, the whole Bill, and nothing but the Bill'.

The most spectacular and telling aspect of this support was the series of vast Newhall Hill meetings, which began in May 1830, and which, as the parliamentary battle over the bill dragged on from impasse to impasse, became ever more magnetic in their popular appeal. These demonstrations were superbly organized, with bands, banners and processions attracting not only members and participants but tens of thousands of excited spectators. The day of a meeting began with a ringing out of all the town's bells. As the various contingents reached Newhall Hill, which lay to the west of St. Paul's Square and commanded a sweeping view of the town, they were greeted with prolonged cheering. The men carrying banners bore them to the top of the ridge, and this line of colourful bunting, together with the backcloth of nearby buildings, helped to create an enclosed, almost amphitheatre-like effect. A semi-circle of wagons at the foot of the slope served as the platform on which the leaders assembled, wearing their Union medals and carrying white wands.

According to Tom Presterne, Attwood often had his carriage 'drawn with ropes' from his home in Harborne to Newhall Hill by the 'horny-handed men from Birmingham'.

And Presterne goes on:

> When he stepped forward to address the crowd at this place, the magic of his personality quelled the tumultuous behaviour. He raised his hand, and began, 'Men of Birmingham, Peace, Law, Order.' Immediately there was silence . . . He spoke with the voice of his city, and his utterance was confirmed by the multitudes . . . making Newhall Hill re-echo with the song of freedom lifted heavenward . . .

> > God is our guide! No sword we draw;
> > We kindle not war's fatal fires;
> > By union, justice, reason, law,
> > We claim the birthright of our sires.
> > We raise the watchword — Liberty:
> > We will — we will — we will — be free!

The medal of the Birmingham Political Union.

It is thought that over 100,000 people were present at the October 1831 meeting, including 20,000 from the Black Country. The 'Great Gathering of the Unions' which was staged on 7 May 1832, during the final crisis, could well have consisted of almost twice that number. Band and banner accompanied contingents converged on Birmingham from the Black Country towns between Wolverhampton and West Bromwich; from Stourbridge, Dudley and Halesowen; from Coventry, Leamington and Warwick; and from Stratford, Droitwich and Worcester. The final procession is said to have extended for 4 miles. Horton wrote:

> Who that witnessed those vast assemblages of people, comprising the might and energy of the district . . . can forget the emphatic impress of the picture, or hesitate to acknowledge that it is entitled to a place among the most triumphant exhibitions of moral power ever recorded?

Before the campaign was over, aided by the obduracy of the Duke of Wellington and the House of Lords, the organizers of the Union had succeeded in uniting virtually the whole town behind its cause. Parkes had taken his group of Whig radicals into the movement directly the Union had decided to support the Whig government's bill. More dramatically, three days after the 'Great Gathering' — recalling 1791 perhaps, and fearful for their property — some 500 'merchants, bankers, solicitors, surgeons, master manufacturers and other influential men' went in procession from the News Room in Bennett's Hill to the Union Rooms in Great Charles Street 'to hand in their adhesion to Mr. Attwood'. 'I ran to Mr. Barlow's', recalled one participant, 'and wrote a placard, "Great and important political movement. The entire middle classes are joining the Political Union."'

On 7 June 1832 the First Reform Bill received the royal assent. Six months later Attwood, president of the Union, and Joshua Scholefield, deputy president, were returned unopposed to represent the new parliamentary borough of Birmingham. 'The two members', we are told, 'were publicly paraded through the town, in a handsome chariot drawn by four horses, and preceded by a band of music'.

Inevitably, the almost total unity of classes which the Political Union had eventually achieved on this one burning

issue of parliamentary reform was not destined to last very long. Most of the upper middle class members conveniently forgot to renew their subscriptions. Many small manufacturers and shopkeepers, having once secured the vote for themselves, saw no reason to agitate for further extensions of the franchise. Nor was it long before the unenfranchised radicals began breaking into splinter groups: some organizing meetings of non-electors in the hope of building up support for further reform, others becoming more involved with the new trade unions which were now springing up in the town. Against this background, and with rapidly falling membership, it is hardly surprising that in June 1834 the leaders of the Union decided to suspend the society indefinitely.

However, by 1836, after three years as an M.P., Attwood had realized that there was no greater prospect of converting the new House of Commons to his economic policies than its unreformed predecessor. To a man of his remorseless logic, this meant that the only remaining hope lay in the creation of a truly radical House of Commons. And the only way to achieve that was by again resorting to 'the union of classes' and 'moral action' — this time to secure the vote for 'the mass of the people'.

So in 1837, the year of the Queen's accession, Attwood found himself president of a revived Birmingham Political Union — a Union which was so radical this time, that it served as one of the main pace-setters for what became the nationwide Chartist movement. In fact, its programme included five of the six points which later appeared in the People's Charter, while the meeting held at Holloway Head in August 1838 was regarded as 'the beginning not only of local but of national Chartism'. As before, Attwood urged other towns and districts to follow Birmingham's example by reviving their unions in support of the new movement; and he also urged the calling of a National Convention to direct and co-ordinate the whole campaign.

But Attwood's cause was now one which had little appeal for the middle classes, and at the same time was bound to attract extremists. When the National Convention met, it was rapidly taken over by the northern 'physical force' radicals under Fergus O'Connor, with Edmonds and other moderates walking out in disgust. Meanwhile, back in Birmingham unfamiliar speakers exhorted workers to arm in defence of their rights. And at what turned out to be the last Political Union meeting, held in April 1839, a letter from Attwood urging friendship between the working and middle classes was 'received with laughter and dissatisfaction'. A short while later, when the National Convention moved to Birmingham, the town became 'full of anger and suspicion', with rioting in and around the Bull Ring, soldiery on stand-by, and two detachments of London policemen patrolling the streets.

In June 1839 Attwood presented the 'monster Chartist

petition' to the House of Commons. But this was 'the last prominent act of his political life'. At the end of the same year he resigned his parliamentary seat and left his Harborne home for Jersey. In a farewell address to the electors of Birmingham he confessed that there was now no prospect of achieving currency reform, and that the moral action for which he had always stood had degenerated into hopeless exhibitions of physical force.

Yet despite Attwood's despair, this was by no means the end of his political influence – at any rate in Birmingham. During the early 1840s the local 'revolutionary' Chartists gradually lost ground to the more moderate Christian Chartists. Meanwhile, Joseph Sturge, having re-affirmed Attwood's viewpoint in a pamphlet called *Reconciliation between the Middle and Labouring Classes,* went on to found the Complete Suffrage Union. Although this at first received nationwide support from less extreme Chartist leaders, the rift between classes had gone too far in the country at large to be healed by appeals to reason. Within the town itself, however, Sturge's well-judged campaign to make the extension of the franchise an accepted part of local Liberal policy proved more successful.

At the general election of 1847 artisan radicals formed a Committee of Non-Electors to campaign actively on behalf of the town's two Liberal candidates, G. F. Muntz and William Scholefield, both of whom had declared themselves 'favourable to the enfranchisement of the working classes'. Thereafter, the holding of polls among non-electors became an accepted part of the endorsement procedure for all Liberal parliamentary candidates.

Meanwhile, first the Reformers' Union and then the Birmingham Reform Association were recruiting 'men of all shades of liberal opinion, enfranchised middle class and non-electors'. 'We have agreed', said a representative of the Association, 'to sink all minor differences and work together to obtain an extension of the franchise, vote by ballot and redistribution of seats'. All this helped to restore that belief in the 'thorough union' of classes which was to so sharply distinguish mid-Victorian Birmingham from many other big industrial towns.

According to John Bright's most recent biographer, the fact that 'ideas of class co-operation rather than class conflict were present' was one of the things that encouraged that much sought after Lancashire politician to accept the offer of a Birmingham parliamentary seat in 1857. And in commenting on Bright's decision at the time, Richard Cobden wrote of 'the social and political state' of Birmingham being 'far more healthy than that of Manchester'. 'There is a freer intercourse between all classes', he added, 'than in the Lancashire town, where a great and impassable gulf separates the workman from

The Market Hall, from the Bull Ring, c.1930. This was built 1833-5 to the design of Charles Edge. Gutted during the war, its foundations have been preserved in a small public garden.

The Town Hall, from the top of New Street. Begun in 1832, the principal architect was J. A. Hansom (inventor of the Hansom cab), who modelled its Corinthian colonnade on that of the Temple of Jupiter Stator at Rome.

the employer'. So, despite the calamity which overtook the Political Union itself, 'the language of "union"' remained Birmingham's 'favourite mode of political expression'.

As we shall see, too, Attwood's faith in 'the efficacy of moral action' was to become no less characteristic of Victorian Birmingham, and exemplary to the nation.

Incorporation and the Moral Mission

The original Political Union had played a major role in the securing of parliamentary representation for Birmingham. Before it was overtaken by the Chartist *débâcle,* the revived Political Union played an equally important part in initiating municipal reform.

Ever since 1769 the Street Commission had been the most powerful local government body in the town, and by the 1830s it was making considerable progress in bringing cleanliness, orderliness and safety at any rate to the main streets, and in wrestling with the many other urgent environmental problems. Meanwhile, with the erection during the 1830s of two fine Classical buildings — the Market Hall in the Bull Ring and the Town Hall at the top end of New Street — Birmingham's appearance and public facilities were at last beginning to be transformed, under its aegis, into those of a major regional centre.

Though dominated by wealthy, public-spirited Whig families, the Street Commission's sole concern had always been with administrative efficiency, in the interests of which it regularly elected Tories and radicals to its membership and endeavoured to keep out of politics. Nevertheless, in the eyes of working and middle class radicals, the undoubted efficiency of the Street Commissioners did not compensate for the fact that they comprised a closed corporation, 'chosen by themselves... appointing their own officers, levying taxes at their pleasure and distributing them, without check or control'. If 'distant oligarchs' had been made to bow, why should their local counterparts be spared?

The Municipal Corporations Act of 1835 provided that a Charter of Incorporation could be granted to unincorporated towns on a petition of the inhabitants. In 1837, therefore, the revived Political Union took the initiative in petitioning Parliament for such a measure, the main effect of which would be to establish a representative Town Council elected by the ratepayers of the borough. Initially the only administrative function of this new body was to be the control of a police force. But it would bring a new democratic voice into the affairs of the town; and eventually, as William Redfern, one of its most forceful advocates, correctly foresaw, it would lead to 'the concentration of all powers in one body and their administration by one set of officers'.

The Tories of the town, together with some Whigs, organized a counter petition, and this brought about a bitter polarization of local opinion. Members of the two parties, according to J. T. Bunce, Birmingham's first municipal historian, 'refused to meet in public or in private, to engage in united action of any kind, to join in the same assemblies . . . even business relations were not conducted without strain'.

But in November 1838 the Privy Council granted a Charter of Incorporation to Birmingham. And at a dinner to celebrate this victory William Redfern called upon his fellow radicals never to rest satisfied 'until every oligarchical system throughout the town was utterly abolished and all its rights, powers and authorities were transferred to the Town Council'.

William Scholefield – Charter Mayor, 1838; Birmingham M.P., 1847-67.

This ultimate triumph was to take a further 13 years, but at least the Liberals made a good start. Partly because of the clever way in which the 13 ward boundaries had been determined, every one of the 48 councillors returned at Birmingham's first municipal election was a radical or Liberal. The resulting Council then proceeded to elect a bench of 16 Liberal aldermen, together with a Liberal mayor – William Scholefield.

Nor was this thrustful and determined political radicalism confined to municipal affairs. It reached right down to the level of vestry politics, where otherwise unenfranchised working class supporters were particularly active. With their aid, during the 1830s, radicals and Liberals took over the administration of the poor law by gaining control of the Board of Guardians. Similarly, what the Conservative *Aris's Gazette* called 'the indecent contention and disgraceful clamour' of radical dissenters ensured that after 1831 the church rate – until then levied on all ratepayers for the benefit of Birmingham's Anglican churches – could never again be collected. George Edmonds chided in the same year:

> Messrs. Churchwardens, have you not found that you are responsible for your acts, and that you must yearly give a faithful account of your stewardship? Messrs. Constables, have you not discovered that you cannot commit wrong without being brought to the bar of public opinion? . . . Messrs. Guardians of the Poor, has not the Political Union purged your body by the introduction of some of its members and enforced a principle of purity in your proceedings?

In the face of this all-out radical assault, the once popular Tory cause was reduced to such a poor pass that in 1840, when Conservative candidates scored successes in the churchwardens' elections and temporarily regained control of the Board of Guardians, a local Tory paper hailed it as 'a glorious victory'. And indeed this momentary shift in political opinion, which must have been due to anti-Chartist reaction more than anything else, did gather sufficient momentum for Richard

THE BRUMMAG

John Bright. "I HAVE NO FE—FE—FEAR OF M

Above: John Bright, Birmingham M.P., 1857-89. Below: A rather cruel Punch comment on Bright's 1866 'Reform Crusade'.

FRANKENSTEIN.

IOOD SUFFRAGE!"—*Mr. Bright's Speech at Birmingham.*

Spooner—Attwood's erstwhile banking partner but political opponent—to be returned to Parliament in 1843 as Birmingham's first Tory M.P.

However, Showell's *Dictionary of Birmingham,* published in 1885, is still recording Richard Spooner as Birmingham's *only* Tory M.P. And this means that—unlike Manchester and Liverpool, for instance, where Conservatives enjoyed substantial periods of ascendancy—right down to Joseph Chamberlain's break with Gladstonian Liberalism in 1886, Victorian Birmingham remained, to all intents and purposes, an 'hereditary borough' for the Liberals—and indeed, 'the focal point of official Liberalism' for the whole country.

In what E. P. Thompson calls 'a tribute impressive from so stern a critic', a contemporary radical, James O'Brien, wrote of the Birmingham Union:

> To this body, more than to any other, is confessedly due the triumph (such as it is) of the Reform Bill. Its well-ordered proceedings, extended organization, and immense assemblages of people, at critical periods in its progress, rendered the measure irresistible.

Recent research has suggested that the influence of the Birmingham Political Union on the campaign for the First Reform Bill has been rather exaggerated. But so far as the town itself is concerned—not to mention the folklore of English radicalism—the myth counted for more than the reality.

And locally, that myth was to remain inviolate throughout the Victorian epoch. Still more to the point, it was to remain a myth which the leaders of Birmingham opinion repeatedly brought back to mind, and challenged both the town and themselves to live up to. For Horton in the early 1850s:

> The spirit of the Political Union meetings lives around us. It pervades the atmosphere of our moral being, and is embodied in the institutions that are springing up on every side.

A few years later, when John Bright made his first speech in the town after his election as a Birmingham M.P., he concluded by crying excitedly:

> . . . do not my eyes look upon the sons of those who thirty years ago shook the fabric of privilege to its base? . . . Shall their sons be less noble than they? Shall the fire which they kindled be extinguished with you?

The answer was 'no'; and Bright went on to use Birmingham as the catalyst in yet another movement for parliamentary reform—a movement which, this time, was eventually to secure the Second Reform Bill of 1867, with its extension of the right to vote to all male householders.

Moreover, alongside this reform campaign, and indeed as an integral part of it, Bright found himself working no less vigorously for the extension of that 'thorough union' of classes throughout the nation, which had been such an essential aspect of Attwood's original 'moral mission'.

Thanks largely to the inspiration of a remarkable nonconformist minister, George Dawson, and to the outstanding political abilities of Joseph Chamberlain, it was only a few years later that Birmingham's 'moral mission' was to culminate in its celebrated 'civic gospel', a new approach to municipal administration which was to affect countless other cities far into the future. For understandable if not wholly excusable reasons, the achievements of the Birmingham Town Council lagged far behind those of Manchester, Liverpool and Glasgow during the 1850s and '60s. Yet regarding 'the group of men around Joseph Chamberlain in the Birmingham of the 1870s', one authority on the history of English local government has recently written, 'Their concept of what a council should be has proved long-lived, dominating thought on the subject almost down to the present'.

And in the popular imagination of the Victorians themselves, all this linked back to what R. K. Dent in 1879 called 'that great battle for political liberty which was fought in Birmingham during the second, third, and fourth decades of the nineteenth century, and has caused Birmingham ever since to be the great centre of English Radicalism'.

But if the political *persona* of Victorian Birmingham was given some of its most distinctive characteristics during the 1830s, the same decade also brought an absolutely fundamental development so far as its economic future was concerned. In 1837 the first railway train steamed into Birmingham.

The 'Iron Cross'

On Monday 9 July 1837 the Directors of the Grand Junction Railway made what *Aris's Gazette* described as 'an experimental trip'. This brought 'two carriages and thirty-six passengers the whole distance from Liverpool to Birmingham in three hours and seventeen minutes'. The following day:

Vauxhall Station today – from 'the bridge which crosses the railway at its entrance'. Few people realize that this is Birmingham's oldest railway terminus.

... the whole town was in a state of great commotion and excitement, owing to the public opening ... Soon after five o'clock the streets leading in the direction of Vauxhall, where the Company's temporary station is situated, were crowded with persons of all ranks ... By six o'clock ... the bridge which crosses the railway at its entrance into the station yard, and indeed, every eminence that commanded the least view of the line, was covered with persons awaiting the starting of the carriages ...

At seven o'clock precisely, the bell rang, and the opening train, drawn by the *Wildfire* engine, commenced moving. The train consisted of eight carriages, all of the first class ... [it] started slowly, but upon emerging from the yard, speedily burst off at a rapid race ... the immense multitude as far as the eye could reach, gave expression to their admiration by loud and long continued huzzas, and the waving of hats and handkerchiefs.

It was as early as 1824, before even the 22 mile long Stockton and Darlington line had been completed, that Birmingham businessmen had optimistically launched a two-part project to build a railway linking together 'the three great capitals of England' – London, Birmingham and Liverpool. So keen was the interest that when the shares came on to the

The Adderley Park cutting, from Bordesley Green Road. The station was inserted in 1860.

Below: The Grand Junction Railway's 'Birmingham Viaduct'. Right: The London and Birmingham Railway's viaduct, photographed from Lawley Street, with 'The Viaduct' pub to the left, and the 'Birmingham Viaduct' beyond.

market in the following year all Birmingham's allocation for the London line were subscribed within two days. However, this was so premature as to be almost like speculating on regular moon flights today. Only in 1833 was parliamentary approval finally obtained for the London and Birmingham Railway; and also for the Grand Junction Railway Company to construct a line linking Birmingham to the already existing Liverpool and Manchester Railway.

The amount of labour which was involved in these undertakings is mind-boggling. 11,000 navvies are said to have worked on the Grand Junction Railway, while on the London and Birmingham a labour force of 20,000 is reckoned to have displaced 400,000,000 cubic feet of earth — an average of 20,000 cubic feet each. Horse-drawn wagons and pulley systems were available, together with the occasional use of gunpowder. But otherwise everything was done with picks and shovels. Recalling these facts while looking at the great Adderley Park cutting, for instance, can still evoke a sense of wonder.

Nor is it difficult for Birmingham people to appreciate that the Victorian town's railways involved remarkable feats of engineering — if only because of the amazing series of mid-nineteenth-century viaducts that can still be seen striding across the Rea valley in the area of Deritend and Duddeston. The one carrying the Grand Junction line was designed by Joseph Locke, who had learned his trade with George Stephenson on the Liverpool and Manchester Railway. Of this structure, which originally carried the track from Vauxhall to Curzon Street, the 1851 *Rail Road Book of England* says:

> The Birmingham Viaduct is the most important and stupendous work, challenging comparison with almost any ancient or modern art. It is built of brick with stone groins and dressings . . . and consists of twenty-eight segmental arches of upwards of thirty feet span, and thirty-two feet wide, the length extending for about one thousand feet, the whole built on a curve of three-quarters of a mile radius.

The London and Birmingham Railway, after emerging from the Adderley Park cutting, also had to be carried to Curzon Street by means of a viaduct. Indeed, this crosses

Lawley Street, by 'The Viaduct' pub, only about 50 yards from its Grand Junction counterpart.

The London and Birmingham Railway was George and Robert Stephenson's first major combined undertaking, and they conceived it entirely in terms of superlatives. At 112½ miles, it was to be the longest railway the world had thus far seen. Its tunnels were to be longer than anyone then believed possible, its embankments higher, its cuttings deeper. As it turned out, too, the determination and character required to complete the London and Birmingham Railway were to reach almost epic proportions. Ten men were lost in the making of the Watford tunnel. Then, during the cutting of the 1½ mile Kilsby tunnel in Northamptonshire, a subterranean lake burst into the workings from above. This happened so suddenly that the gang of navvies only just managed to reach a vertical air shaft in time. So serious was the inundation that for a while it was touch and go whether the company would decide to abandon the project altogether. Only after the Stephensons had kept a battery of pumping engines working day and night for 9 months was it eventually possible for work to be resumed. Writing of this critical phase in the building of the railway line along which today's crowded Inter-City expresses ply safely and constantly back and forth, Christian Barman says:

> The Kilsby tunnel is entered just before the trains to Birmingham reach Rugby. As the traveller passes the bottom of each of the two tall shafts, there is a flash of pale blue daylight and the roar of the wheels is momentarily hushed. It would be fitting if at that moment he were to spare a thought for this dramatic incident in the long battle waged against earth and water by England's greatest engineer.

Compared with the opening of the Liverpool line, the departure of the first train from Curzon Street was something of an anticlimax. This was partly because 'the novelty was beginning to wear off'; but also because — since Kilsby was still uncompleted — the early trains could only run as far as Rugby anyway, with a lengthy road detour for those going on to London. It was not until 17 September 1838 that the *Gazette* announced 'This morning the entire line of Railroad . . . will be opened to the public'.

The stone entrance building which the London and Birmingham Railway erected at the front of its Curzon Street sheds and platforms was designed by Sir Philip Hardwick in the Classical style. At the time it must have accorded well, both in architectural idiom and monumentality, with those two other imposing public buildings of the 1830s, the Town Hall and the Market Hall. Today the Ionic-columned portico looks almost pathetic in down-town Duddeston. Yet it is undoubtedly among Victorian Birmingham's most important relics, marvellously epitomizing what Barman has called 'the bold faith and imperturbable daring' of those early railway years.

Despite the fact that the London and Birmingham Railway — for obvious reasons — cost almost twice as much to

Above: 'Entrance to Birmingham Station' – from an engraving of 1839. Right: The Curzon Street portico today. This building originally contained 'the board room of the directors, the secretary's offices . . . a refreshment saloon, &c.'

Time-table and fares of the Grand Junction Railway, from an advertisement in Bridgen's Directory of the Borough of Wolverhampton, 1838.

build than had originally been intended, it was an immediate and unqualified success. By 1841, 11 trains were running between London and Birmingham daily, with passengers paying £1. 10s. (£1.50) for first class accommodation, £1 for third, and taking under 5 hours on their journey. Against an initial outlay of £5½ million, the London and Birmingham receipts from passenger traffic in that year amounted to £577,000, with a further £137,000 from goods. The Grand Junction Railway, whose time-table and fares can be seen in a contemporary advertisement, took gross receipts in 1839 of

BIRMINGHAM TO LIVERPOOL.

Published by J. Bridgen, Wolverhampton.

BIRMINGHAM TO LIVERPOOL. STATIONS.	Distance to Birmingham.	FIRST CLASS. 6 o'clock, A.M.	SECOND CLASS. $8\frac{1}{2}$ o'clock, A.M.	FIRST CLASS. $11\frac{1}{2}$ o'clock, A.M	FIRST CLASS. $2\frac{1}{2}$ o'clock, P.M.	SECOND CLASS. 5 o'clock, P.M.	FIRST CLASS. 7 o'clock, P.M.
	Miles	H. M.	H. M.	H. M.	H. M.	H. M.	H. M.
BIRMINGHAM		6 0	8 30	11 30	2 30	5 0	7 0
PERRY BAR	$3\frac{1}{2}$		8 38			5 8	
NEWTON ROAD	$6\frac{3}{4}$		8 51			5 20	
BESCOT BRIDGE	$9\frac{1}{2}$		9 0			5 30	
JAMES'S BRIDGE	$10\frac{1}{4}$		9 3			5 33	
WILLENHALL	12		9 16			5 46	
WOLVERHAMPTON	$14\frac{1}{2}$	6 35	9 26	12 5	3 5	5 56	7 35
FOUR ASHES	20		9 43			6 13	
SPREAD EAGLE	$21\frac{1}{2}$		9 47			6 17	
PENKRIDGE	24		10 0			6 40	
STAFFORD.	$29\frac{1}{4}$	7 10	10 13	12 40	3 40	6 43	8 10
BRIDGEFORD	$32\frac{3}{4}$		10 27			6 57	
NORTON BRIDGE	35		10 39			7 9	
WHITMORE	$43\frac{1}{4}$	7 53	10 59	1 23	4 23	7 29	8 53
MADELEY	46		11 11			7 41	
CREWE	54	8 24	11 29	1 54	4 54	7 59	9 24
COPPENHALL	56		11 40			8 10	
MINSHULL VERNON	$58\frac{3}{4}$		11 48			8 18	
WINSFORD	$61\frac{1}{4}$		11 57			8 27	
HARTFORD	$65\frac{3}{4}$	8 59	12 7	2 29	5 29	8 37	9 59
ACTON	$68\frac{1}{4}$		12 18			8 48	
PRESTON BROOK	$72\frac{1}{2}$		12 31			9 1	
MOORE	75		12 36			9 6	
WARRINGTON	78	9 36	12 44	3 6	6 6	9 14	10 36
NEWTON JUNCTION	$82\frac{3}{4}$		1 2			9 32	
MANCHESTER and **LIVERPOOL**	$97\frac{1}{4}$	10 45	1 45	4 15	7 15	10 15	11 45

FARES

FROM LIVERPOOL OR MANCHESTER TO BIRMINGHAM,

Or vice versa.

	£	s.	d.
First Class Coach, six inside, whether in First Class or in Mixed Trains	1	1	0
Mail Coach, four inside	1	5	0
Bed-carriage, in Mail Coach	2	0	0
Second Class Coach	0	14	0
Children under ten years of age, half-price.			
Gentlemen's Carriage, four wheels	3	0	0
Ditto ditto, two wheels	2	0	0
Passengers, if belonging to and riding in gentlemen's Carriages, each	0	15	0
Servants, ditto ditto, each	0	10	0
Grooms in charge of Horses, each	0	10	0
One Horse	1	10	0
Two Horses	2	10	0
Three Horses	3	0	0
Dogs	0	3	0

ON SUNDAYS,

The four First Class Trains only, with the addition of Second Class Coaches, will start at the same hours as on the week days, but will not take up and set down passengers at any but the six principal stopping places.

£281,125 from passengers and £66,457 from goods.

Although the railways to London and the north-west were the most promising commercially, lines to the south-west and north-east were to follow with remarkable rapidity. In 1840 trains from Gloucester, having first been hauled up the Lickey Incline by a stationary steam engine, began unloading their passengers and freight—somewhat discordantly perhaps—beside the timber-framed Stratford Place at Camp Hill, then the home of Mrs. Ann Simcox. A year later the line had been extended—across the Stratford and Coventry roads—to Curzon Street. Two years after that the Birmingham and Gloucester Railway was proudly announcing the extension of its services to Bristol. Meanwhile, the Birmingham and Derby Railway, opened in 1842, by connecting Birmingham to the North Midland Railway, had in turn provided the possibility of through rail travel to Leeds, Hull and other north-east ports.

Scarcely a generation had passed since Birmingham had found itself at the centre of James Brindley's 'silver cross' of canals; now it was at the centre of a comparable 'iron cross' of railways. Moreover, whereas it had taken a full 30 years for local

The early railways of Birmingham, as shown in Allens' Pictorial Guide of 1852. The full name of the 'Stour Valley Railway' was the 'Birmingham, Wolverhampton and Stour Valley Railway'.

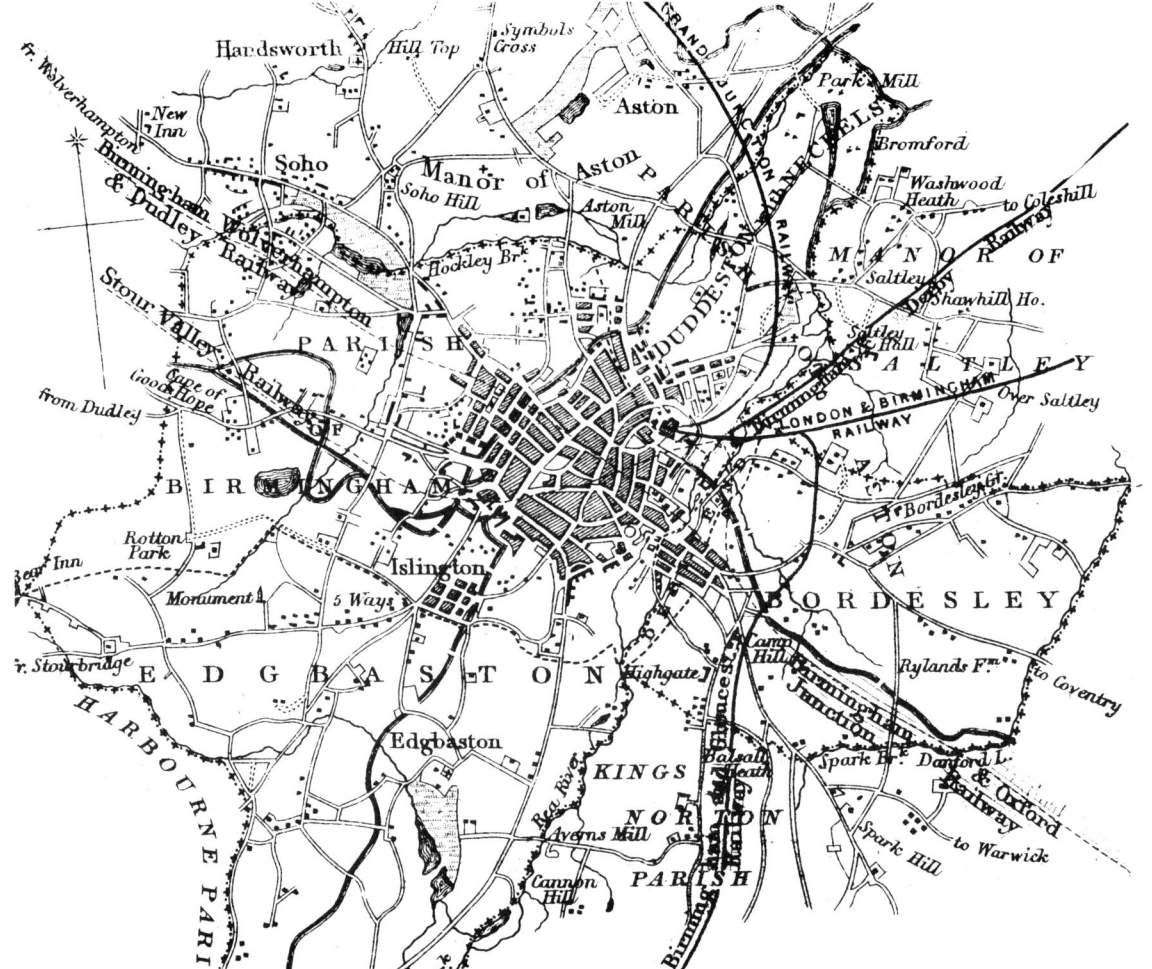

merchants to gain access to Liverpool, Hull, Bristol and London by water, their successors were provided with equivalent rail facilities in a mere seven. Already in 1841 Granville was remarking in his *Spas of England* that Birmingham had 'by fortuitous circumstances . . . been converted into a centre of almost numberless radii of conveyance or railroad-tracks to every part of the kingdom':

> If anyone, either from the north, or the north east, or the north west, desires to visit the capital or proceed to the south, how can he do it better, at a cheaper rate, or more expeditiously, than by going through Birmingham? And if the Londoner or any other traveller from the south, the south east, and the south west, desires to reach the opposite points of the compass, how can he carry his intention into effect more advantageously than by going through Birmingham?

It is often thought that there was only one early railway station at Curzon Street, but this is erroneous. The Birmingham and Gloucester Railway did indeed run its trains into the London and Birmingham station. But when the completion of the Birmingham Viaduct enabled the Grand Junction to extend its line to Curzon Street, this railway established its own separate terminus on the opposite side of the road. Similarly, in the interests of independence, the Birmingham and Derby Railway opened a separate low-level station at Lawley Street, with provision for lifting its carriages up on to the London and Birmingham tracks.

Apart from this somewhat untidy dispersion of facilities, the main disadvantage with Curzon Street was the fact that it lay about a mile away from the centre of the town. Horse omnibuses had been operating in Birmingham since 1834, and horse cabs were always available to carry those who could afford the fare of 1 shilling (5p.) from the station to the town and *vice versa*. But to reach High Street or New Street meant either a lengthy drive round two sides of a triangle, or a difficult journey through narrow back streets and alleys which were often blocked.

The Street Commissioners had been mindful of this problem of access from the start; and they were also concerned that the existing routes were bound to give visitors an unfavourable first impression of the town. With characteristic decisiveness, therefore, by the end of 1838 the Street Commissioners had drawn up an ambitious proposal for making a 'new and commodious' half-mile long 'railway boulevard', which was to cut diagonally across existing streets, from the junction of High Street and New Street directly to the great Curzon Street portico. However, this scheme, which would have been immensely complicated and costly, met with so much opposition from affected property owners that it had to be dropped in favour of a more simple solution. This alternative plan amounted, in effect, to a continuation of Curzon Street itself right up into the middle of the town. Named Albert Street, after the Prince Consort, the Street

Commission survived long enough to see the making of the lower part of this extension — i.e., from Park Street to Moor Street — by the Free Grammar School, whose land it was. But with the demise of the Street Commission in 1851, the Borough Council dragged its feet to such good effect that the section of Albert Street between Moor Street and Dale End was not finished until 1862. And that was ten years after travellers had grown accustomed to ending their railway journeys in the middle of Birmingham anyway!

In almost every town, railway stations were initially situated on the edge of the built-up area — much as airports are today. Not infrequently, too, even in major cities like London and Manchester, it proved impossible subsequently to establish them right at the centre. However, with its conviction that 'vast benefits cannot fail to result to all classes of inhabitants' from the railways, peripheral termini were not to prove good enough for Birmingham.

The case for a central station was being actively canvassed from the mid-1840s. Apart from the problems of dispersion and remoteness, it was by then plain that 'the business of railways' had so much increased 'that the space which was formerly deemed sufficient ... has since been found to be quite insufficient'. There was also the question of developing rail routes on the other side of Birmingham. The trains to Manchester and Liverpool called at Wolverhampton, but otherwise the Black Country — despite its crucial industrial involvement with the town — remained solely dependent on road and canal transport throughout the 1840s. Nor would it have made much sense to bring lines from the middle of the Black Country into Curzon Street.

The prospects of Birmingham acquiring a central station were greatly improved in 1844 and 1846 by company amalgamations. In the former year the Birmingham and Derby merged with the Birmingham and Gloucester to form the Midland Counties Railway. In the latter the London and Birmingham and the Grand Junction came together as the London and North Western Railway. Just as importantly, from the start, the Midland Railway and the L & NWR, which was Britain's largest amalgamation, favoured a policy of friendly co-operation.

It was in its inaugural year that the L & NWR decided to build New Street station, at the same time agreeing to allow Midland Railway trains to use it. The parliamentary act sanctioning this development also provided for the recently formed Birmingham, Wolverhampton and Stour Valley Railway to use New Street as its terminus; and within a year, the L & NWR had bought out this company, thereby securing for itself a railway which ran across the Black Country alongside the Birmingham and Wolverhampton Canal.

But it was not merely commercial initiative, inter-company

New Street – the west tunnels.

The L & NWR section of New Street Station in the early 1900's.

co-operation and common sense that enabled Birmingham to secure a central station when so many other big towns failed. This was also due to Birmingham's peculiarly fortunate geography. During the canal age, the fact that it stood on a sandstone ridge which had been partially breached to the north by the Tame valley, had enabled canals to be cut round all but the southern side of the town, thus providing a ring waterway, as it were, with lead-offs in all directions. Now the railways were about to exploit the same unusual topographical situation in a completely different but no less beneficial manner. Having crossed the Rea valley on their separate viaducts, the lines already gathered together at Curzon Street could be taken into the sandstone ridge on one side and out at the other by means of tunnels. Since they would then run under the town centre, no great swathes of property would need to be purchased and cleared to make way for them. The only buildings which would have to be demolished would be those on the site of the station itself. In the case of New Street the site really chose itself. It was a natural bowl—almost a natural amphitheatre—which was located close to the professional quarters, shopping streets, markets and best hotels. As luck would have it, too, the desired area was occupied by 7 acres of perhaps the worst slums that were then to be found in Birmingham—and certainly, as a contemporary declared, by 'a collection of streets and houses that it would be advantageous to Birmingham altogether to get rid of'.

New Street, with its east and west tunnels, and other necessary works, took 7 years to complete, though some use was being made of it from 1852. At the time of its construction, it was said to have the largest iron and glass roof in the world—1,080 feet long and with a single span of 212 feet. The station was enlarged to cover almost 12 acres in the 1880s; and was of course completely re-styled and refurbished in the 1960s. The platforms still lie at their original level, however, some 25 feet below New Street; yet, because of the bowl-like topography, more or less on the same level as Station Street.

When the lines from the east were brought into New Street the tracks had to be raised considerably, and one can still see graphic evidence for this on the Birmingham Viaduct for instance (page 27). Here a viaduct has been built on top of a viaduct. The lower one represents the original Joseph Locke structure that took the Liverpool line into Curzon Street. The blue-brick arcade above dates from c.1850, and carries the present-day track towards New Street.

In the event, Birmingham was to have not one but two central stations. This was a development which was bitterly resisted by the L & NWR. But it was argued that New Street, although convenient for 'the carriage traffic', would not be able to cope with the small masters bringing in manufactures 'on their backs and in carts' from the workshops and factories of the north-west. Snow Hill was higher in the town, but otherwise its site was remarkably similar to that of New Street. Lines coming in from the west would be able to approach the terminus by tunnel and viaduct, and then pass under the town for the east by means of a tunnel. Again, although from half way down Livery Street or Snow Hill one could walk directly on to a platform, from the main entrance in Colmore Row it was necessary to descend a long flight of steps.

Two companies, the Birmingham, Wolverhampton and Dudley Railway, and the Birmingham and Oxford Junction Railway, received parliamentary permission to use Snow Hill as their terminus in August 1846. But by the end of the same year both companies had sold out to the Great Western. This railway, which was already second to the L&NWR in size and importance, thereby posed a direct threat to the latter, not only by acquiring a rival Black Country service, but because of its ability to develop the Oxford line as an alternative route to London.

As well as challenging the L&NWR's commercial supremacy, the sudden advent of the GWR brought the 'Battle of the Gauges' to Birmingham. While George Stephenson was building his first railway, the Stockton and Darlington, he had decided the width of his track by taking about a hundred farmers' carts and establishing the average width between their wheels. This worked out at 4′ 8½″, and thereafter Stephenson, and indeed all his successors save one, automatically used this gauge for their railways. The exception was Isambard Brunel, the chief engineer of the GWR, who adopted the much wider gauge of 7′.

There can be little doubt that in purely engineering terms Brunel had a good deal of merit on his side. Yet many hundreds of miles of railways had already been built to Stephenson's specification, and so long as there were two gauges a fully integrated national railway network would obviously be impossible. This was a conflict which was perhaps bound to

Left: Snow Hill Station, c.1930. 'For many years', Showell tells us, 'a monstrous wooden shed did duty as Snow Hill Station'. A brick structure was first erected in 1871, only to be replaced 30 years later by the building so many still remember. Below: Snow Hill Station under demolition in 1977.

The Duddeston Viaduct, from Upper Trinity Street.

come to a head at the centre of the 'iron cross'. After a protracted commercial and legal battle, Parliament decided that the Oxford line must be provided with the narrow gauge — albeit alongside the broad. Moreover, in order to preserve the case for a unified railway network, and to placate the L&NWR still further, the GWR was required to construct a link line between its own Oxford Junction Railway and the L&NWR's London and Birmingham.

The result was the Duddeston Viaduct, carried on 58 blue-brick arches a distance of 1,100 yards between Upper Trinity Street, Bordesley, and Banbury Street, Duddeston. Though built by and belonging to the GWR, neither broad nor narrow gauge rails were ever laid along it, and no connection was ever made at the L&NWR end. Yet 130 years later the Duddeston Viaduct still lours over houses and factories — at once the city's most preposterous Victorian folly, and the nation's most eloquent and enduring monument to the 'Battle of the Gauges', a battle which was not finally settled until the uprooting of the last stretch of 7' track in 1892.

By the 1850s the railways had come to dominate the long distance transport of Birmingham. Although hackney coaches and private carriages were more plentiful than ever, the stage coach was virtually banished, while wagon haulage over long distances was much reduced.

Canals, on the other hand, still had an important part to play. Even as late as the 1860s over a million tons of coal came into Birmingham by canal each year. With its intricate network of waterways, too, much of the town's factory-to-factory traffic continued to be boat-borne. At the very beginning of the railway epoch the canal companies had fought fiercely against their upstart competitors. But despite lowering tariffs drastically there was no way the canals could sustain their former volume of business. This impotence, plus the fact that railways often found it economic and convenient to lay down their lines along canal routes, and also to make use of central canal warehousing and wharfage facilities, gradually led to the integration of the two services. By 1870 a report of the Birmingham Chamber of Commerce concluded that 'The Birmingham Canal Company is just another name for the L&NWR'. Similarly, the Midland Railway eventually took control of the Worcester and Birmingham Canal. One result of this eminently sensible policy was the development of special interchange basins, like that at Hockley Port, where loads could be switched from water to rail and *vice versa*.

The construction of the railways could have a considerable topographical impact on the rural parishes of the Greater Birmingham area through which they passed. The Great Western's Oxford Railway, having crossed the Rea valley on its arrow-straight ¾ mile long viaduct, was able to proceed through Small Heath at ground level. But after entering the parish of Yardley, a deep cutting had to be made through Tyseley Hill, and five high, narrow brick bridges constructed to preserve rights of way.

A dozen years before, when the Gloucester railway was cut and tunnelled through the Moseley ridge, a brick bridge was built to carry the Alcester Road over the cutting. Half a mile nearer Birmingham, however, where the deeply sunken track intercepted what was then little more than a fordrough, a timber structure was considered adequate, and this survived down to 1908. The timber bridge became known as Woodbridge; and, predictably so soon after the accession of Queen Victoria, the brick bridge as Queen's Bridge. Both in turn provided road

Bottom: Hockley Port in its hey-day, as depicted on a recently painted mural at the site. For the location of this interesting survival see map on page 98. Below: the GWR's 'Oxford line' viaduct, photographed from the top deck of the Park Street multi-storey car park.

names that are still familiar.

In the eyes of some, a railway could enhance the rural scene. The Aston Viaduct, on the Grand Junction Railway, was described in 1851 as:

> . . . one of the great ornaments of this line, which, with the embankments and the general aspect of the country of this locality, presents the most beautiful and picturesque scenery, heightened by the presence of a reservoir or inland lake, and a belt of noble elms, from which emerges the elegant spire of Aston church.

Disruptive and scenic effects aside, however, the railways had comparatively little immediate influence on rural parishes. This was because all the emphasis for the first decade or so was on long distance traffic. Only a handful of suburban stations were to be found in the Greater Birmingham area in 1850. These were at Stechford on the London and Birmingham line; Vauxhall and Perry Barr on the line to Liverpool; Castle Bromwich on the line to Derby; Camp Hill, King's Heath, Lifford and King's Norton on the line to Gloucester.

Above: 'Aston Church and Viaduct', from a print published in Drake's Grand Junction Railway, 1838. The track in the foreground is Holborn Lane, and the stone-faced viaduct arches can still be found at the point where this meets the Lichfield Road.

Once the railways could carry people into the heart of the city, the development of suburban services became a more attractive proposition. During the 1850s and 1860s the GWR provided its Oxford line with stations at Acock's Green (1852), Bordesley (1855) and Small Heath (1863). From its opening in 1854, the same company's Wolverhampton line offered stations at Hockley, Soho and Handsworth. The only early stations on the L&NWR's route to Wolverhampton were at Monument Lane and Smethwick. But its Grand Junction route was given additional stations at Aston (1854) and Great Barr (1862), and its London line at Adderley Park (1860). Similarly, the Midland Railway opened extra stations at Saltley (1854) on the Derby line, and at Moseley (1867) and Northfield (1869) on the line to Gloucester.

Of greater importance than the development of passenger services, though, was the undoubted success of the railway companies in handling the ever growing quantities of provisions, raw materials and finished products which had to be brought into and sent out of the town. By the end of the nineteenth century, Curzon Street, Lawley Street, Camp Hill, Hockley and other goods yards occupied no less than 390 acres, and in addition there were innumerable private industrial sidings. Victorian London, Manchester and Liverpool experienced tremendous logistical problems in dealing with their goods traffic. Yet Birmingham equipped itself so well for this purpose that the railway enquiries which investigated such difficulties never so much as mention it.

This efficiency in the movement of raw materials and finished products, along with Birmingham's position as a focal point 'of almost numberless radii', must have had a highly beneficial influence on the industrial development of the Victorian town.

Brass, Guns, Jewellery and Buttons

So far as Birmingham's industrial history is concerned, the first half of Queen Victoria's reign was at one and the same time a period of great continuity and also of great change.

It was a period of continuity because the town's industrial structure continued to be dominated by the brass, gun, jewellery and button industries—or in other words, by the same four industries that had been pre-eminent in late Georgian times. Just as importantly, in these and other trades, a very high proportion of the labour force continued to be skilled craftsmen working in outbuildings, garrets and 'nests of small shops', as their forefathers had done for centuries.

Previous historians have generally put most emphasis on these long established aspects of early Victorian industry, arguing with G. C. Allen that this was a period 'of development on the lines laid down in the later eighteenth century rather than an era of transformation'.

This may be a mistake. And certainly it would be a mistake if we allowed the admittedly strong elements of continuity to blind us to the fact that there was also massive technological development. Perhaps the most obvious sign of this is the wide range of new industries which managed to establish themselves between 1830 and 1870. Among the more important were the electro-plating and chemical industries, the manufacture of metal bedsteads, of steel pens, cut nails and wood screws, plate glass, hydraulic machinery, railway rolling stock and sewing machines. In the majority of cases, too, these new industries were organized from the start on a factory rather than a workshop basis, and employed a great deal of steam-driven machinery.

Despite appearances to the contrary, the same period also brought big changes in the traditional Birmingham trades. These had been relatively unaffected by technological innovations down to 1830. Of the three lines of development which together transformed production methods during the first industrial revolution, only the sub-division of labour could be said to have made major progress by that date. With the other two—the introduction of machinery and the application of steam power—this was not the case. Nor, perhaps, is it difficult to appreciate why. The textile industries of the north could be—and were—dramatically transformed by the introduction of half a dozen machines, which were first water- and then steam-driven. But with the countless highly complex operations involved in the Birmingham hardware trades hundreds of new machines would have been required to achieve anything like the same effect. It was only to be expected therefore that the process of full mechanization should have moved forward much more tentatively in Birmingham than in

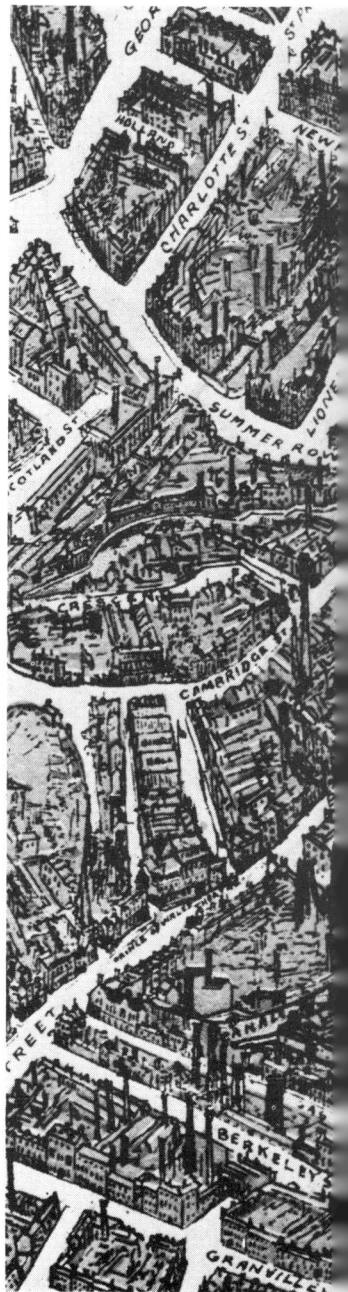

Manchester; or, to put the same point the other way round, that the widespread use of 'pre-industrial' craft skills should have persisted a great deal longer.

However, the 1830s seem to have been a watershed in this respect, as in so many others. And from then down to 1870, it could well be that the pace of technological change was as hectic as at any time either before or since. This is suggested, for instance, by the spate of patents that were taken out by Birmingham inventors and businessmen. In the 1810s and 1820s there had been 71 and 83 respectively. But between 1831 and 1840 the number of patented inventions went up to 170, and in the next decade to 265 — which was equivalent to one every fortnight.

Still more striking is the alacrity with which local firms were now at last adopting steam power. In 1836 Birmingham had possessed 169 steam engines, producing a total of 2,700 horse power. By 1849 the town's horse power had doubled to 5,400, a figure which enabled *Allens' Pictorial Guide* of 1852 to claim that 'though the steam engine is not autocratic here, as at Manchester and Leeds, the amount of steam power in requisition is very considerable'. By 1870 there were 814 engines and the horse power was up fivefold on the 1836 figure, to 11,272 h.p.

Using a conversion factor of 16, a contemporary estimated that the 5,400 horse power of 1849 was 'equal to the labour of 86,400 men'. On that basis the steam power available in 1836 must have been equivalent to the labour of 43,200 men. By 1870 the equivalent figure had increased to 180,325. Bearing in mind that Birmingham's total industrial labour force (including children) in 1871 has been reckoned at not more than 150,000, these are staggering figures. Indeed, superficially at least, they would seem to imply that by this time steam power alone had more than doubled the town's industrial capacity.

Moreover, in addition to steam power, the many light manually operated machines which had been brought into use by 1870 must also have been making a considerable impact on output and on unit costs. Two examples of this may be cited. When Joseph Gillott adapted the hand press to the making of steel pens he is reported to have found that 'unassisted, he could produce as many pens as twenty pairs of hands, working under the old system could turn out'. Similarly, it was claimed that the use of dies and hand- or foot-operated presses in the jewellery industry could so increase the output of ear-rings and lockets that 'twenty are produced in the same time as one was formerly made'.

This double-pronged technological development of the early Victorian period needs to be borne in mind when we turn to look at the performance of particular industries. It has repeatedly been suggested, for instance, that the button trade was in decline during these years. In *Birmingham and the*

Left: Birmingham factory chimneys, as shown on a section of the 1904 Bird's-eye View of Birmingham. In 1882 the Borough had 1,671 registered chimneys. Today factory chimneys are becoming almost as rare as water wheels, while many of those which remain have been truncated. The examples shown were photographed from Morton Street, Lichfield Road and Allison Street.

Midland Hardware District, the detailed review of local industry which Samuel Timmins edited in 1866, even John Turner, a prominent contemporary button maker, asserted that the trade at that time could 'scarcely be said to maintain its ground'.

One of the reasons Turner gave for this was the strong foreign competition which had resulted from Sir Robert Peel's abolition of import controls on buttons. Another was the fact that, whereas until the 1840s 'gentlemen wore gilt buttons on their coats, vests and leggings', by high Victorian times they preferred 'the quietest possible buttons . . . and as few of them as is consistent with decency and convenience'.

To some extent, however, these negative factors would presumably have been offset by the steady growth both of national population and of spending power which took place during the middle decades of the nineteenth century. In any case, a good deal of capital investment must have been going into the button industry at this time. We may infer this, in the first place, because as the trade in the traditional gilt 'Brammagem buttons' fell away, a whole series of new lines were developed. Foremost among these were the cloth, figured silk and linen buttons in which a piece of fabric was stretched over a metal frame; and also the vegetable ivory button. This last was made from imported corozo nuts, and as gentlemen's long coats passed out of vogue it came to be much favoured on the short jackets that replaced them.

An even more obvious pointer to unflagging industrial initiative is the fact that such buttons — as well as those made of jet, glass, bone, horn, box wood, rubber and leather — were increasingly being produced in large factories 'where steam power and machinery, more or less complicated, is generally used'. Of the 20 or so big firms of button makers, one of the 'best conducted establishments' in 1852 was W. Elliott and Son in Regent Street, where according to *Allens' Pictorial Guide,*

A foot-operated stamping press being used in the making of buttons.

Left: Elliott's Regent Works, Regent Street – a remarkable survival. The 1839 edition of Wrightson's Directory is already giving William Elliott's address as Regent Street. Below: Button making on the top floor of Elliott's factory, as shown on a mid-nineteenth-century engraving. The women working along the side walls are operating hand presses for the cutting out of blanks.

'upwards of 300 persons' were employed in the making of 'metal, Florentine, silk, and other buttons'. 'Each species', we are told, 'has its own department, so that . . . the sub-division of labour is too minute for us to follow'. But among the processes involved were 'the punching of the disc — the making and fixing of the shank — the gilding or silvering — the stamping of those for livery or other uniforms, &c.' In the Florentine department 'two bits of thin sheet iron, a bit of pasteboard, a bit of thick canvas, and a bit of lasting or silk, are cut out by stamping each circular disc, and all adjusted by a most beautiful machine, and fixed together by two movements of a press, without the aid of glue, rivets, or any other fastening'. All these operations were 'performed with incredible rapidity by females, and although to put together a single button, fourteen pairs of hands and a number of machines are employed, a set of fourteen buttons can be sold for 1d. or 1½d.' (about ½p.). 'Not least striking' to the visitor of mid-nineteenth-century Elliott's was the rapidity with which the finished buttons were 'finally placed upon cards and made up in packets'; 'by one girl, as many as 3,600 buttons could be sewed on in one day, or upwards of 21,000 per week'.

Clearly, the marked contraction of the numbers employed in the button industry — from perhaps 17,000 in 1830 to a mere 6,000 in the 1860s — needs to be viewed against the background of the technological changes that are here apparent. And this is all the more true since we know that by the 1860s there was only one section of the trade which had not been extensively mechanized. This was the making of the ever popular pearl button which, because of the frailty of the material, still had to be turned by hand on a foot lathe. Here a 'few pounds' of capital would be enough to 'enable a respectable workman to commence on his own account'. So pearl button manufacture remained mostly in the hands of small masters and highly skilled workshop craftsmen. Of these there were no less than 2,000 still at work in the 1860s, as against the 4,000 men, women and children employed in all the mechanized branches of the trade.

In terms of the number of workers, and of what those engaged in the industry could hope to make out of it, the mid-Victorian button trade may well have looked in the doldrums. Writing of what he ruefully called 'the Augustan age of button-making in Birmingham' (i.e., before 1840), John Turner claimed that 'both employers and artisans were well off, for . . . while the latter was frequently enabled to earn his £2 to £4 per week, the former was obtaining his £2,000 to £3,000 a year'. Turner does not say how much big employers were making in the 1860s. But he does tell us that, although a few special workmen could still earn '£2 to £4 per week', the average male wage was 25s. (£1.25), while the two-thirds of the factory labour force who were women and young children earned as little as 7s. — 9s. (35p. — 45p.) and 1s. — 1s. 6d. (5p. — 7½p.) respectively.

On the other hand, although we have no figures, the likelihood is that Birmingham—which was virtually Britain's only production centre—was turning out considerably more buttons in 1860 than the 600,000,000 per annum it is said to have produced 20 years before. In fact, the main problem with this mid-Victorian industry could well have been one of over-production, which in turn had been induced by over-competitiveness and over-capitalization. How could the wages of button makers be otherwise than low at a time when porcelain buttons are reported to have been wholesaled for 11d. (under 5p.) and glass buttons at 2d. (under 1p.) per gross (144)!

What we seem to have here then, is an industry which, far from merely developing 'on the lines laid down in the later eighteenth century', was very much in the throes of a major technological transformation. And that transformation, however necessary if the Birmingham button trade was not to disappear altogether, no doubt brought many difficulties to the majority of people concerned.

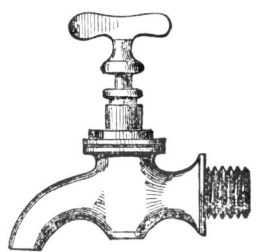

STUFFING BOX BIB COCK.

Brass was Birmingham's pre-eminent mid-Victorian trade, employing about 10,000 workers by 1870. Indeed, Timmins's correspondent, W. C. Aitken, boasted that 'What Manchester is in cotton, Bradford in wool, and Sheffield in steel, Birmingham is in brass'.

Broadly speaking, we may think of this industry operating on three levels. These were the actual making of the alloy; the conversion of the resulting metal into sheets, wire, tubes, etc.; and thirdly, the production of finished articles, either by cutting, stamping, piercing the above, or by direct casting from brass ingots.

The finishing end of the industry was in turn divided into several branches. The 'cabinet' trade made such things as hinges, castors, knobs and window fastenings; the 'lighting' branch, candlesticks, oil lamps and gas fittings; the 'plumbers' branch, water taps, plugs, pumps; and the 'engineering' section, steam cocks, gauges and whistles for machinery.

As in the button trade, technological innovation had wrought major changes in all sections of the brass industry by the 1860s. From 1830 a new method of making brass had been rapidly adopted. This was by the mixing of copper and zinc directly in a crucible, which was much quicker and more efficient than the old, complicated 'cementation' process. It was in the same decade, too, that the brass trade began using iron moulds, instead of the traditional sand moulds, for the casting of standardized products. This development helped to reduce costs, firstly by rendering it unnecessary for fresh moulds to be made after each operation, and secondly by producing more finely finished articles and thereby cutting down on the amount of filing necessary to remove irregularities.

Meanwhile, 'in establishments for the production of sheet metal, wire, tube, &c.' steam power was being introduced, so

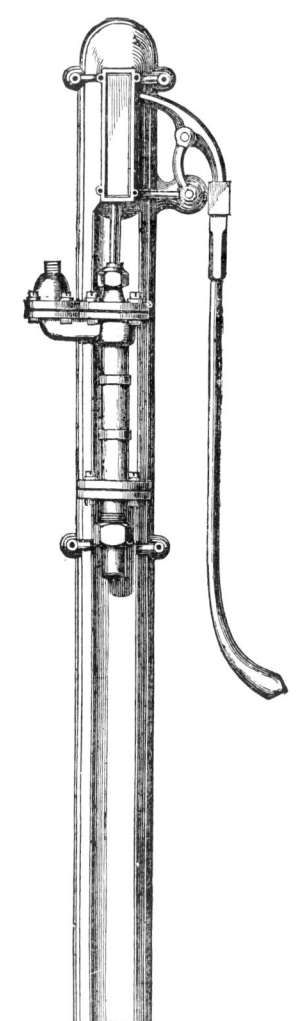

BREEDEN'S PATENT LIFT AND FORCE PUMP.

Two products of J. & W. Breeden and Booth as advertised in the 1874 Kelly's Directory. Their 'Cheapside Works' is shown on page 11.

42

that in Aitken's words:

> . . . rolls of great size and power . . . draw-benches with admirably fitting trains of wheels . . . and wire-drawing blocks . . . revolving truly and silently . . . demonstrate the advantage taken of improved mechanical skill to facilitate producton and lighten labour.

In the finishing branches of the trade, according to the same source, most manufactories had formerly been 'dwelling-houses converted into workshops' where 'some 20, 30 or 40 workmen . . . treddled the turning lathe'. But 'within the last twenty years manufactories have been specially built'; 'shafting, worked by steam power, is led into the shopping to drive the lathes', with special departments being provided for such processes as 'dipping' and 'lacquering'. As a result the small workshop was gradually giving way to the big factory.

Says Aitken:

> Cabinet Brass-foundry establishments, which ten or twelve years ago employed each about 60 or 80 hands, now employ from 150 to 200 each; and one house which embraces several branches of the Brass trade, and which in 1835 employed not more than 100 workmen, now numbers 800.

If only because of the quite exceptional complexity of its products, one would have expected gun making, which employed about 6,000 people in the 1860s, to have been much less amenable to technological progress than the button or brass industries. Yet even here the foundation in 1862 of the Birmingham Small Arms Company by an initial group of 16 local firms went a long way towards mechanizing at least the military side of the trade. For this venture was based on the American system of, in effect, mass producing rifles with interchangeable parts — a method which had been successfully introduced at the British government's Enfield factory some 8 years before.

The key to this system was the use of lathes or milling machines for cutting irregular forms with such accuracy that, once the burs and marks of the cutting tools had been filed off by hand, each part would be exactly alike and therefore interchangeable. Such machines consisted of two lathes placed side by side, the one containing an exact copy in hardened steel of the object required, and the other the block of material out of which the replica was to be cut.

Covering 6 acres, the B.S.A. works at Small Heath was powered by two 180 h.p. steam engines, and the way it functioned was outlined by John Goodman in the Timmins volume. The making of the barrels began on the 'forging machines, American drops, steam hammers, and steam drops' of the Smithy. They then passed to 'a room containing the furnaces for annealing and hardening', followed by others for 'pickling', 'browning', 'rifling', and for 'the milling of the barrels, locks, bands, &c.' Meanwhile, on the first floor of the factory there was a room which contained 'the milling machines for some of the lighter parts of the gun', together with departments for 'the hand-filing of the locks, sights, &c., the

"viewing" of the parts of the gun in all the several stages', and for putting together and packing.

Some traditional craftsmen were required for the finishing and assembling operations. In order to save on the 'outlay for machinery', too, the B.S.A. bought in certain standard components from specialist outworkers. But otherwise the new approach, which alone enabled Birmingham to retain a competitive place in the military small arms market, gave this section of the industry a heavily capitalized and essentially factory-based organization. And from the manufacturer's point of view, its great advantage was that it required, not only a relatively small labour force, but also a relatively unskilled and therefore inexpensive one. Nor was the B.S.A. on its own. Westley Richards, the firm which originated the breech-loading gun, developed a highly integrated factory, while in 1864 Charles Reeves was employing 400 in the making of rifles and swords.

Even in traditional gun manufacture, by the mid-Victorian period, mechanization was far from unknown. Gun polishers were using steam power; and so were firms which specialized in the making of barrels for cheap sporting guns and African muskets. The machine for 'making gun barrels by means of grooved rollers' is said to have been invented during a strike of barrel welders—who thereafter tried to prevent its adoption by Luddite threats on the home and mill of the inventor, a Mr. Osborne. However, by 1874, at least 5 of the 28 gun barrel makers listed in *Kelly's Directory* are known to have

An early photograph of the B.S.A. at Small Heath, built in 1862 to the round-arched Italianate design of T. W. Goodman.

The remains of the B.S.A. today—as interesting in their way as medieval monastic ruin.

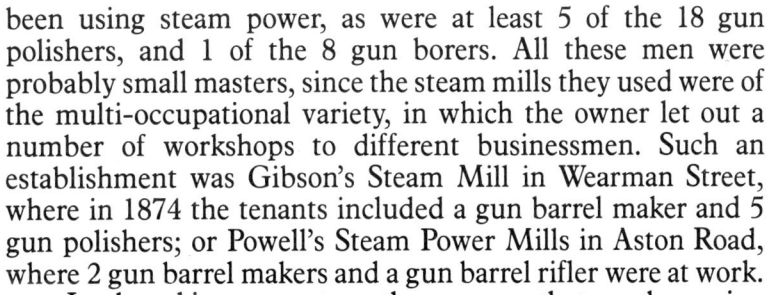

The making of barrels at the works of Messrs. Sargant. A William Lucas Sargant, gun maker, is listed in the 1874 Kelly's at 33 Whittall Street. The illustration shows a barrel's edges being hammered together after it had been pre-formed or 'curled' by means of grooved rollers. The rolling must have been done elsewhere, but there is a supply of half-formed barrels resting against the side wall.

been using steam power, as were at least 5 of the 18 gun polishers, and 1 of the 8 gun borers. All these men were probably small masters, since the steam mills they used were of the multi-occupational variety, in which the owner let out a number of workshops to different businessmen. Such an establishment was Gibson's Steam Mill in Wearman Street, where in 1874 the tenants included a gun barrel maker and 5 gun polishers; or Powell's Steam Power Mills in Aston Road, where 2 gun barrel makers and a gun barrel rifler were at work.

Lock making was yet another process that was becoming mechanized by the 1860s. Goodman tells us that 'till within the last few years locks were entirely the production of hand labour, the several parts were forged on the anvil by men whose wonderful skill became proverbial'. However, 'at the present time', he goes on, 'the steam hammer and stamp are superseding the forge'.

Gradually, therefore, mechanization was having its effect even in Birmingham's oldest surviving traditional industry. Indeed, according to an official report of 1868, steam power was by then being used in the gun trade at the rate of 20 h.p. per 100 workers, as against 5 h.p. per 100 workers among brass chandlers and 4 h.p. among button makers.

Despite this, however, even in the 1860s, and indeed for long afterwards, the most prestigious section of the industry, the 'birding trade', or manufacture of high class sporting guns, remained almost exclusively the prerogative of traditional craftsmen.

This was the part of the trade that was concentrated in the famous Gun Quarter, where it had already been accommodated for over a century, and where — despite the fact that most of it was obliterated by the Inner Ring Road Scheme — a small

remnant has miraculously survived to the present day. Centred on St. Mary's Church, the ancient Gun Quarter was a tightly packed rectangular area bounded by the Fazeley Canal in the north, Snow Hill in the west, Lichfield Street in the south, and Lancaster Street in the east. Its twentieth-century remnant consists of parts of four of the quarter's northern streets — Price Street, Loveday Street, Bath Street and Princip Street.

To all intents and purposes, in the making of high quality sporting guns mechanization and steam power counted for nothing. The division of labour, on the other hand, was of supreme importance. For the skills of not far short of 50 different sorts of highly specialized craftsmen might be involved in the manufacture of a single fowling piece.

Such craftsmen fell into two main categories: the 'material makers' who produced the various parts of the gun, and the 'setters-up' who were responsible for assembling and finishing it. Among the former were barrel makers, lock makers, sight stampers, trigger stampers, ramrod makers, and gun-furniture makers. Among the 'setters-up' were the jiggers who worked on the breech end of the gun, the stockers who shaped the stock and let in the lock and barrel, the strippers who prepared the gun for rifling and proof; the hardeners, polishers, borers and riflers; the barrel setters who straightened the barrel; the engravers, browners, and the lock freers who adjusted the working parts.

Many of these operations called for 'the very highest skill'. Goodman gives an example:

> . . . the degree of straightness required in a gun barrel is nothing short of absolute perfection. The practised eye of a barrel setter can detect a deviation from the straight line which no mechanical contrivance can discover. He accomplishes his object by looking through the barrel, while standing in front of a window, and causing the shade of the upper edge of the window to traverse up and down the tube. The irregularities in the outline of the shade show him where the inaccuracies exist. These he removes by well directed blows of a hammer, the perfecting blows being given with a light wooden mallet.

Both material makers and setters-up could be individual outworkers, small masters employing half a dozen assistants, or quite substantial firms with 30 or 40 workers. In any case, their 'materials' were purchased, or their 'setting-up' paid for, by the so-called 'gun makers'. These were the factors and merchants of the industry. But whereas in some local trades such people were little more than wholesale dealers, in the gun business they had the more complex role of actually initiating and controlling the activities of the material makers and setters-up; or in other words, of organizing, co-ordinating and financing what were in effect long, complicated chains of production.

No doubt it was this unusual organizational structure of the traditional gun industry which had encouraged its concentration in a single area from as long ago as the mid-eighteenth century. The constant need to be sending parts

Map: The Gun Quarter in 1852 — from Allens' Pictorial Guide. Above: Gordon Walker, Price Street. The hanging sign reads 'Importer of French Walnut Gunstock Blanks'. Above centre: Bailons Gunmakers Ltd., Bath Street — still manufacturing firearms in the Gun Quarter today. Above right: M. A. Lloyd & Son, Princip Street. In 1874 this was the works of W. & W. Scott, 'gun and pistol makers'. Below: A Georgian house in Price Street used by gun makers throughout the Victorian period, and for long afterwards. Below centre: New Buildings, Price Street, erected before 1874. Below right: New Buildings from the rear, showing the proliferation of shopping.

from one workshop to another would alone have made this desirable, to say nothing of the gun maker's need to keep in regular touch with large numbers of workshop proprietors and individual craftsmen. Moreover, this proximity of work places would be particularly important at the assembly and finishing end of the trade. Parts might well be manufactured elsewhere in Birmingham, or even be brought in—as many gun locks were—from the workshops of the Black Country. But even as late as 1874 we find that of the 329 gun makers, gun stockers, polishers, engravers and finishers whose addresses are given in *Kelly's Directory,* no less than 210 (or 64%) had their premises in the Gun Quarter itself. One can therefore almost think of this unique complex of workshops—some of them accommodated in purpose-built units by the mid-nineteenth century, but many still in small converted houses—as a vast industrial co-operative; and as such, it may well have functioned as efficiently in its way as the B.S.A., or any other large factory.

A typical corner of the Gun Quarter about 1860 was characterized by G. C. Allen as follows:

> A passage from a main street communicates with a courtyard, from which two blocks of three-storied buildings rise facing one another, and at intervals staircases lead up from the courtyard to the workshops . . . Each shop consists of one or two small rooms, in which various operations in connection with the 'setting-up' of the guns are performed. In one shop two women will be found engaged in barrel-browning; in another a single workman is shaping the gun stocks from a pile of roughly cut wooden blocks . . . Elsewhere a lock-filer is working with one assistant, and in another shop leading from the same staircase an engraver and his sons carry on their trade . . . Each craftsmen works for one of several gun-makers, and receives the materials and parts from them; but he hires his own workshop, and pays his own assistants. In 1860, not only the 'setting-up' but much of the 'material-making', which has since passed into factories, was carried on in this way.

Goodman helps to complete the picture:

> At any time, in the neighbourhood of St. Mary's Church . . . the lads may be seen, one with half a dozen stocked guns on his shoulder, conveying them from the stocker to the screwer; another with a tray full of locks for the polisher; a third on his way with a few barrels to the Proof-house, and so on.

Standing in front of the entrance to the 'New Buildings' in Price Street, with its board of 'Shopping Tenants' to the left of the drainpipe, it is perhaps not too difficult to vizualize such a scene even today. Working here in 1874 were a pistol maker, a gun maker, a gun barrel maker, a gun barrel filer, a gun barrel rifler, a gun action filer, two gun implement makers, two gun stockers, a stock finisher and three engravers.

It is interesting, too, that one of the gun implement makers listed was Thomas Lightwood & Son, and this business certainly seems to have flourished. For its name still runs along the whole of the first floor of the building. Nearby in Loveday Street is a pair of early nineteenth-century houses which bear sign boards reading 'G. E. LEWIS & SONS, GUN & RIFLE MAKERS'. However frail and ephemeral it now seems, this

Above: The 'shopping entrance' to New Buildings. Right: G. E. Lewis & Sons, Lower Loveday Street. A wide range of name plates and wall inscriptions provide evidence of many years of sub-letting and multi-occupation.

sight cannot have changed much in a hundred years. In the 1874 *Kelly's* we find 'Lewis, George Edward, gunmaker, 33 Loveday Street'. And the same firm can still be found in today's telephone directory, trading from the same address. Thomas Lightwoods, too, are still in business, with their works in nearby Fleet Street.

Although jewellery had been gradually emerging alongside — and to some extent, out of — the declining buckle and toy trades from the mid-eighteenth century, it was not until around the accession of Queen Victoria that it became a trade of major importance. From then onwards, though, as J. S. Wright tells us in Timmins:

> The discovery of gold in Australia and California, the vastly increased wealth of England and her Colonies, together with the desire for personal adornment . . . united to give an unparalleled prosperity to this branch of industry.

Yet if jewellery was the newest and arguably the most consistently prosperous of nineteenth-century Birmingham's four staple trades, it was also the one which proved the most resistant to technological change, and in that sense the most obdurately traditional. By the 1860s, according to Wright, such things as gold ear-rings could be made by means of 'dies and machinery'. 'Steam power and elaborate machinery' were also employed 'to a small extent' in the making of gold, silver, and gilt chains. Even more significantly, at the bottom end of the market there were manufacturers who used 'the press and the stamp' to turn out 'imitations of the more elaborate and delicately finished jewellery', so that 'a locket, which in gold might be worth from 15s. to 30s., is produced in metal gilt for a penny'. By the mid-Victorian period, therefore, steam power was being used to a minor extent, while in a few branches of the trade small factories employing unskilled or semi-skilled labour were to be found. Indeed, Messrs. Goode & Bolland, manufacturers of gold and silver chains, constructed a 'roomy and substantial factory' in 1853 to house 400 workers.

Nevertheless, even the cheap stamped and pressed wares had to be assembled and finished by skilled manual workers. And 'the class of best work', which included such things as gold and silver necklaces, brooches, rings and bracelets, often set with precious stones, depended entirely on highly skilled craftsmen.

'Probably nine out of every ten of the master jewellers', Wright tells us, 'were originally themselves workmen':

> All that is needed for a workman to start as a master is a peculiarly-shaped bench and a leather apron, one or two pounds worth of tools (including a blow-pipe), and for material, a few sovereigns, and some ounces of copper and zinc. His shop may be the top room of his house, or a small building over the wash-house, at a rent of 2s. or 2s. 6d. per week, and the indispensable gas-jet, which the Gas Company will supply on credit. With these appliances, and a skilful hand, he may produce scarf-pins, studs, links, rings, lockets, &c., &c., for all of which he will find a ready market on the Saturday among the numerous 'factors', whose special business it is to supply the shopkeepers throughout the country.

So, as Wright himself pointed out, jewellery was the trade *par excellence* to illustrate that 'peculiarity which places Birmingham in favourable contrast with every other town and centre of industry in the country — namely, the great number of independent manufacturers it supports'.

Apart from the almost continuously advantageous economic conditions, it was no doubt the heavy emphasis on skilled craftsmanship, rather than on machines, that caused the numbers engaged in the industry to increase so steadily. By 1860 there were 7,000 — 7,500 working in the jewellery, silver tableware, electro-plating and other subsidiary trades. A decade later the equivalent figure was not far short of 10,000.

The factors in this industry were merely responsible for marketing, leaving the master jeweller or workshop owner to control the entire production process. Nevertheless, these factors obviously earned their keep. 'London now depends mainly on Birmingham for the supply of articles suitable for the middle classes', says Wright, adding 'it is only necessary to walk from the Bank to Hyde Park to enable any person to form an idea of the ingenuity, skill, and taste of the Birmingham artisans'. But then by the 1860s most of Britain's jewellery, both cheap and of high quality, came from Birmingham — rival centres like Derby having been virtually shut down. And the

Right: Early villa houses in Frederick Street. The second from the right, with its impressive Doric façade, remained a private dwelling in 1874. But the nearest (No. 26) was then occupied by 'Simeon Greenberg, goldsmith'. The legend 'Goldsmith' can still be seen, cut in relief, above the doorway. Far right: Later jewellers' villas on the Vyse Estate – Plantagenet Buildings, Spencer Street.

'merchants', who specialized in 'exportation', had meanwhile built up a flourishing foreign and colonial trade.

The products of the jewellery industry were a great deal more varied than those of the gun trade. Yet all its wares called for the application in various ways of a common range of skills. It is not surprising therefore that many of these skills should have developed into distinct sub-trades, with master jewellers farming out work to specialist diamond cutters, gem setters, engravers, polishers, and so on. Given such practices, it was also natural that — as with the gun trade — those concerned with jewellery should eventually tend to become concentrated in one part of the town.

The process began early, with toymakers and jewellers moving into the recently built houses of the Newhall Estate during the latter part of the eighteenth century. By 1830 a marked concentration was to be found in the streets immediately north of St. Paul's — which was eventually to become known as 'the Jewellers' Church'. It so happened, too, that the Vyse Estate, which lay immediately north of this district, was being developed during the years immediately following the gold discoveries of 1849-51. Here the properties were rather larger than the usual house-workshop complex. And this fact, plus their proximity to the St. Paul's area, and the boom conditions which the industry was then enjoying, ensured that by 1865 most of the Vyse Estate had also been taken over by members of the various jewellery trades.

Happily, despite a good deal of demolition and redevelopment, a considerable proportion of the resulting Jewellery Quarter is still intact today. Indeed, it has recently been accorded 'Improvement Area' status.

Perhaps no comparable stretch of local Victorian townscape is more worthy of preservation than this 'Hockley Square Mile',

Above: John Betts & Sons Ltd., 'Precious Metal Smelters and Refiners', Charlotte Street. Established in 1760, this is the oldest surviving firm in the Jewellery Quarter; it also occupies one of the oldest surviving buildings.

which is roughly speaking bounded by Graham Street/Newhall Street/Charlotte Street/St. Paul's Square in the south; Legge Lane/Carver Street/Icknield Street in the west; and Key Hill/Great Hampton Street/Constitution Hill in the north-east.

Here we have something that must be virtually unparalleled elsewhere in twentieth-century Britain. For the Jewellery Quarter is an efficiently functioning modern industrial zone in which, not only are there whole streets of workshops and small factories which look much as they must have looked a century ago, but in a considerable number of cases they are still being used in much the same way.

True the larger firms of the quarter — employing 40 or more workers — tend now to have adopted modern mass production methods. But alongside these there are innumerable one-man or small businesses, quite frequently specializing in a single aspect of jewellery manufacture. And most of the jewellers of this sort, as well as occupying the same workshops as their Victorian counterparts, are still employing virtually the same tools, materials and techniques.

Moreover, an appreciable number of both the small and larger firms can themselves be traced back into the Victorian past, comparison with the 1874 *Kelly's Directory* not infrequently showing that they have occupied the same accommodation for over a century. This is continuity indeed: a living museum which, because even today high-class jewellery remains essentially a handicraft, is also a thriving contemporary industry.

Map: The Jewellery Quarter, from Murray's Warwickshire, 1899. (Mount Street is now regarded as part of Newhall Street). Below left: 3–7 Warstone Lane. Below: The doorway of No. 7. Among its name-plates are those of a 'diamond mounter', a 'brazing and soldering' company, an 'art engraving' service, a 'jeweller' and a 'jeweller and mounter'. Below right: 22-46 Vittoria Street. An interesting progression of properties, from 22-4 which were back-to-back houses in origin, to the large, purpose-built Unity Works. Far right: The door-plate of the Unity Works. In 1874 this property is listed as 'Jenkins, Henry & Sons, die sinkers (Unity Works)'.

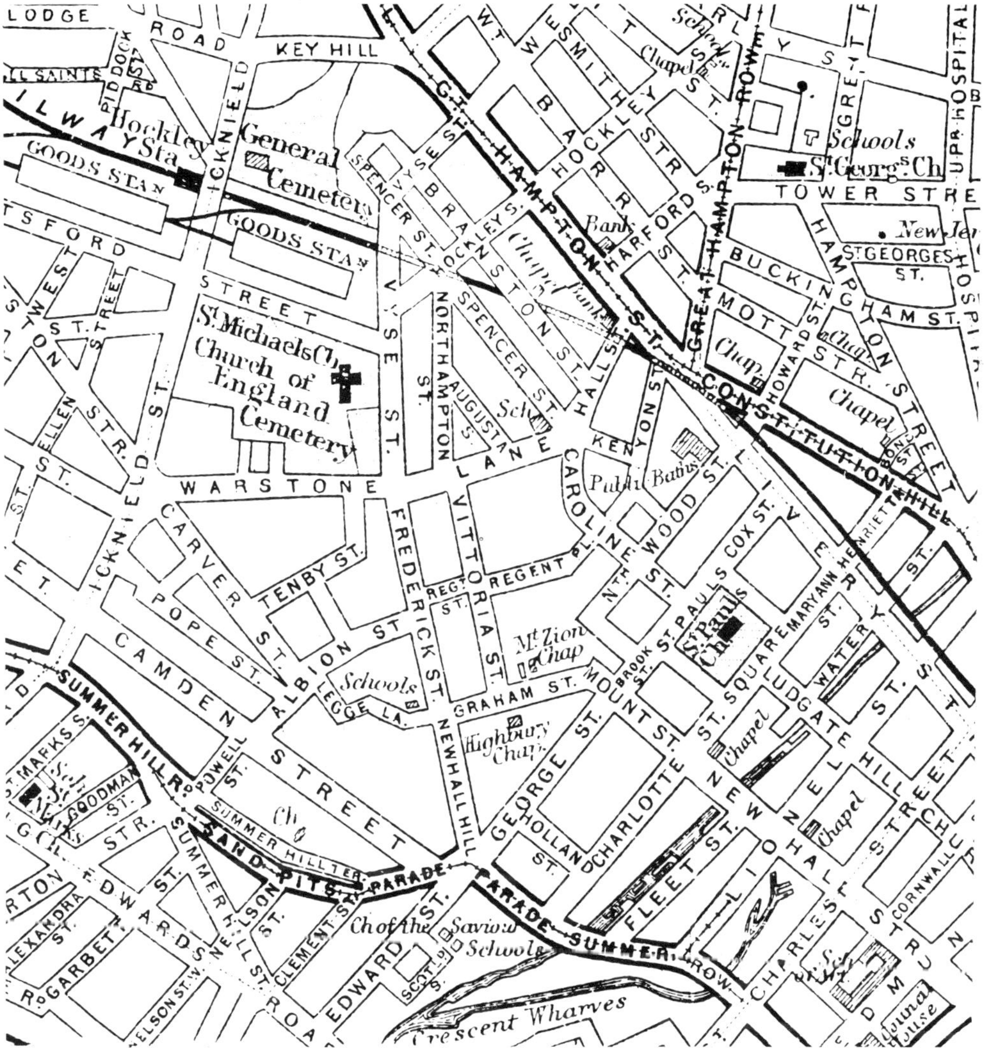

The Thousand Trades

Sheffield plating, by means of which thin strips of gold or silver were laboriously soldered on to copper articles, had been an important branch of the toy and jewellery trades since the days of Matthew Boulton. However, by 1840 Henry and G. R. Elkington had totally revolutionized this branch of manufacture by taking up an invention of the Birmingham surgeon John Wright, and introducing the electro-plating of 'German silver' or nickel.

In an article commemorating the fiftieth anniversary of the Elkington-Wright patent, a local journalist described how cutlery, tableware and ornaments of all kinds, having first been made in nickel by various casting and stamping processes, were then transformed in 'the magic trough with its solution of nitrate of silver and cyanide of gold':

> All that was necessary was to place the article to be plated in this solution, suspended in it by a copper wire which served also to carry the electric current to it, then whenever the wonder working current was turned on, the electricity attacked the nitrate of silver or cyanide of gold, broke up the chemical combination which held the component parts together, seized the liberated silver or gold and forced it into chemical combination with the surface of the German silver. In absolute silence, without a ripple on the surface of the bath, all this went on. Such was the mystery of electro-plating in 1840, when Messrs. Elkington patented it, and without change it is carried on now.

At first, in fact, the new process confronted the Elkingtons with many technical, managerial and commercial problems. But with the help of the pen maker Josiah Mason, who became a partner in 1842, these were gradually overcome. In particular, although the prices of electro-plated goods were originally even higher than those of Sheffield plate, 'by the division of labour and the introduction of machinery', production costs were slowly reduced until 'articles of elegance and luxury which great wealth alone could once afford' had been brought within the reach of middle class families everywhere.

The statue of Sir Robert Peel, cast by Messrs. Elkington & Mason at a cost of 2,000 guineas. Unveiled in 1855, this is currently located outside the Police Training Centre, Pershore Road.

Subsequently the Elkingtons adapted the same principle of electrical metallurgy to the making of massive bronze statues. Only in this case the electro deposit, instead of coating the outer surface of an otherwise finished article, was induced to settle on the inside of a hollow plaster mould until it had produced bronze walls about ¾" thick. Among the public memorials designed and made by the Elkingtons in this way was Birmingham's own 7' high statue of Sir Robert Peel which originally stood at the top end of New Street.

With a payroll of 500 workers by 1850, and perhaps 1,000 by 1870, Elkington's supremacy in the electro-plating trade was absolutely beyond challenge. Nevertheless the mid-Victorian town had over 80 other 'electro-platers and gilders', as against a mere handful of firms persisting with the traditional method.

By the late 1840s the splendid Elkington Factory, which stood in Newhall Street alongside the Fazeley Canal, had

been put into its final form, reputably by Josiah Mason. From then onwards it became famous as a showplace; 'the whole establishment', Elihu Burritt tells us, was made 'accessible to all who wish to visit it'. So perhaps it is appropriate that, although stripped of its elegant Classical façade, this important building today provides the core of the Museum of Science and Industry, and as such is still in the business of attracting visitors.

Electro-plating was one of the new 'wonder' industries of early Victorian Birmingham. Another was pen making. It was about 1829 that Joseph Gillott, a Sheffield immigrant, successfully adapted the ubiquitous hand press to the making of steel pen nibs. Thereafter, despite the friendly rivalry of Josiah Mason and the Mitchell brothers who began making steel pens at about the same time, Gillott remained the pace-setter, until he was eventually able to build the renowned 'Victoria Works' or 'Gillott's Manufactory' which still stands in Graham Street.

With the ever-growing emphasis on letter writing, record keeping and education, the demand for pens seems almost to have become insatiable. Moreover, by 1866 Samuel Timmins is claiming that Birmingham had established itself as 'the great

seat of this manufacture', 'the pen shop of the world'. There were then 12 pen factories in the town, which together employed 2,410 workers.

For the better quality pens a succession of hand presses continued to be used: 'to cut out the blanks, to pierce the hole, to form the nib, to emboss the pattern, and to make the name'. But it is also clear from Timmins that, as in other industries, steam power was becoming increasingly important. Indeed, apart from its use in the rolling down of Sheffield steel strip to the required gauge, 'the commonest export pens' were already being made on 'self-acting machinery'. As always, too, mechanization led to a tumbling of prices. In the 1830s the cheapest nibs had cost 5s. (25p.) per gross. By the 1860s, steam power, the growth of the market, and 'the pressure of mutual competition', had brought the bottom price down to 1½d. (under 1p.) per gross.

Hockley Tools Ltd., Alma Street – described on the 1886 25 inch Ordnance Survey map as a 'Bedstead Factory'.

The beginning of the Victorian predilection for ornamental iron and brass bedsteads, and the discovery of how to make them by dovetailing the parts together, seem more or less to have coincided with the accession of the Queen. Again, Birmingham became the principal centre for their manufacture. By the mid-Victorian period between 20 and 30 firms, many employing 100 workers or more, were producing perhaps 5,000 bedsteads per week, of which at least a third went for export.

Another new industry that arrived with the new monarch was the manufacture of railway rolling stock. As well as representing the town's first major incursion into the production of wheeled vehicles, this industry developed a practice which was later to prove so effective in the car trade: namely, that of getting its wheels, axles and other components made for it in the nearby Black Country. About 1,200 men and boys worked as smiths, carpenters, painters, etc. at the Metro

The Midland Works, Landor Street. In 1874 this was the works of the 'Midland Wagon Company', railway carriage and wagon builders'. The photograph illustrates the factory's location, between the Birmingham—Warwick Canal (near bridge) and the railway line to Derby (far bridge).

Left: Hay Mills today. The entrance to Webster and Horsfall can be seen on the left, and part of a row of mid-nineteenth-century workers' cottages on the right. In between are the school and church (St. Cyprian's) built by James Horsfall in 1863 and 1873-4 respectively. Below: Hay Mills in 1856, from a contemporary painting (by kind permission of Webster & Horsfall Ltd.). Right: Making the wire for the Atlantic Cable—from the Illustrated London News, 1866.

Carriage and Waggon Company's massive plant at Saltley. And with 2 of the 3 other big rolling stock works situated among the viaducts, stations and goods yards of the same area, this north-eastern sector of the Victorian town might well have become known as the 'Railway Quarter'.

Alongside Birmingham's staple trades, on the one hand, and her completely new ones on the other, there were many industries which, although they had long existed in the town, were now being transformed and expanded beyond recognition. The 1841 census lists only 380 wire workers. By 1871 there were 2,630; and this sevenfold increase in the labour force had occurred despite the fact that, with an average steam capacity of 81 h.p. per 100 workers by the latter date, this was far and away the most extensively mechanized of all Birmingham trades.

Among the principal wire-drawing firms was that of James Horsfall, who, following many years of secret experimentation, patented an incomparably strong high-tensile steel wire in 1847. After moving from Digbeth to Hay Mills, Yardley, and amalgamating with the Websters of Penns Mill, Sutton Coldfield, this firm secured a virtual monopoly of the European piano wire trade. It also became a major supplier of the Redditch needle and fish-hook industry, and of the heavier steel wires that were now in such demand for engineering, machinery, colliery winding ropes and ship's rigging.

Despite the fact that Webster & Horsfall had already supplied the French with a telegraph cable which successfully linked Marseilles and Algiers, the order for the first Atlantic Cable of 1863 did not come their way—or indeed, to Birmingham. However, having so much stirred the popular imagination, this first direct link between England and America went dead within a month; and Webster & Horsfall's

Patent Steel Wire had to be used to recover it. The firm was then commissioned to supply the replacement, completing the 1,600 tons of cable involved, ahead of schedule, in 11 months. The same company, occupying the same premises, is still receiving orders for Atlantic Brand Spring Wire from all over the world today.

Not only steel, but iron, copper and brass wires were produced in Birmingham, and together these gave rise to a bewildering variety of subsidiary industries. In most of them, according to Timmins's correspondents, machinery had transformed 'the old handicraft character of the trade'. This applied to wire weaving, net making and chain making. 'A machine tended by a child can make an endless chain', we read, 'at the rate of nine feet per minute, thus doing in one minute the work that formerly took a good workwoman at least half an hour'.

In the same way, 'nails, pins, staples, cotters and many similar articles' were 'no longer made by hand'. Even bird cages, instead of being produced in 'the old tedious slow style', were 'turned out with astonishing rapidity and simplicity'. With umbrella furniture, on the other hand, 'the greater part' of which 'had long been manufactured in Birmingham', although 'steam is applied to the production of various parts . . . they continue also to be made by hand with lathes and hand-work presses'.

The screw industry is interesting because it seems to have undergone two technological revolutions within a few years. Describing 'the laborious and tedious process' by which screws were made in the early nineteenth century, Joseph Chamberlain wrote:

> The wire was first cut into the required lengths, then the head was forged on the shank by the smith. A slot for the screw-driver to work in, called the 'nick', was then cut by a hand saw with fine teeth; and lastly the thread or 'worm' was filed out by hand.

The London Works, Cranford Street, Smethwick – formerly the headquarters of the Patent Nut and Bolt Co. Ltd., now the Group Head Office of GKN.

The Cornwall Works. Left, in the 1880s; below, in the 1960s; right, to-day.

The cost of such a screw can be imagined, and it is no wonder they are so rarely found in antique furniture! Only extremely minor improvements occurred in the trade down to the late 1840s. But then the adoption of German methods enabled steam power to be introduced, with women operating a series of machines that successively headed, turned, nicked and wormed the screws. In 1854, however, J. S. Nettlefold and Joseph Chamberlain Senior paid £30,000 for the English rights in newly invented American machinery. This made pointed screws from nickel wire in two entirely automatic operations: and with such efficiency that one woman could attend many machines.

Joseph Chamberlain, the future mayor and politician, joined the firm in 1854, at the age of 18, and his flair and initiative, plus the take-over of two big rival companies, soon established Nettlefold and Chamberlain as Britain's — as well as Birmingham's — leading firm of screw makers. Meanwhile, in a closely related trade, the adoption of American methods and accompanying amalgamations were producing yet another national giant. This was the Patent Nut and Bolt Company Limited, whose headquarters was at the still extant London Works, Smethwick.

Like the wire trades, the engineering sector of Birmingham industry, apart from increasing the output of steam engines, weighing machines, scientific instruments and other established lines, was constantly extending the range of its products. Perhaps the greatest innovator here was Richard Tangye, who came to Birmingham from Cornwall in 1852, closely followed by his two brothers. Within fifteen years they were employing 1,000 men at their massive Cornwall Works, Smethwick, had opened a warehouse in London and built up a world-wide export trade. 'Very few firms have introduced more "novelties" than we have', wrote Tangye in his autobiography:

I believe that four-fifths of our business, including pumping machinery, hydraulic machinery generally, lifting tackle, and, to a large extent, steam engines, is not only new to Birmingham, constituting a distinct addition to its manufacturing industry, but is also the result of new inventions, or adaptations, previously unknown.

A similar innovative role was played by Chance Brothers in the until then relatively unimportant glass trade. This firm took over a crown glass factory at Smethwick in 1824, began making sheet window glass in 1832, then pushed into the manufacture of optical glass, lighthouse lenses and — from the 1850s — of rolled plate glass. By this time it was the largest firm of glass makers in Britain, with the proud boast that it had supplied nearly a million feet of window glass for the Crystal Palace.

Novel in a different way was the work of F. & C. Osler of Broad Street, who established a high reputation for their cut and ornamental flint glass. Among this firm's most exotic products were the 'lofty crystal fountain' for the Great Exhibition and a candelabra for Mohammad's tomb at Mecca. Samuel Sidney wrote in his *Railway Rides* of 1851:

The changes of fashion and the discoveries of science always find Birmingham prepared to march in their van, and skilfully execute the work needed in iron, in brass, in gold and silver, in all the mixed metals and in glass . . . and when England demands a Palace to hold the united contributions of 'The Industry of the World' a Birmingham banker finds the contractor and the credit, and Birmingham manufacturers find the iron, the glass, and the skill needed for the most rapid and gigantic piece of building ever executed in one year.

We miss an essential aspect of the Victorian experience unless we bear in mind the tremendous sense of wonder which was evoked, not only by the endless stream of new industrial products, but also by the wholly unprecedented manufacturing processes that were producing them. This becomes clear from a glance at *Allens' Pictorial Guide* of 1852, for instance, where Birmingham's leading factories are presented to the middle class traveller as major tourist attractions. He is told that R. F. Sturge's manufactory in Broad Street, where 'a great variety of British plate and Britannia metal articles' are produced, 'is at all times open for persons of respectability'; that 'strangers are liberally permitted to inspect' Clifford's Rolling Mills in Fazeley Street; or Phipson's Pin Manufactory in Mott Street, where 10 million pins are made weekly and the 'great variety of ingenious and complicated operations must excite the pleasure and astonishment of the stranger'. And of course, as in the eighteenth century so in Victorian times, among the strangers who came to see Birmingham at work were some who needed — or who should have needed — no introduction. Showell wrote in 1885:

From the grand old days of Boulton and his Soho, down to today, there has been hardly a Prince or potentate, white, black, copper, or coffee coloured, who has visited England, but that has come to peep at our workshops, mayor after mayor having the 'honour' to toady to them and trot them round the back streets and slums to where the men of the bench, the file

The visit of the Prince of Wales to Gillott's Pen Factory, 1874.

Below: The Midland Bank, New Street. Birmingham gave Britain two of its 'big five' banks, Lloyds (originally Taylors & Lloyds, founded in 1765), and the Midland (originally the Birmingham & Midland, founded in 1836). This fine Classical building was opened in 1869 and is the oldest surviving Midland Bank in the country. Right: The Birmingham Exchange. Formerly facing the Midland Bank, across Stephenson Place, this Gothic building was erected 1863-5 and demolished about a century later. Apart from the main hall, or Exchange proper, it incorporated offices, a restaurant and shops.

and the hammer have been diligently working generation after generation, for the fame and the name of our world-known town.

The middle fifty years of the nineteenth century have been called 'the classic era of the expanding, competitive, capitalist economy'. But this expansion did not only depend on inventive ability, 'the men of the bench', and constantly improving production methods. Businesses had to be financed.

In the early nineteenth century capital was scarce in Birmingham, if only because—with dozens of small masters competing fiercely against each other—returns on investment tended to be extremely low. By the late 1820s there were 6 banking houses in the town, and these firms were playing a pivotal role in the smooth running of its economy. Apart from aiding transactions of all kinds by the issue of paper notes, each bank tended to specialize in the lending of money to a particular branch of trade, so that it acquired an intimate knowledge of the risks and rewards involved.

The castastrophic run on the banks in 1825, however, had revealed the insecurity of private 'country' banks, and over the next thirty years the banking services of the town were strengthened and improved in two main ways. To begin with, the Bank of England established a branch here in 1827, and by the mid-1850s this institution—with its unassailably safe gold reserves—was supplying almost all the paper money that circulated in the town. Indeed, its notes had virtually come to be regarded—as they are today—as 'national currency'. Meanwhile, the amount of capital available to Birmingham industry was enormously increased by the development of bigger 'joint stock' banks. Between the opening of the Birmingham Banking Company, which was the town's first joint stock bank, in 1829, and the closing of Spooner & Attwood's in 1856, all the town's private houses either disappeared or transformed themselves, leaving the provision of capital in the hands of 7 more broadly based joint stock banks.

Other institutions which helped to facilitate the growth and smooth running of local business were the Chamber of Commerce and the Birmingham Exchange. After a fitful early history, the former was established on a permanent basis in 1855. The Exchange Building, Stephenson Place, was opened ten years later as a central venue where merchants and manufacturers could undertake their transactions. The 1874 *Kelly's Directory* tells us:

> There is a large commercial class in Birmingham, many merchants, factors, accountants, agents, and stockbrokers, and a great body of clerks. The merchants and factors form the chief means of distributing the productions of the town, the merchants by their agencies and correspondents abroad, and the factors by their travellers, who carry samples of hardware and solicit orders from every town in Great Britain.

By the 1860s industrial joint stock companies, like the Patent Nut and Bolt Company or the B.S.A., were beginning to make their appearance. Protected by limited liability and able to raise large amounts of capital, they were gradually to surpass the privately owned and directed business. But down to this time virtually all Birmingham's big firms were the creation of able and resourceful individuals. Such a man was the great brass founder Robert Winfield, who started his business about 1820. 'Old men', wrote W. J. Davis in 1892, 'remember the little stucco building . . . where that eminent manufacturer commenced business in a very small way; saw it gradually over-topped by huge piles, which from time to time were added, till the place became, as it was said, "a little town"'. 'In addition to his brassfoundry trade', another nineteenth-century writer tells us, 'Winfield gradually added the manufacture of brass, copper and tin tubing, gas-fittings and chandeliers, iron and brass bedsteads, ship's fittings, brass fittings for shop fronts . . . and he was for forty years largely engaged in the coal business'.

Another much admired early Victorian industrialist was George Frederick Muntz. Born in 1797, after spending one year at school in Small Heath, he entered the family's modest metal rolling business at the age of 13. Four years later he had suddenly to take it over, on his father's untimely death. It was in 1832—the same year as he succeeded Thomas Attwood as chairman of the Birmingham Political Union—that Muntz patented the alloy of copper and zinc which proved so much better, as well as cheaper, than copper for the sheathing of timber ships. But to establish the superiority of his new 'yellow metal', Muntz had to sell it without profit at first, as well as guaranteeing shipowners against any loss that might be caused by its failure. It was a gigantic gamble, the outcome of which remained in doubt for several years. Fortunately by 1844 about 400 London ships were fitted with Muntz metal and soon the shipowners of Liverpool and other ports began to follow suit. Meanwhile, Muntz—as well as being elected an M.P. for Birmingham—had established a new and bigger works at

John Yates's Exchange Works, Aston, 1858.

George Frederick Muntz, 1797-1857.

Smethwick, where he soon had a workforce of 200. A stubborn, rough-mannered man, but with a high sense of integrity, on his death in 1857, Muntz left an estate worth £600,000.

Most of the industrial activity down to 1870 remained within, or corseted up against, the town itself. But, particularly where there were canals and railways, bulges and promontories extended beyond the confines of the borough. To the north-east there was the railway dominated incursion into Saltley, together with a ribbon of industrial development aligned on the Birmingham & Fazeley Canal and the Lichfield Road. Except in this last area, where John Yates, edge tool manufacturer, was the biggest concern, industry was surprisingly slow in penetrating the 943 acre Aston Manor. Nevertheless, by the 1860s a scatter of workshops and small factories were to be found in the districts abutting on to Birmingham, while the local brewing industry was already in evidence.

Joseph Ansell bought the plot of land on which the present brewery stands in 1851, together with several others in Aston Manor that were to accommodate the earliest of his chain of public houses. However, since it was then usual for inns to brew their own beer, Ansells traded at first merely as maltsters and hop merchants, thereby providing publicans with their basic raw materials. It was not until 1881, following Gladstone's reimposition of the Beer Duty, that this firm turned its attention to brewing. Meanwhile, from 1853 Frederick Smith was building up a rival business which by 1865 had become 'The Model Brewery' in Queen's Road. Yet as late as 1875 the *Aston Chronicle* could still write of Aston Manor that it had 'no large business establishments'.

Once the famous Boulton and Watt factory had been shut down and demolished (1862-3), the industrial probe into the predominantly rural parish of Handsworth at Soho amounted to little more than 'two small breweries, two corn mills, and a red lead manufactory'. But things were different in adjacent Smethwick—which, although destined ultimately to become an independent county borough, was widely regarded in early Victorian times as being wedded to Birmingham. Here, aligned on the canal and railway lines between Birmingham and Wolverhampton, was a district 'studded with works and manufactories of great extent and importance'. Apart from Tangye Brothers, Chance brothers, Nettlefold & Chamberlain, and Muntz's Metal Company, other 'leading establishments' included the Birmingham Plate Glass Company, the Patent Nut & Bolt Company, 'the Patent Tube works, the Crown iron works . . . the Patent Rivet works', and Henry Mitchell & Co., brewers.

Several similar if smaller industrial pockets were flourishing elsewhere by 1870. In addition to the B.S.A. at Small Heath and Webster & Horsfall at Hay Mills, Kynoch &

Co. Ltd., which was eventually to become IMI, started making their world-famous cartridges at the Lion Works, Witton in the 1860s.

But perhaps the most surprising outposts of mid-Victorian industry were in the remote parishes of Northfield and King's Norton. A chemical works had been established on the banks of the Worcester canal at Selly Oak before the Queen's accession. This factory was taken over in 1853 by Elliott's Patent Sheathing & Metal Co., who then expanded their business until they were employing many hundreds of people. Meanwhile, other important new industrial enterprises were being established in the neighbouring King's Norton parish. These included G. R. Wilson's india rubber works at Lifford Mills, James Baldwin's Sherborne paper mill, and Nettlefold & Chamberlain's second big screw works, on the Worcester canal at Stirchley.

Even in the relatively non-industrialized parishes of the Greater Birmingham area, it is clear that Birmingham-based industries were by now having a profound influence both on their population size and industrial structure. The parish of Yardley in 1861 had 168 males engaged in the metal and allied trades, as against 77 farmers and 193 farm servants and agricultural labourers. Among the metal craftsmen were 41 wire workers, 17 gun workers of various kinds, 17 needle makers, 8 white (or silver) smiths, 5 steel workers, 4 scale-beam makers and 4 bedstead makers. The great majority of such people would have been employed in nearby factories and workshops — the wire workers at Hay Mills, the gun workers at the B.S.A., and so on. But the 8 white smiths, for instance, together with the 2 locksmiths, a silver chain maker and spectacle maker, could well have been working on a domestic basis.

In any case, there is one industry which we know was still being carried on in this way in the rural parishes on the south-western side of Birmingham. This was nail making, which, despite the growing competition from cut and machine wrought nails, managed to hang on in the domestic workshops of King's Norton, Northfield and Harborne right through to the 1880s and beyond. Recalling the nail makers of Harborne, Tom Presterne wrote in 1913:

> The houses in Harborne Terrace all had nail-shops; also 'Murphy Row' — now called Vine Terrace — had them. These nail-makers, the men and the women, worked very hard during the first five days of the week, from early morning till bed-time. On Saturday morning each man would trudge off to town with the stock of nails he had made during the week. He would carry them — a very heavy weight sometimes — in a coarse sack on his shoulder, to his employer. On his return, he would carry the bundle of iron on his shoulder for the next week's work. This was in my day. Before this time they were employed chiefly by the nail-masters of the village . . .

A recent analysis shows that 355 different types of firm were listed in the 1830 edition of *Wrightson's Directory*. In 1849

Elliott's Works, Elliott Road, Selly Oak — all that remains after recent and extensive demolitions.

Robert Rawlinson wrote:

> There are about 520 distinctly classified manufacturers, traders, or dealers, and about 20 separate professions in Birmingham, and each trade may certainly be divided into five branches, which will give 2,600 varieties of occupation.

By 1870 *Kelly's Directory* is listing no less than 953 types of firm.

This ever-growing diversity of occupation marked Birmingham off sharply from the immediately abutting Black Country, with its extremely restricted range of products and trades; and also from the big towns of Lancashire, say. 'Look here', exclaimed a Birmingham businessman in 1896, 'if the shipping trade isn't good, Liverpool's all awry; if there's a dispute in the cotton trade, Manchester suffers keenly; but nothing upsets us. You see, we've all sorts of trades, from guns to pens and buttons.'

Birmingham differed from the industrial towns of the north in another way. Bradford and Manchester were not only heavily concentrated on one type of industry, by the mid-nineteenth century they had to a large extent become factory towns. True Birmingham was moving in the same direction. 'Fifty years ago', wrote Joseph Chamberlain in Timmins, 'there were very few factories in the town of great size or importance . . . Of late years these have grown with extraordinary rapidity . . .' Yet, as the mid-Victorian directories show, thousands of small businesses still existed alongside the factories — in the high quality sections of the gun and jewellery trades, in the pearl button industry, and in innumerable other largely unmechanized industrial activities. Official factory returns made in 1871 give a total of 92,799 workers in 4,873 establishments, which is an average of 19 per firm. And since premises too small to be subject to the factory acts were excluded, the true average number of workers per workplace must have been considerably lower even than this. Marjorie H. Tiltman began her 1920s novel *Quality Chase* as follows:

> Birmingham in the '70s. You may still talk with those who remember it. A honeycomb of artisans in a hive of hovels. Every man Jack for himself and the devil take the hindmost. Hundreds, thousands of them — smiths, chain-makers, brass-founders, cutlers, bit- buckle- and button-makers . . . A big town of little men. The toyshop of Europe, growing — growing — growing . . .

Hockley Terrace, 69-73 Great Hampton Street — a palimpsest of 'The Thousand Trades'. Among the enterprises decipherable from its no doubt doomed walls are a silver manufactory, a silversmith, a metal polisher, a jewellery repairer and a printer, together with others which produced cutlery, 'screws, turned parts and rivets', and 'pressed metal smallware'.

The Land of Goshen

Many of the problems of the first industrial revolution can only be properly understood in the context of the transition from a domestic or workshop to a factory system of production. In the Manchester cotton industry this transition was so stark and sudden that it is difficult even today to think of the evils that accompanied it except in terms of inhumanity and ruthless exploitation. Because the change was so much more hesitant and gradual in Birmingham — an evolution in fact, rather than a revolution — the sufferings of early industrialization here, though abhorrent enough, were by no means so extreme.

Moreover, it could be cogently argued that the problems and malpractices which characterized early Victorian industry in Birmingham belonged at least as much to the old order as to the new. At Quarry Bank in the Black Country the firm of Noah Bloomer continued producing hand-welded chain right down to 1977. The proprietor owned the large brick-built workshop with its dozen or so hearths, and provided fuel and raw materials. But each chain maker, being paid for finished chain on a piece-rate basis, was free to come and go more or less as he pleased. If he had wanted to employ a lad to help him, that would have been his affair, and he would then himself have settled the lad's rate of pay and hours of work.

Noah Bloomer's might be thought of as a semi-factory, and the individual chain makers as semi-factory workers — or alternatively as semi-masters. Throughout the early Victorian period this kind of half-way situation was to be found in most of the traditional Birmingham industries. Factory proprietors made piece-rate contracts with experienced workers who were variously called 'sub-contractors', 'butties', 'piece-masters', or 'overhands'. The overhand was then responsible for engaging

Noah Bloomer's chain works, Quarry Bank, photographed in 1975.

and supervising his own group of workers. He was also responsible for paying them — usually on a day rate — out of his own piece-rate earnings. Even the women in the button factories — or semi-factories — each had a few girl assistants, and it was said of that trade in 1850, '. . . the manufacturer has merely a nominal control over the large proportion of his workpeople. He neither engages them, pays them nor dismisses them. They are the servants of his servants.'

In essence this was a survival of the old domestic or workshop system into the factory context. No one had ever told the domestic pearl button maker at what age he could begin employing his own or his neighbour's children, what hours they and his wife should be allowed to work, or what wages — if any — he should pay them. The domestic worker or garret master undertook to produce buttons for a given factor at a given price — the rest was up to him. Initially at least, the adult factory worker expected the same 'freedoms'.

In the past many women and children would have worked in the home. But in the 1860s, W. C. Aitken assures us, 'the proportion of married women who work in factories, away from home, is undoubtedly increasing', while mothers 'deliver over the child of six or seven years of age to the foreman or other operative for a paltry sum of 1s. 6d. or 2s. per week'. In marked contrast to the Black Country, where women sweated beside their menfolk on the pitbanks or in the brick yards and chain shops, Birmingham women rarely toiled in heavy labouring occupations. Nevertheless, many contemporaries agreed with Aitken that the employment of young mothers represented a serious evil:

> Birmingham operatives marry early: the girl-wife becomes a mother, but, from early associations, she likes the manufactory better than her home — likes the company of the workers, and her earnings 'help to keep the house'. As soon as she can go to the manufactory after her confinement she goes (the absence on these occasions rarely exceeds one month), and the infant is left the greater part of the day to be fed on artificial food, and is usually attended to by a child not more than six or seven years of age.

On child labour Aitken was equally adamant:

> Experience shows . . . that the tender years of youth should not be passed within the walls of a factory, or the frame subjected to labour during its growth; that youth is the season when the elements of education are best imparted . . .

The *Children's Employment Commission* of 1843 stressed 'the general good usage of children in Birmingham'. All the same, in 1862 about 2,000 under the age of 10 were employed in the Borough of Birmingham alone. Seven years later an educational survey found that out of a sample of 37,122 children aged 5-15, 6,337 were at work.

Youngsters were employed in the brass foundries, where the atmosphere was so poisonous that the adult worker might well be dead by 45. Boys helped the casters, while both girls and boys pumped the bellows. In the button trade many children came to work 'as young as six years old', though between that age and 12 they were mainly employed 'as attendants on older hands, or doing such work as is merely mechanical'. Among the 'little lads' in some of the bigger factories were the 'nutcrackers', who were engaged in 'breaking the shells of the vegetable ivory nuts, ready for the workman who saws them up'. As helpmates, children inevitably tended to have the same working hours as adults. A 12 hour day was not uncommon, and in 'the shops of very small employers', where conditions were at their worst, children might even be expected to work round the clock during the latter part of the week.

Parliamentary legislation had no effect on the local situation at first, the early factory acts being confined to the textile trades. Even the Factory Act of 1867, which did seek to regulate the hours and conditions of female and child labour in all types of factory, counted for little until well into the 1870s. Meanwhile, it could not have helped that, alongside the factory labour force, countless people were still working under the old totally uncontrollable domestic system anyway. It could not have helped either that in the traditional industries at least it was virtually impossible for a businessman to start with a clean sheet. A factory in the brass, button or gun trade generally evolved as a small master built up his own business, or when a factor gathered his outworkers together in a steam-powered factory. Either way, apart from accepting new manufacturing techniques, key employees would expect to go on working with much the same 'customary practices' as before.

No doubt this is why the best working conditions were generally to be found in the new industries, which also tended to be the most highly mechanized and capitalized ones. Firms of this kind often closed for a week or fortnight at Christmas, as well as giving one or two days off at Easter, Whitsun and at the time of the Onion Fair. We read in Timmins that at Elkington's 'the occupation is pleasant, the labour light, cleanly, and remunerative'; that the 'principal steel-pen makers have been deservedly famous during the past twenty years' for 'the generous treatment of work-people and the cultivation of their powers'. Similarly, Robert Winfield, Tangye Brothers and Chance Brothers were noted as good employers, while Nettlefold and Chamberlain 'practised modern management methods with great emphasis on the health and welfare of employees'. Some of the leading factory owners would not permit the employment of children under 12, and many of them established schools for their young workers.

On the other hand, the new-style firms tended to take on as much female labour as possible. The number of women in the steel pen trade, for instance, went up from 125 in 1841 to 2,050 in 1866 — with a mere 360 males at the latter date. Semi-skilled female labour predominated wherever the hand

Work at Elkington's. Top, on the small stamp; centre, soldering; below, enamelling.

press was to be found; and also in the screw trade and other 'machine minding' industries.

There had been much cyclical unemployment in the 1830s and '40s. But throughout the mid-Victorian period, despite frequent and sometimes alarming recessions in individual trades, Birmingham enjoyed a generally high level of industrial activity. Average wage rates, however, seem not to have altered much prior to the 1870s, when 'the cyclical inflationary boom of 1870-3' brought sharp increases of from 20 to 35%. It was probably cut-throat competition, and the constant need to expand markets, that held back wages until this time. Certainly, for several decades the benefits of ever rising productivity appear to have been mainly devoted to the lowering of prices. The effects of this tendency in the button, steel pen, and electro-plating trades have already been noted, and many other graphic examples can be found in the Timmins volume. In the brass industry, for example, manufacturers sold 'A stiff bracket, straight, 12 inches long' at 5s. 0d. in 1820, but at 1s. 9d. in 1866. Over the same period, 'One-inch main taps' were brought down in price from 14s. 0d. to 2s. 11d.

A statistical survey carried out for the British Association in 1839 estimated average earnings for males and females at different ages as follows:

	Males	*Females*
7−13	3s. 1d.	2s. 4d.
14−20	5s. 9d.	5s. 2d.
Above 20	24s. 3d.	8s. 0d.

In the mid-1860s unskilled manual labourers, such as the 'men who simply raise and ram the press' or those who 'attend annealing and pickling' in the brass trade, could expect to earn from 15s. 0d. to 18s. 0d. per week. The wages of semi-skilled males, such as 'stampers', or 'reducers' and 'finishers' in the wire industry ranged from 20s. 0d. to 30s. 0d. Overhands and highly skilled craftsmen might take home anything from £2 to £5 per week.

If one thought of 1s., or 5p., as being worth about £2, this might give a very rough idea of present-day equivalents. But in any case, the mid-Victorians themselves—or at least mid-Victorian employers—obviously regarded Birmingham wage rates as relatively high. Thus, in comparing the local gun trade with that of Belgium, John Goodman says that 'the better paid, and better fed English workman can accomplish an amount of work considerably in advance of his Belgian workfellow'. And indeed, according to the same writer, the high level of wages was one of the main factors which encouraged 'the more extended application of machinery' here, whereas in Belgium technological advance was 'discouraged by the cheap rate at which hand labour can be obtained'.

By the same token, although only limited use was made of child workers in the best run factories, one of the great advantages of female labour from an employer's point of view must have been its relative cheapness. Semi-skilled women, such as 'women stampers', 'women solderers', 'women lacquerers', would earn between 7s. 0d. and 12s. 0d. per week—or rather less than half as much as semi-skilled males.

But apart from being cheaper to employ, women were also preferred as more reliable, more ready to adapt to factory discipline and more regular in attendance. Under the old workshop system Birmingham men had been notorious, like their counterparts in Sheffield, the Potteries and elsewhere, for the irregularity of their working hours; and this was yet another carry-over into the early factories. Of the artisans in the pre-1840 silver plating trade, we read in Timmins:

> As a class they were about an average with other trades, never setting bodily to work till Tuesday or Wednesday morning. Of course there were always exceptions, and those were generally the men who in time saved money, and began business for themselves.

But many Birmingham workers, particularly those who were highly skilled and therefore highly paid, had long been accustomed to 'playing away' on 'St. Monday'—and sometimes on Tuesday as well—concentrating their whole week's labour into the remaining four or five days. Some did not mind the reduction of earnings that threatened, others would secure a full week's remuneration by working day and night until late on Saturday.

In a domestic workshop efficiency may hardly have been affected by this alternation of leisure and concentrated labour. But in factories the absence of key men could delay whole chains of production. Big industrialists in the new trades, or in the old trades where craft skills had largely been replaced by mechanization, could often minimize this problem by opting for female labour. The manager at Elkington's freely admitted that his firm had employed women 'upon a branch of work which was formerly done by men, because the latter were so much more difficult to keep steady at their work'. But in many firms, particularly in the male dominated brass and gun industries, the practice of St. Monday proved incredibly difficult to eradicate.

At least two employers resorted to lock-outs, declaring 'If you will not come on Monday you will not come on Tuesday'. But more effective than the stick, perhaps, in the long run, was the carrot of the 5½ day week. It was by this means that from 1851 onwards, aided by a well organized publicity campaign, manufacturers tried to shift the workers' 'playing away' habits from Monday to Saturday. By June 1853 over 10,000 workers from 'thirty of the largest manufactories in the town and neighbourhood' had been released from Saturday afternoon working. As it turned out, however, this often amounted to a mere re-arrangement of hours rather than a genuine reduction of the 52-58 hour working week. Nor did it necessarily produce the desired result. As late as 1864 it was reported that at one large works only 40 to 50 out of 300 to 400 men were in on Monday, that few factories were fully operational on that day, and that casters in a big brass foundry were not reporting for work until towards midday on Tuesday.

Nevertheless, the inexorable advance of mechanization and the steam engine ensured that by 1870 the vast majority of workers had — however begrudgingly — accepted the 'time discipline' that was an inevitable part of the new production methods. In his account of the bedstead trade for Timmins, Edward Peyton intones solemnly:

> In this, as in many other departments of production . . . a great object must always be that all shall work together as nearly as possible as though moved by one will, and it may therefore be reasonably hoped that the value of steadiness and regularity will be more and more recognized by both masters and workmen. Such a recognition cannot fail to prove one of the most cogent . . . influences in the improvement of the moral and social condition of the labouring classes.

Joseph Chamberlain made a similar point more brightly when he declared that the factory system, with its 'regularity of hours', might prove 'an almost unmixed good', bringing with it 'healthier work-places . . . economy of labour, increased demand, lower prices, and at the same time higher wages'.

In the past, Birmingham has generally been regarded as the classic illustration of the Webbs' theory that early industrial society 'was still divided vertically trade by trade, instead of horizontally between workers and employers'. However, a recent attempt has been made to argue that class consciousness was already playing a significant role in early nineteenth-century Birmingham. At least 103 strikes have now been catalogued between 1800 and 1849, involving 43 different trades — an average of just over two each in half a century. If only because of the paucity of documentation, this must be a gross under-estimate. It has therefore been thought safe to conclude that there was 'a constant trade presence', though it is also admitted that most of the industrial activity was opportunist, ephemeral and lacking in organizational continuity. Trade societies languished, or perhaps even vanished, and were later revived, the 'periods of activity' being 'characteristically those of better trade'.

It is further argued that the growth of trade unionism in those Birmingham trades where it occurred stemmed directly from the pressures created by rapid industrialization. As the factory system advanced, trade societies struggled not only to safeguard and improve wages but to maintain 'customary practices', like recruitment through apprenticeship, the 'overhand' system, and St. Monday. According to their employers, the Operative Screw Locksmiths in 1835 wanted 'to get as much money in three days as will support their families and supply them to get drunk and attend men fights, dog fights, etc., on the other three days of the week'.

The point at which the advocates of class consciousness find it most easy to flesh-out their case is naturally at the time of the widespread Chartist agitation. Granville complained in his *Spas of England* (1841) of 'artisans grumbling and dejected . . . parading the streets and other public places in Birmingham, with minds poisoned by demagogues, murmuring at the superior comforts, better means of living, and display of wealth . . . by which certain other classes of society, apart from themselves, are distinguished'.

The brass cock founders supported the Chartist Convention in 1839, struck for 15 weeks in 1840, and after reorganizing themselves, were successful in a wages or 'discount' strike in 1845. The pearl button makers, cabinet makers and tailors were also active during these years, while new societies were formed among the edge tool makers and fire arms makers. More unusually, in 1845 John Mason, a Chartist lecturer and president of the local boot makers and shoe makers society, instituted the Central Committee of Trades which aimed to co-ordinate strike activity in the town. Thereafter, as well as organizing several walk-outs in his own industry, this northern, O'Connorite radical intervened in strikes involving wire, pin, building, and glass workers. The wire workers in 1845 even called upon 'the working men of all trades to combine to secure proper and just protection for labour'. With typical common sense and neglect of dogma, however, they also specifically suggested that this should be in alliance with 'those employers who acted reasonably'.

On the traditional view, the long term ineffectiveness of trade unionism in early Victorian Birmingham is thought to have been due to the 'smallness and intimacy' of a high proportion of workplaces; to the option which at least all skilled workmen had of changing their employer, or setting up in business themselves; and to the fact that the owners of workshops and small factories had often built up their business in this very way, and therefore knew what it was like to be a wage-earner. And so indeed did many of the big factory owners, like Richard Tangye who claimed that his firm was 'remarkably free from disputes with our men; for, having sprung from their ranks ourselves, we knew their wants and

Left: The Tangyes' first workshop – 4s. a week rent'. Below: 'Our second workshop – 10s. a week rent'. Reproduced from Richard Tangye's autobiography, "One and All" (1889).

feelings, and tried to meet them as far as possible'. Then there was the paternalistic tradition among the town's principal employers, which from the days of Matthew Boulton seems to have encouraged them almost to vie with one another, not only in providing what they considered fair wages, but also the best available environmental and social conditions in their factories.

But possibly of greater significance than all this was the fact that, compared with textiles or mining, say, the Birmingham hardware trades, by their very nature, produced an almost incomprehensibly fragmented labour force. And one which was not only split vertically into hundreds of different industries, but also horizontally by the varying degrees of skill and therefore of remuneration and status which were to be found within the individual industries themselves.

Then, too, both the old workshop system and the new factory system as it gradually evolved in Birmingham tended to obscure the realities of the situation at any given time, as between capital and labour. Under the former system the small master had to strike a bargain, on the one hand with the factor, and on the other with his workers. And the overhand in one of the new factories found himself in a virtually identical position. In hard times factors could be ruthless in forcing down prices, and the small master might then have no alternative but to do the same with the earnings of his workers. Even in good times, in the face of unrelenting competition, it was customary for a businessman to offer 'discount' to prospective customers, and this led in turn to the widely practised 'discount' system of reducing wages. But who was the exploiter when such manoeuvres were afoot? The factor had to be able to sell his goods, the master to keep his business afloat. Should the artisan strike against his master, or with the master against the factor?

In practice what generally happened is that factors and masters gave wage increases in times of good trading, and masters and men accepted reductions when times were bad. As a rule in Birmingham this was done without the intervention of a trade society. Even the secretary of the extremely active Flint Glass Makers Society went on record as saying in 1867 that 'in nineteen cases out of twenty' industrial disputes were 'settled by the men and employers amongst themselves and we do not hear anything about it'.

Of course there were both fair and unfair factors, masters and factory owners. And some working men were more aggressive in the face of the unfair ones than others. A scale-beam maker received a letter from one of his workers in 1834 which read as follows:

Sir — of all the bloody rogues that ever I herd tell of you are the biggest. You rob your men you rebell against God and you are no better than a murderer . . . I believe you are going to turn your men out next Saturday but we will murder you. We have a plan to work upon that can blow your bloody branes out and it shall be done there is twenty of us united together and we shall cach you on the bonce. I thought I would lett you know because you will know what it is for.

One of the Witfield men.

Yet in general there was not only 'a popular acceptance of industrialization in Birmingham'—but of all, or most, that went with it. With a perspective that it is not too difficult for us to understand these days, Tangye was proud that in a time of massive national and local population increase he and his brothers had been 'enabled to build up a concern which has given continuous employment to thousands of people for more than a quarter of a century'. He also tells us that:

> One dark night I was walking home behind two of our workmen, when I heard one of them say to his companion, 'Another Cornishman come to the land of Goshen'. Well, I was glad there was a land of Goshen for my fellow Cornishmen to come to, for employment had become increasingly scarce in the old county, and many had been dispersed over the face of the globe.

Though some might envy Richard Tangye the Cornish estate to which he was eventually able to retire, the overriding probability is that, like him, the majority of Birmingham workers were 'glad there was a land of Goshen'.

MR. RICHARD TANGYE, F.R.G.S.
(From a Photograph by Tuttle & Co., George and Market Streets, Sydney.)

Slums, Arcadia and Aston

It was as long ago as the 1840s that Friedrich Engels showed how the social structure of a great town could be deduced from its physical appearance. Indeed, he argued that 'the separation of classes' had been built into the very layout of Manchester. For the 'fairly extensive commercial district' at its centre was surrounded by 'a pure working class district', with 'the villa-like houses' of 'the upper and middle classes' beyond. Moreover, since the main streets leading into Manchester were 'occupied almost uninterruptedly . . . by shops, which are kept by members of the middle and lower-middle classes', the villa dwellers could travel 'to their places of business . . . without even noticing how close they are to the most squalid misery which lies immediately about them on both sides of the road'.

Although Victorian Birmingham's social structure was a great deal more complex than that of Engels's Manchester, this also was given full physical expression in its townscape. The reason is simple: each of the community's principal socio-economic groups had its own characteristic type of housing.

Throughout early Victorian times most of the ever growing multitude of Birmingham workers were accommodated in new or fairly new terraces and courts of back-to-back houses. In the long established parts of the town, and also in the recently industrialized parts like Duddeston and Saltley, 'small capitalists' and speculative builders were constantly infilling any available building plots with such dwellings. But by the 1870s the great grid of streets that stretched northwards from the Jewellery and Gun Quarters as far as New John Street, and in an east-west direction from Nechells to Spring Hill, was almost entirely devoted to them. Meanwhile, similar housing development to the south, from Ladywood, through Lee Bank to Highgate, Deritend and Bordesley, was all but completing the town's encirclement of 'pure working class' housing.

The population of Duddeston and Nechells went up from 20,079 in 1841 to 45,986 in 1871. That of Ladywood increased even more sharply over the same period, from 8,787 to 42,779. And the large scale maps of Victorian Birmingham show that the vast majority of newcomers must have moved into back-to-back houses.

Essentially a back-to-back terrace consisted of a long double row of cell-like dwellings, arranged back-to-back under a single roof. This meant that all but the end houses had three party walls, leaving only the fourth for access, light and ventilation.

Lots of back-to-backs survived until the wholesale inner-ring redevelopment of the 1950s, and from field surveys it appears that there were three main types. The smallest was of two stories, with a living room or kitchen on the ground floor, measuring perhaps 10 feet by 12 feet, and a second floor divided into two tiny bedrooms. Then there was a three-storey version occupying a similar ground area but having two larger bedrooms on separate floors. The third type resembled the second but was wide enough to accommodate a narrow hall on the ground floor, with a stairway that rose from this, instead of from a corner of the living room. Sometimes these less cramped examples also had a basement.

Seen from the road, back-to-back terraces could well be mistaken for more commodious houses and—as the observations of Engels may have led us to anticipate—particularly along main roads, this illusion of artisan prosperity was often reinforced by the practice of embellishing their fronts with stone dressings, fanlights and other decorative features.

Back-to-back houses in Benacre Street, photographed in 1965. In Court 14 (right) both the two- and three-storey versions can be seen. At some stage the ground-floor accommodation was improved by converting the tunnel entries into doorways and hall passages, with an additional window being inserted where the old door had been. Benacre Street, which has now disappeared altogether, was situated between Bristol Street and Sherlock Street, and was almost entirely lined with back-to-back courts.

Unfortunately the tunnel entries between alternate front doors usually led, not merely to architecturally sterner rear houses, but to still further blocks of back-to-backs immediately behind. And more often than not in Birmingham these last were arranged around courtyards, with the dwellings on three sides and the communal privies, ashpits and water pump on the fourth.

It has to be borne in mind that meeting the housing requirements of a population that was increasing so remorselessly must have presented a tremendous challenge to the local building industry. To roof the thousands upon thousands of new dwellings some 15 to 20 local slate merchants transported an endless stream of Welsh slate into the town by canal and railway. Many of the house bricks for the western side of Birmingham — not to mention the blue engineering bricks required by the railways and industry — were brought by canal from the Black Country. But the eastern side of the town must have been mainly constructed from the red clays of Yardley, Small Heath and Saltley. In 1874 the former had six brick and tile makers spread over the parish from Yardley village to Sparkbrook and Billesley. The Small Heath-Saltley brick works were much more concentrated. There were no less than eight of them in an intensively quarried square of roughly 100 acres at the top of Kingston Hill and immediately north and east of St. Andrew's. In fact, the Birmingham City football ground itself utilizes the site of one of these brick works.

In terms of the materials that went into them, Birmingham back-to-backs were infinitely superior to many nearby farm labourers' cottages, let alone the mud hovels that were then to be found all over the Black Country. Despite their minimal size, minimal facilities for cooking, water supply and sanitation, the same could be claimed for the accommodation they provided. Nor is it clear how the alarmingly high density of such housing could have been avoided. The majority of workers could only afford a weekly rent of 3s. to 4s. and had to live close to their workplace, while suitably located building land was bound to be exorbitantly expensive.

Bearing in mind the circumstances, then, a considerable proportion of Victorian builders probably did a reasonably honest job. And indeed, unless this had been the case it is difficult to see how such a large stock of Birmingham back-to-backs could have survived — even as sub-standard housing — for upwards of a century. Nevertheless, without any agencies or procedures for controlling standards, it was perhaps inevitable that there should have been a good deal of inferior workmanship or 'jerry building'.

Official reports of the 1840s commend many of the newer courts, with their small gardens, or yards of 'carefully laid blue brick' as being 'excellent in their arrangement'. But they also

Late surviving back-to-backs off Princip Street, only recently demolished. The position of the doorways indicates that these houses represented the third and 'best' type of back-to-back, being wide enough to accommodate a narrow hall and hall stairway.

tell of houses where the capital costs were kept down to as little as £60 by making load-bearing walls 'only 4½ inches thick, and supporting floors on joists measuring 5½ by 1½ inches which were placed 17 inches apart'. Such 'slight' buildings could have 'a clean and cheerful appearance' and let readily. But it was not long before cracks, dampness and leakages began to appear and the properties declined into slums.

Although back-to-backs had to suffice for the majority of manual labourers and semi-skilled factory workers, the higher incomes of top craftsmen in the gun, jewellery, engineering and other skilled trades enabled them to live in decidedly better accommodation. All over the town, therefore, blocks of superior artisans' 'cottages' were to be found. These were also built in terraces, but unlike back-to-backs, they were 'through-houses' two rooms in depth, with a front parlour, back kitchen and hall on the ground floor, two large bedrooms on the first floor, and sometimes two attic bedrooms above them. Such houses, which could be bought for £100-£150 or rented for 5s. - 7s. 6d. per week, often also had a back garden which included a wash house as well as a private external toilet.

Representing the other extreme of the working classes were the casual labourers, pedlars, paupers and drop-outs who formed the 'forgotten poor', or as John Bright called them, 'the sunken sixth'. These were the slum-dwellers who, by defi-nition, had descended to the very bottom of the pile so far as housing and everything else was concerned.

In general, the 'cruel habitations' available to these people were of two sorts. Firstly there were those terraces and courts of back-to-backs which had so much deteriorated and been 'put out of condition' that their original, more respectable occupants had fled from them to live elsewhere. Typical housing of this sort was to be found, for instance, in the triangle of land bounded by the New Street and Snow Hill railway lines and the Duddeston viaduct—an area which, although only developed in the 1840s, was by 1884 being singled out as 'the worst

Superior artisans' cottages, Adderley Road, Saltley. Below: front view of Belmont Terrace, dated 1865, and of similar houses nearer the camera. Right: the rear view of the left-hand terrace, with the back doors indicating that these are 'through-houses'. A fair number of mid-nineteenth-century houses of this type are still providing acceptable accommodation.

extreme of jerry building in Birmingham'.

But the very grimmest slums were located in the old alleyways and courts at or near the centre of town. Often such areas had originally been devoted to good standard merchant houses. As industrialization advanced, however, the middle classes departed, leaving their high-walled gardens to be filled up with small workshops or 'shopping', and as many miserable dwellings as could be crammed into them. Writing of the 1840s, William White, a Quaker councillor who became mayor in 1882, tells us:

> From Worcester Street and Smallbrook Street up to the Town Hall, and crowding the hill closely behind New Street, these discreditable slums existed under the names of the Old Inkleys, the New Inkleys, Tonk Street, Peck Lane, the Froggery, King, Queen, and Pinfold Street . . . and our noble Town Hall itself was hemmed in on three sides by buildings in a similar condition.

In such areas, White goes on, were to be found:

> . . . a network of streets, lanes and courts of the meanest character, and the abode in many instances of the more vicious and criminal classes of the population, their intricacy often enabling such to resist the vigilance of the police.

The making of New Street and Snow Hill stations led to the sweeping away of some of the worst of this old slum housing in the middle years of the century, with the Artisans' Dwellings Act of 1875 eventually leading to the demolition of the remainder.

Even before this, however, and indeed from the 1840s onwards, all contemporary reports were unanimous in stressing that working class housing in Birmingham was better than in most other industrial towns. For at least here the general rule was to have 'each family living in a separate dwelling', with relatively few people having to be accommodated in 'lodgings' or 'tenements', and none at all in the damp unwholesome cellars which were so prevalent elsewhere.

Insanitary houses, c.1875. Left: No. 2 Court, John Street. Right: No. 1 Court, Steelhouse Lane. Reproduced from Dent's Old and New Birmingham (1880).

Turning now to middle class housing, many prosperous families had obviously hankered after 'social segregation' – or at least to be away from the din and stink of industry – since the beginning of industrial expansion. Yet this proved difficult to achieve, and even more to sustain, in nineteenth-century Birmingham, where the rapid deterioration of select residential areas became a constantly recurring theme of the town's development.

Apart from the older central properties which had long since become slums, the Colmores, for instance, had laid out their Newhall Estate in the second half of the eighteenth century as 'an exclusive area for merchants, with good houses, large gardens, a fine view of the country . . ? But in the absence of leases precluding industrial use, the majority of 'backlands' had been filled up with 'offices', 'manufactories' and 'other premises' long before the accession of Queen Victoria. The same thing happened on the Wearman, Gooch and Inge estates, while by the 1840s the spread of industry and working class housing was even beginning to threaten the more distant 'first generation' suburbs like Ashsted and Bordesley. Only in one area was this process of industrial advance at the cost of environmental and social amenity completely blocked. This was on the Calthorpe Estate at Edgbaston, which in consequence emerged as the early Victorian town's only sizable middle class retreat and bastion.

With remarkable foresight, as it turned out, and a landholding that occupied 85% of the entire parish of Edgbaston, the late Georgian Calthorpes set themselves the objective, not only of attracting the wealthy merchants, factory owners and professional *élite* of Birmingham, but of attracting them in large numbers.

Their estate formed a 2,500 acre wedge, mainly between the Hagley and Pershore Roads, which ran west and south from the town centre respectively. As such, like the premier middle class suburbs of other great towns — Kelvinside, Headingley, Hampstead — although geographically convenient, Edgbaston was to windward of the noise, dirt and 'noxious vapours' produced by industry.

However, in order to be sure of tempting those who had 'basked in the sunshine of commercial prosperity' to build £2,000 houses on their land, the Calthorpes and their agents realized that, as well as laying out a tastefully planned rural suburb, they had to be able to guarantee that this would remain secluded and sacrosanct more or less in perpetuity. And that in turn meant the total exclusion of sub-standard housing and all forms of industrial and commercial activity from their jealously guarded acres.

The Calthorpes had granted their first leases as early as 1786, and systematic development dated from the 1810s.

Nevertheless, the great bulk of the estate was built up during the opening 40 years of Queen Victoria's reign — which, so far as the wealthy were concerned, was a period of almost uninterrupted commercial prosperity and expansive optimism. Between 1841 and 1881 Edgbaston's population increased from 6,609 to 22,760, while by the latter date the Calthorpes' gross annual rental had soared to almost £30,000.

By this time, too, from being a working agricultural parish, much of Edgbaston had been transformed into what Francis Brett Young described as 'a region of tree-lined roads and exquisitely tasteful houses, with their libraries and music rooms, tennis courts and croquet lawns, rose trees and rhododendron bushes'—or in other words into that almost perfect suburban arcadia for the wealthy which has persisted in the popular imagination ever since.

Not all Birmingham's top people moved to the Calthorpes' 'West End'. On the contrary, isolated suburban residences remained as popular as they had been in the eighteenth century. Richard Tangye lived at Winson House, Winson Green, and later at Gilbertstone House, Sheldon; Joseph Nettlefold at Kingsfield, King's Heath; Sir Josiah Mason at Norwood House, Erdington. Other big factory owners and merchants bought themselves a manor and became the squire of a country estate, as James Horsfall did at Penns, Sutton Coldfield, or G. F. Muntz at Umberslade. Nevertheless, a list of early and mid-Victorian Edgbastonians might quite easily be mistaken for a Birmingham *Who's Who* of the period. Here were to be found great industrialists like Joseph Gillott and R. L. Chance; great preachers like George Dawson and R. W. Dale; and above all, so many representatives of the Avery, Barrow, Cadbury, Chamberlain, Kenrick, Martineau, Pemberton, Ryland and Sturge families that, in a very real sense, late nineteenth-century Edgbaston might be described as 'but the council house at home'.

Despite all this success, however, there was one respect in which the Calthorpes' tasteful and remunerative piece of environmental planning inevitably had to be compromised. As early as the 1860s, with only about one-third of the estate leased out to the top people, it was rapidly becoming clear that even booming mid-Victorian Birmingham could not produce a sufficient number of upper middle class families to take over all of Edgbaston's 2,500 acres. The Calthorpes were left with no alternative but to move down the social scale and begin admitting lower middle class and even respectable working class families to their once exclusively aristocratic domains.

Yet, as the recent fascinating study by David Cannadine has shown, the Calthorpes and their agents were clever enough to turn even this unfortunate necessity to the advantage of their more prosperous and distinguished tenants. They did this by skilfully placing the humbler housing, like cotton wool pad-

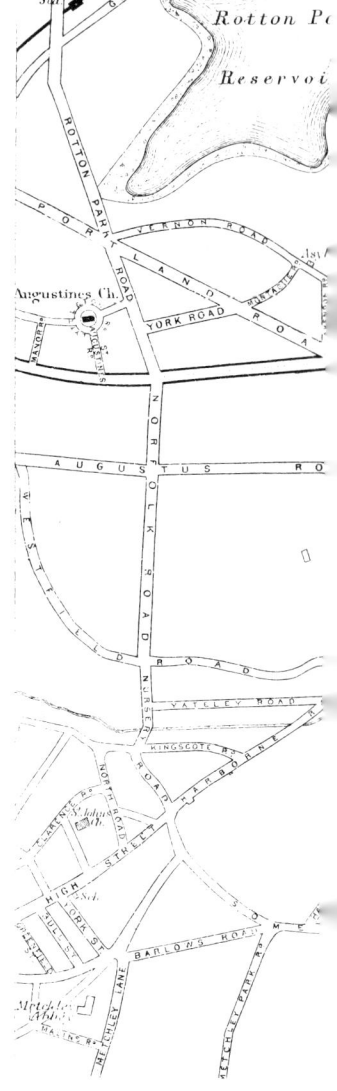

ding, along the entire eastern and northern boundaries of the estate, where it eventually stretched for over 4 miles. Building controls, covenants and strict estate supervision did the rest, effectively excluding not merely industry and inferior housing, but shops and trading, taverns and off-licences, even nonconformist chapels. Thus a protective barrier of respectability was erected against the working and working-class part of the town, and the upper class enclave at the estate's centre was made, if anything, even more secure, secluded and elysian than it had been before.

In fact, Cannadine distinguishes four types of property which a Victorian visitor might have passed if he had walked from town towards the centre of Edgbaston—along Balsall Heath Road and Wellington Road, say, or along Wheeley's Road and Carpenter Road. First he would see the comparatively

Edgbaston, from a map in Murray's Warwickshire, 1899.

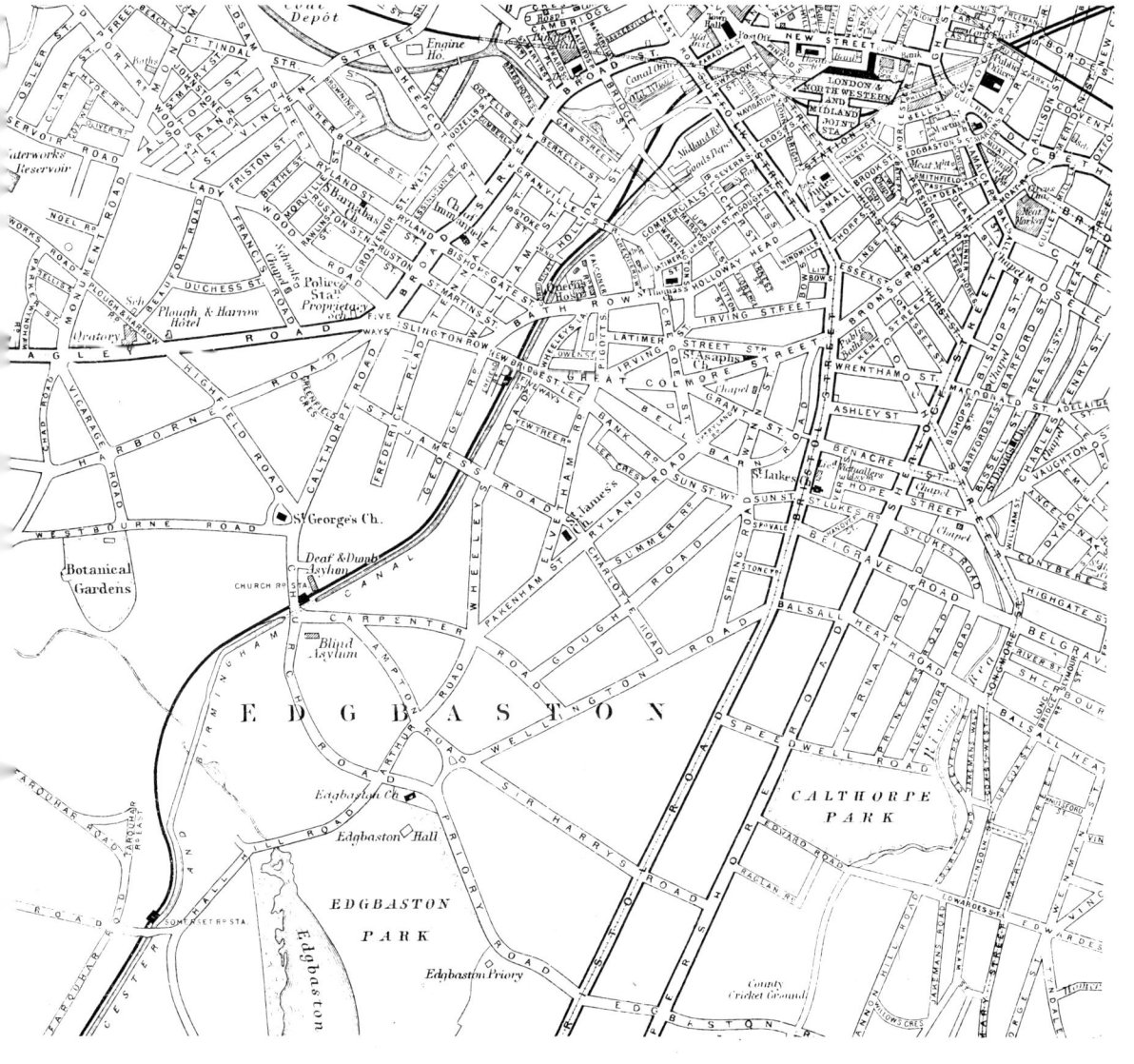

modest terraces occupied by what Cannadine calls the 'labour aristocracy and lower middle class'; then would come the decidedly more enviable houses of the 'middle middle class'. These in turn would give way to the big, impressive villas that signified 'upper middle class' status; and finally—if he were brave enough—the intruder might penetrate to the magnificent mansions which then belonged to what Cannadine dubs the '"aristocracy" of Birmingham'.

In 1851 there were 1,665 households in Edgbaston. A collation of the 1851 Census with an Edgbaston Poor Rate Book for the same year has shown that 121 of these, or 7.3%, occupied residences with a rateable value of £60+, and might therefore be equated with Cannadine's '"aristocracy" of Birmingham'. A further 577, or 34.7%, could be considered 'upper middle class', having properties rated between £20 and £59. Apart from housing, another indication of varying middle class status was the extent of servant-keeping. In 1851 Edgbaston householders with a rateable value of £20-£29 had an average of 1.2 living-in servants, whereas those whose properties were rated at £80+ averaged 3.9 each. This gave the former a mean household size of 5.4 persons, as against the latter's 8.3.

We have now identified two absolutely exclusive kinds of residential area in mid-Victorian Birmingham; and significantly, they were to be found at either extreme of the social spectrum. On the one hand, there was the carefully cocooned upper middle class arcadia of inner Edgbaston; and on the other, the hidden, unspeakable slums of the old, decaying town centre, which were the exclusive preserve of the very poorest of the poor. It has also been seen that, as in Engels's Manchester, a belt of recently built 'pure working class' housing surrounded much of the town: so that between the main radial roads in many directions, we have to visualize dreary, more or less uninterrupted stretches of back-to-back territory—or back-to-back territory which was interrupted only by the workshops

Left: Lower middle class houses at the town end—and lower end—of Wheeley's Road (Nos. 10-14). Above: 22 Wheeley's Road—a middle middle class property, with its coach house. Near right: 18 Carpenter Road—an upper middle class villa, four bays long and three bays deep. Far right: 8 Carpenter Road, the 'mansion' of a member of the '"aristocracy" of Birmingham'. In 1874 the New Street printer and stationer, Alderman Edward Corn Osborne, lived here.

and large factories that had been set down in its midst.

But if Engels's 'separation of classes' was built into the layout of Victorian Birmingham to a certain extent, there were nevertheless many districts where one would have been struck rather by the intermixture of housing and inhabitants of differing types and status. Indeed, by the 1870s, for reasons that are worth exploring, such seems to have been the case over virtually the whole of the 943 acre Aston Manor.

On the break-up of the Holt estate in 1818, the Hall, park and other manorial lands were acquired by a firm of Warwick bankers. By the 1830s they had begun developing an estate of middle class villas immediately north of Hockley Brook, and so only about a mile from the centre of Birmingham. This estate was marked on the Aston tithe map of 1848 as 'Aston New Town', and the road name New Town Row still points to the area in question.

It was no doubt the New Town estate, together with the building of well appointed properties along the Lichfield and Walsall roads, around Aston village and at Lozells, that pushed up the population of Aston from 922 in 1831 to 6,426 in 1851. So thus far, it would seem, the urbanization of this manor had proceeded along very similar lines to that of Edgbaston—albeit at a somewhat slower rate.

However, if the Calthorpes were eventually compelled to lower their 'status threshold', it is hardly surprising that the more detached financiers who had invested in Aston should have found it politic to do likewise—nor indeed that they came to that conclusion a good deal sooner.

By 1851 the value of land at Aston had appreciated enormously, with the best plots in the Park commanding almost £3,000 an acre. The time had come for the bankers to take their profit, and in a series of 20 sales over the next 10 years they disposed of virtually all their holdings. After the first sale advertisement 'Aston New Town' was never again mentioned. At the second sale, lots were said to be 'Suitable for Villa and

General Building Purposes', but by the next even the word 'Villa' had been dropped.

The floodgates were now open for the wholesale urbanization of Aston. Between 1851 and 1861 the number of houses went up from 1,437 to 3,562, and the population from 6,426 to 16,337. Moreover, if only because the land was sold freehold — unlike the Calthorpes — the vendors had no means of controlling the type or quality of development.

Yet, as it happens, the majority of new dwellings were built for people of some status. There was as yet little large-scale industry in Aston, and therefore little immediately local employment for manual or semi-skilled labour. Because of its high density, back-to-back housing could probably be as remunerative for the speculator, builder or landlord as better class property. But for a variety of reasons, only the more prosperous and respectable artisans seem then to have been prepared to travel any distance to and from work. So having started as a largely middle and upper middle class suburb, Aston Manor now became a place where lower middle class people and skilled craftsmen tended to settle — a process which was no doubt further encouraged by the opening of Aston railway station in 1854.

Nor was the Edgbaston ideal entirely lost sight of, if only because of the activities of the Freehold Land Society. This organization was the foremost of several Birmingham friendly societies which concentrated on the provision of houses for their members. Founded in 1847, largely due to the inspiration of George Dawson and of Joseph Sturge's Complete Suffrage Union, the aim of the F.L.S. was partly political. For in providing subscribers with a 'respectable dwelling and outhouse', it also made them into 40s. freeholders. Among the F.L.S. slogans, therefore, was not only 'Freeholds for the People', but 'County Votes for Working Men'. (Aston and other districts outside the Borough of Birmingham were of course represented by county M.Ps.)

For propaganda reasons, the Freehold Land Society chose this road name in connection with its second piece of property development – at Perry Barr.

Between 1855 and 1860 the society purchased the so-called 'Wheeler Street Estate' at Lozells, together with three plots between Victoria and Albert Roads, overlooking what was left of the 320 acre Aston Park. As on all its sites, it then proceeded to regulate development with almost as much punctilious care as the Calthorpes. At Wheeler Street, for instance, it stipulated that all buildings had to be set back 6 feet from the road, that no 'back houses' were to be constructed, 'and no front houses of less value than £200'. The resulting dwellings were generally built in terraces on the so-called 'tunnel-back' layout, with front parlour, living room, scullery, three first-floor bedrooms, and outside offices.

Needless to say, since weekly subscriptions ranged from 5s. 2d. up to 15s. 6d., only the most prosperous 'Working Men' could aspire to home ownership through the F.L.S. The 1861

census shows that among the 64 heads of household in Victoria Road, were not only many skilled artisans and small Birmingham manufacturers, but a surgeon and superintendent of police. Indeed, 16 of the 64 households included 1 or 2 servants. Yet for all that, such houses — a high proportion of which are still in use today — set a new standard for working class accommodation, and eventually provided the prototype for the 'bye-law' tunnel-backs which became the norm in artisan dwellings during the last quarter of the nineteenth century.

It is doubtful whether back-to-backs were built on any scale in Aston until the 1860s. But with increasing industrialization, the majority of the 5,000 odd houses erected between 1871 and 1881 took this form. And when Aston Borough — as the Manor had by then become — finally banned their construction in 1883, back-to-backs were said to account for 29% of all Aston dwellings.

However, arriving so late on the scene, much of the back-to-back building here inevitably took the form of infilling. So in many parts of high Victorian Aston cramped courts of inferior dwellings stood cheek by jowl with substantial tunnel-backs or even large villa houses. Some of the latter were ideal for conversion into business premises. All the same, the enormous variation in house types meant that it was quite common to find middle class families and unskilled labourers

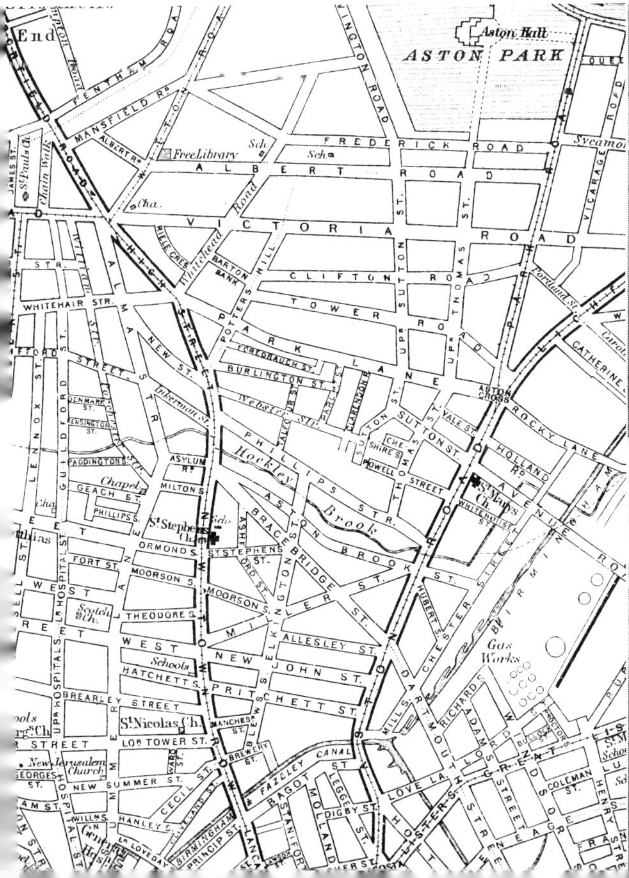

The Trustee Savings Bank in Aston Road North (above) is the only surviving property connected with Aston New Town. This development occupied the rectangle bounded by High Street, Park Lane (formerly Park Wall), Aston Road and Phillips Street. The Barton Arms of 1901 (left), in the triangle between High Street, Park Lane and Potters Hill, today serves as a prominent western marker. Top right: Swansea House, Camborne Villas and other big F.L.S. houses in Victoria Road, Aston. Bottom right: comparatively small F.L.S. tunnel-backs (Cambridge Villas, Mayfield Place) in Albert Road — recenty refurbished.

living together in the same street. To cite just one specific example, the 1871 census shows that in Berner Street a builder who was employing 40 workers had a nightsoil man as his next door neighbour.

Although three small private estates were involved, the urbanization of Balsall Heath was similar in many ways to that of Aston. Lying half a mile on either side of the Moseley Road between Moseley and Highgate, this district originally formed the extreme northern end of the 12,000 acre King's Norton parish. The 1840 tithe map and schedule show that most of the area was then still under pasture and meadow. To the west of the Moseley Road, however, the east-west running thoroughfares, Sherbourne Road, Balsall Heath Road, Edward Road and Homer Street, had already been laid out. So too, had the north-south running St. Mary Street, Wenman Street, Vincent Street and Tindal Street. Down to this date, development was almost entirely restricted to big villa houses — in Edgbaston Road, Tindal Street and Homer Street, for instance, as well as along the pre-existing Ladypool and Moseley Roads. But by 1871 the population of Balsall Heath had swollen to 13,615; virtually all available land to the west of the Moseley Road had been built up, while a matrix of new streets was now under development to the east of it.

As with Aston, Balsall Heath attracted little industrial activity at first, and therefore little early lower working class housing. Through-houses and tunnel-backs, on the other hand, of the kind favoured by skilled artisans, were built in considerable numbers. Moreover, by 1871, the arrival of industry and of a substantial industrial labour force had produced many mixed neighbourhoods, where the mansions of professional and business men, the through-terraces of clerks and craftsmen, and the back-to-backs of manual and semi-skilled factory workers, were all to be found in close proximity.

Contrasts in nineteenth-century housing at Balsall Heath. Left: early middle class villas in Ladypool Road, still extant. Below: a 'half' back-to-back terrace off Turner Street, photographed in 1973, prior to demolition.

An inspection of the late Victorian 25 inch Ordnance Survey maps suggests that a similar course of development took place in parts of Smethwick, Handsworth, Winson Green, Rotton Park, and in several other areas.

So, taking the housing stock of Victorian Birmingham as our guide, it might seem reasonable to conclude that the town's social structure consisted of, say, six principal socio-economic groups — with both the 'middle classes' and the 'working classes' falling roughly into three sub-sections. These were, on the one hand, the lower, middle and upper middle classes, the latter being headed by Cannadine's 'aristocracy of Birmingham'; and on the other, the skilled artisans, the manual labourers and semi-skilled factory hands, and 'the sunken sixth' or 'forgotten poor'.

From the residential point of view, the two extremities — or in other words, the upper middle class and the forgotten poor — tended to live a hidden existence, apart from the rest. And a considerable proportion of the town's manual labourers and semi-skilled factory workers were obviously housed in large, exclusively back-to-back estates. Yet there were also many neighbourhoods — particularly in the fringe areas, immediately beyond the Birmingham borough boundary — where the middle and lower middle classes, and the skilled and semi-skilled working classes were very much mixed up together.

With housing and social structure, then, as with so much else in Victorian Birmingham, things never seem to have become quite so black and white as they apparently did in Manchester, and perhaps in many other large industrial towns.

Public Health and Public Utilities

It would be a mistake to suppose that the vigorous growth of Birmingham's population during Victorian times was due mainly to the influx of strangers. On the contrary, by the mid-nineteenth century natural increase — or the excess of births over deaths — had become the key factor in the town's continuing expansion. Before the industrial revolution virtually all large urban centres witnessed an alarming excess of deaths over births, and were therefore in need of constant replenishment from outside. In 1865, however, the Borough of Birmingham's birth rate was 38.9 per 1,000, its death rate 24.5. So with births outnumbering deaths by over 50% — unlike ancient Rome, medieval Paris or eighteenth-century London — Victorian Birmingham was perfectly capable, not merely of sustaining itself, but of generating the bulk of its own continuing demographic growth.

Nevertheless, the fact that the death rate was low

compared with the birth rate, by no means meant that it was altogether satisfactory. Over the period 1855-62 Sheffield had an annual average death rate of 27.2 per 1,000, Manchester 31.9, Liverpool 32.3. The equivalent average for Birmingham over the same period was 26.3. Yet the death rate for England as a whole was then 21.8, while the rates for rural parishes in the Birmingham area were lower still, with the 1851-60 figure for Solihull being 18 and for King's Norton 17 per 1,000.

Edwin Chadwick said of Birmingham in his famous 1842 *Report on the Sanitary Condition of the Labouring Population* that 'The houses . . . are on the whole built upon an approved plan . . . and the general health of the population is high, although the occupations are such as are elsewhere deemed prejudicial to health'. Dr. Heslop, though, who wrote on 'The Medical Aspects of Birmingham' for Timmins, insisted that Birmingham's 'reputation of being one of the healthiest large towns in the kingdom' was partly 'a fair image of the fancy'.

One of the main causes of premature death was the prevalence of Chadwick's 'occupations prejudicial to health'. Heslop tells us that Birmingham metal workers were comparatively more healthy than the general population between 15 and 35 years of age. But 'a remarkable change takes place at 45, when a peculiar fatality begins to attend these men'. Most brass workers suffered from 'an intermittent fever which they term the brass ague'. 'Japanners, lacquerers, gilders, people who employ mercury, lead, or arsenic in their work, glass-blowers, and enamellers' were 'also liable to special disturbances of their health', and grinders were 'universally short-lived'. However, the local doctor also conceded that:

> Much has been done of late years to diminish the evils attendant upon all the trades mentioned. ... Many ingenious contrivances have been invented to obviate the effects of the more injurious employments. The shops are larger, and better ventilated ... and there is a constantly increasing tendency to shorten the time passed in the workshop.

Yet despite such measures, the male death rate in Birmingham during the decade 1851-60 was 28 per 1,000, as against a female rate of 25.

Children under the age of 5 provided a second group among whom mortality was alarmingly high, with a Birmingham death rate that was 40% above that for England as a whole. The main killers here of course were the contagious, or 'zymotic', diseases. The louse-borne typhus, and air-borne infections like measles, scarlet fever and tuberculosis seem to have been permanent hazards. Diptheria, Heslop says, had 'displayed itself in full vigour' from 1856 onwards, and during the years 1864 and 1865 smallpox was 'so severe in Birmingham, that great alarm was experienced among the public'. Of the food- and water-borne infections, amazingly, the town had 'nearly complete immunity from cholera'. But the cognate diseases of 'Diarrhoea, Dysentery, &c., are remarkably

The General Hospital, Summer Lane, c.1830.

The General Dispensary, Union Street, established in 1794 for 'administering medical relief to sick and midwifery patients of the poorer classes'.

The Royal Orthopaedic Hospital, Broad Street. This was formerly the Birmingham and Midland Free Hospital for Sick Children, which was founded in 1861, and moved from Steelhouse Lane to Broad Street in 1870.

prevalent', with 'the resources of the hospitals and parochial medical officers' being 'severely taxed' during the second nationwide cholera epidemic of 1849-50.

As one would expect, epidemic diseases and child mortality were particularly rife in the 'squalid filthy slums'. According to his biographer, when William White visited the 'condemned and overcrowded courts,' which filled 'that part of the town lying between New Street and the far end of Steelhouse Lane' in 1875, he found:

> The amount of sickness was enormous. He went from house to house seeing sickly people, hearing such a story of illness and its attendant misery as would, even for this small district, fill a volume . . . In one court [he heard] such statements as: 'Buried four, only one left'; 'buried six, married twelve years'; 'buried two, I wish you would come and smell this cellar'.

St. Mary's Ward, in which this district was situated, had a death rate in that year of 26.8 per 1,000 which was over twice the Edgbaston figure of 13.1. But at the heart of the same slum, Lower Priory produced an average death rate over the three years 1873-5 of 62.5 per 1,000.

Although castigating the Poor Law Guardians for expecting the newly built Workhouse Infirmary's 599 beds to be 'officered by one medical man', Heslop considered that in other respects 'ample provision' was 'made by charity for the sick and hurt of this busy town'. Apart from the 'six district medical officers' whose job it was to care for 'sick paupers, external to the Workhouse', the General Hospital, Queen's Hospital and Children's Hospital were together treating over 3,800 in-patients per annum in the mid-1860s. Their annual tally of out-patients, plus those of the General Dispensary, came to 46,000. This suggests that something like 1 in every 7 of the borough's population could have used the services of one or other of these four institutions in a typical year. In addition, the 'voluntary and very unequal contributions of the rich' were by then

supporting an Eye Hospital, an Ear Infirmary, an Eye and Ear Hospital, an Orthopaedic Hospital and a Lying-in Hospital.

But Heslop knew that hospitals could not make a healthy town, and had forthright views on what made an unhealthy one:

> It would be sufficiently wonderful if a town could be, in any intelligible sense, termed healthy, when the density of the population is such that there were, in 1860, 5.01 persons to a house, and 100 persons to 1.25 acres, containing, too, a population which was increasing from 1851-60, at the rate of 22.23 per cent., while the percentage increase of England and Wales, during the same period, was only 11.93. This is the real explanation of the high death-rate of Birmingham ... Great density of population means a high death-rate, and will probably have the same significance to the end of time.

In fact, Heslop was soon to be proved wrong in maintaining that 'the high death-rate of Birmingham ... can never be abolished'. For, mainly through the carrying out of what Patrick Geddes, with almost biblical awe, called 'great works of prime necessity', before the end of Queen Victoria's reign, such a miracle had been accomplished.

The greatest of all enemies to health in a congested urban environment was human excrement. Yet in the mid-nineteenth century, Bunce tells us:

> ... the town was practically what is called a 'midden' town — that is, there were few water-closets draining directly into the sewers, and the sewerage system was so little developed as to afford no adequate means of dealing with excreta ... The soil and refuse had therefore to be collected from the houses, and when collected it was deposited in heaps at wharves in various parts of the town, and, so far as possible ... sold to the neighbouring farmers as manure; ... [the remainder] being carted away to places remote from the houses, where 'sewage tips' were established.

Robert Rawlinson's 1849 report on the sanitary state of the town describes the consequences of such a system of sewage disposal in Birmingham's '2,000 close courts':

> The common practice is that the manure is mixed with ashes and rubbish ... till it over-runs the seats, runs into the courts, and gives rise to noxious exhalations ... Ordure is ... often kept in the houses, and emptied anywhere at nightfall; in other places, such as the Inkleys, and other Irish quarters, the door is opened, and it is thrown out without the least reference to the spot where it falls, or anything else.

Moreover, Edgbaston was not all that better in some respects than the slums of Birmingham. 'In the Hagley Road the water-closets of some of the houses absolutely discharge themselves into the road.' Elsewhere 'we see ditches and open spaces filled with foul, green-coloured, stagnant water, emitting disgusting odours into the adjoining atmosphere'.

The stink must have been bad enough. Yet the relatively unnoticed pollution of the town's water supply was even more detrimental to health. The porous Bunter Pebble Beds and Keuper Sandstone had once provided a copious and reliable natural reservoir of fresh water. But Rawlinson explains:

> ... when such a district becomes crowded with inhabitants, streets, middens, cesspools, and graveyards, as all large towns are, then open subsoil, full of water, is rapidly converted into a dangerous nuisance. The infiltration from every source of impurity passes into the sand and gravel,

and all the water drawn from such strata is of necessity impregnated with the offensive matter.

In such a predicament there was only one feasible — albeit expensive and technologically challenging — remedy. That was to keep the excrement and the water supply apart, by providing the town with two separate networks of underground piping, the one to distribute pure water to every household, the other to carry the nightsoil out.

This was the foremost recommendation of the Chadwick Report. Nor was Birmingham slow to at any rate embark upon such a difficult and, until then, uncharted course. Indeed, it was the very first big industrial town to acquire a comprehensive system of piped water.

The Birmingham Waterworks Company was established by Act of Parliament as early as 1826, with authorization to raise an initial capital of £150,000 and to supply 'good wholesome water' to 'the parishes, hamlets, or places of Birmingham, Aston, Duddeston, Nechells and Edgbaston'. The company's source of water was to be the River Tame, and by 1831 the Salford Reservoir and Aston pumping station had been opened, with supplies being pumped from there up to the smaller storage reservoir off Monument Lane, Edgbaston.

At first there were few customers, availability was intermittent and confined to certain districts only. But by 1853 water was not merely being raised from Salford Reservoir (297 feet) to that on Monument Lane (532 feet), but also from this last up to the High Level Reservoir on the Hagley Road (602 feet). And this meant that, using gravity flow, a constant water supply was thereafter available throughout the entire borough.

There were soon serious problems with the quality of the River Tame's water, most of which had its origin in the ever more heavily polluted Black Country. But three Acts of

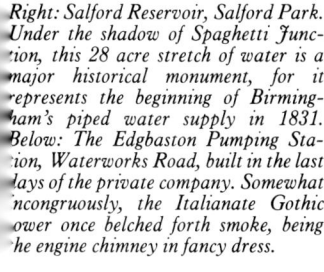

Right: Salford Reservoir, Salford Park. Under the shadow of Spaghetti Junction, this 28 acre stretch of water is a major historical monument, for it represents the beginning of Birmingham's piped water supply in 1831. Below: The Edgbaston Pumping Station, Waterworks Road, built in the last days of the private company. Somewhat incongruously, the Italianate Gothic tower once belched forth smoke, being the engine chimney in fancy dress.

The Birmingham Waterworks Company's Office, Broad Street; and from 1875, the Office of the Corporation Water Department.

Parliament between 1855 and 1870 enabled the company to construct 7 further reservoirs, including one on the River Blythe at Whitacre. Meanwhile, the district it served was expanded to embrace Handsworth, Yardley, King's Norton, Northfield and parts of Harborne. In 1875, on the eve of its purchase by the corporation, the Birmingham Waterworks Company had a gathering area of 190 square miles, 10 storage reservoirs covering 85 acres, 16 pumping engines, and 266 miles of street mains. A further 3 reservoirs, covering 92 acres, were under construction or prospected.

As Bunce, less technologically blasé than ourselves, wrote in 1885, 'an undertaking of this nature and magnitude involved engineering skill of no common order, and required also courage, and forethought, and an intelligent and high-minded recognition on the part of those who provided the capital and directed the operation of the company'. Yet throughout this whole period only the better-off could avail themselves of its services. The remainder had to purchase their drinking water from water-carts; or, in the case of the bulk of the working classes, continue depending on contaminated well water.

The Street Commissioners, who down to 1851 went on acting as the main local government authority for all environmental matters, played an important supportive role so far as the Waterworks Company was concerned. As well as co-operating on such matters as the laying of iron conduit pipes, they regularly purchased 'a vast quantity of water ... for watering the streets and roads' of the town. Moreover, when it came to drainage and sewage disposal, for which the Commissioners themselves bore direct responsibility, far from prevaricating, they set about planning a comprehensive system as early as 1842, the very year of the Chadwick Report.

In essence this system, which still provides the framework of the town's drainage today, was designed by the enterprising surveyor to the Street Commissioners, J. Pigott Smith, with the help of his London counterpart, John Roe. It was based on the installation of 'two great mains', known as the Hockley Brook Main and the River Rea Main (see map on page 165). Both of these were planned to start within half a mile of the highest point in the then borough (615 feet), and to convey the sewage by means of gravity to a single outlet point on the Tame at Saltley (290 feet). The first, which served the north of the town, ran from near Sandon Road for 6¼ miles along the line of the Hockley Brook. The second, sewering the south, started at the borough boundary near the Hagley Road reservoir and followed the Rea for 8¼ miles. In design these mains were egg-shaped, measuring 3′6″ x 2′6″ at their uppermost point, and widening to 5′9″ x 4′0″ at the outlet. Pigott Smith outlined the rest of the plan as follows:

> From these main lines of sewers minor street mains branch off in every direction . . . and as they approach the higher levels they decrease in size

Saltley Road Bellmouth, 1937. Together these converging sewers convey the whole of the sewage from the Nechells Green area into the River Rea Main. The two egg-shaped ones on the right, the largest of which measures 4′ 6″ x 2′ 9″, are of Victorian origin. They are still in service. (By kind permission of David N. Rogers, C.Eng., City Engineer).

to a twelve inch pipe, all well ventilated and capable of being flushed. As a whole, these sewers are calculated to carry off the sewage of twice the present population, and all other water, with the exception of extraordinary rainfall.

Well up with the times, at any rate in intention, Pigott Smith then went on:

In connection with this system of sewers it is proposed ultimately and universally to introduce the water closet with the connected apparatus, and house drainage by means of tubular pipes. This will cause the total abolition of the cesspool retaining organic refuse beneath or near habitations. We shall also be in great measure relieved from the present costly nightsoil department ... together with the foul nuisance of depots which fill our streets nightly with offensive matter...

Clearly, to finance from the rates and to fully implement such a scheme would be the work of several decades. But by 1848 sewers had already been laid along 43½ miles of the borough's 124 miles of roadway.

Another public utility for which the Street Commissioners were initially responsible was street lighting. However, throughout the early Victorian period, the supply of gas for this, like piped water, depended on private enterprise. A John Gosling was the first to erect a gasworks and lay gas pipes in Birmingham, making contracts with the Street Commissioners for the lighting of a number of thoroughfares, as well as supplying business premises and private households. This was in 1817, and two years later an Act of Parliament incorporated Gosling's business as the Birmingham Gas Light & Coke Company.

In 1825, though, with gas still lacking over much of the town, a rival company was sanctioned by Parliament. Known as the Birmingham & Staffordshire Gas Light Company, this operated from the Swan Village Gasworks at West Bromwich, and as well as supplying parts of Handsworth and Aston

Manor, laid its mains throughout the Borough of Birmingham, and indeed was ultimately authorized to extend its coverage to include Yardley, King's Norton, Northfield, Harborne, Smethwick and Sutton Coldfield.

Rawlinson reported that in 1849 the Birmingham company was supplying 805, and the Staffordshire company 1,280 public lamps in the borough. But he also asserted that their charges, particularly to private consumers, were excessive, and suggested that this was partly due to the fact that 'there are two separate establishments, with distinct offices, and two sets of mains'.

Below: Panoramic view of the Swan Village Gasworks, West Bromwich, in the 1920s. This plant dates back to the inception of the Birmingham & Staffordshire Gas Light Company in 1825. Right: Part of Swan Village Gasworks today. Above: John Gosling's gasworks has long disappeared, but this road name still reminds us of its location – in a road off Broad Street, and beside what became known as the Gas Street Canal Basin.

Negative Parsimony

During the first fifteen years of Victoria's reign, and the last fifteen of their own, the self-elected Birmingham Street Commissioners — mainly Whig and wealthy, but also highly efficient and public spirited — were engaged in a veritable fever of activity. Apart from their indirect concern with gas and water, and their own ambitious sewerage scheme, they were responsible for everything to do with the maintenance and improvement of communications as a public utility. This included the control of railway construction, together with the accommodation of the two central stations; the macadamizing of roads and footpaths, which had previously been paved with spiteful 'sharp-pointed pebbles'; the making of new thorough-fares such as Albert Street, and the constant widening of old ones in order to remove bottle-necks and make provision for the ever increasing traffic flow.

Yet while this old oligarchic body was wrestling so bravely with the expanding town's expanding problems, Birmingham's new democratically elected municipal corporation was making an almost unbelievably ineffectual start to its history. Through no fault of its own, having been granted its charter in 1838, it was not until 1842 that the legality of the charter was confirmed, and with it the council's right to raise a borough rate, and to begin discharging its only initial administrative function, the control of the police. Less excusably, this four years of impotence was followed by a further nine of no more than minimal achievement.

The main reason for this was the fact that, despite their political radicalism, most of the early councillors soon showed themselves to be committed, not so much to public service and improvement, as to the opposite policies of economy and *laissez faire*.

Furthermore, however ironically, such an attitude may perhaps be seen as a virtually inevitable consequence of the early borough council's democratic status — or at least of the extremely restricted nature of its democratic franchise. For, although the population of the town in 1841 was 182,922, the number of householders whose rental qualification of £10 per annum (plus 2½ years' residence) qualified them to vote in municipal elections was under 6,000 — or barely 3% of the whole community. And this tiny group of burgesses were not merely the only people who had a say in municipal government. Because of the relatively high rateable value of their properties, and also because the rates of most tenant householders had to be met by landlords out of rents, this same tiny group of inhabitants bore the main brunt of paying for municipal government — or at any rate may reasonably be forgiven for thinking that they did so.

Perhaps a thousand burgesses, being rich merchants, factory owners or professional men, could hardly have had any justifiable worries on this score. But the great majority were small manufacturers, traders and shopkeepers of fairly modest means. Naturally enough, too, the composition of the electoral roll was duly reflected in that of the council itself. Recent research has suggested that in 1839, 11 of the 64 council members (or 17%) belonged to the 'social *élite*' of the town, whereas 35 (or 55%) were 'small businessmen'; in 1842 the corresponding proportions were 14% and 47%.

With such a restricted 'representation of the people', it was almost a case of too little democracy being worse than none at all. The Street Commissioners were not directly answerable to ratepayers, and could therefore ignore their opinions and complaints to a considerable extent, showing as much or even more concern for the interests of the community as a whole. And the Street Commissioners were notoriously big spenders. But a council which was elected, and in large measure financed, by under 6,000 inhabitants was almost bound to find itself tempted to 'leave things alone', and certainly to set the utmost store by economy.

It is a strange paradox, therefore, that Birmingham's 'small masters' and their like, who from the socio-economic point of view helped to bridge the gap between the very rich and the very poor, thereby tending to produce an unusually homogeneous community, seem politically to have had exactly the reverse effect. In any case, it would be difficult to argue that during the period these 'little men' dominated municipal affairs as burgesses and ratepayers they did much to further 'the union of classes', or that local philosophy which Lord Briggs characterized as laying emphasis on 'mutual interests', 'inter-dependence' and 'common action'.

The early council's poor record seems all the more regrettable because between 1838 and 1851 a remarkable series of General Acts of Parliament were encouraging municipal corporations not merely to equip their towns with essential institutions but also to provide a wide range of enlightened social amenities, such as public baths, parks and recreation grounds, public libraries, museums and art galleries.

Dourly, the borough council concentrated on essentials. Easily the most conspicuous surviving monuments to the first thirteen years of Birmingham municipal government, therefore, are the architecturally impressive but socially sobering bulks of the borough prison and asylum out at Winson Green. These institutions were opened in 1849 and 1850 respectively. By 1852 the Board of Guardians' new workhouse had arisen in the same vicinity, thereby completing a bleak, if all too essential, threesome of early Victorian institutions of last resort.

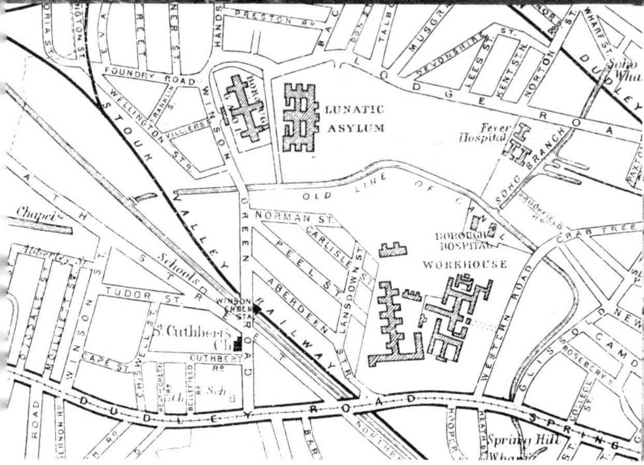

The gaol and asylum together involved the borrowing of £187,086, and unable to escape capital expenditures of this order, perhaps it is no wonder that the council made every effort to economize in other directions. The borough's first Chief Police Superintendent, for instance, was appointed at an annual salary of £250, as against the £800 stipend of his Home Office predecessor. Similarly, the force he commanded was restricted by the Watch Committee to 270 men, as against the previous 310. Despite constant complaints, too, and the obvious fact that a rapidly increasing population was rendering police provision ever more inadequate, no increase was sanctioned until 1849, and then by a mere 10 constables.

Of course, with William Redfern—the man who in 1838 had looked forward to the corporation becoming 'a great instrument of social welfare'—as the borough's first Town Clerk, and such high-minded public servants as Samuel Beale, William Scholefield, and Joseph and Charles Sturge in the council chamber, enlightenment was never entirely absent, either from the council's deliberations or its policies.

One sign of this was the exemplary pains it took to make 'Winson Green Asylum' a place for caring and curing, rather than mere incarceration. Indeed, this much is suggested by the building itself, which, although now known as All Saints

Top left: The Borough Gaol, now Winson Green Prison. Designed by D. R. Hill, Pevsner calls this 'a toy fortress, all castellated and round-arched'. Top right: The Borough Asylum, now All Saints Hospital. Again the architect was D. R. Hill, who this time used the Tudor style. Above: The Birmingham Workhouse, now incorporated into Dudley Road Hospital. Here the somewhat sterner Tudor design was by J. J. Bateman. The map (from Murray's Warwickshire, 1899) shows the close proximity of these institutions, on what had formerly been Birmingham Heath.

98

Hospital, still serves a similar purpose today. Looking almost as grand as a great country house, it is almost as beautifully sited. For it stands on a high bank, with a wide expanse of open land in front of it. This originally served as a 20 acre farm on which inmates could work usefully — and, it was hoped, therapeutically — in the open air. This and other practices of the early asylum might be criticized today. But with its 'care for diet and physical health', and its 'constant efforts . . . to keep patients' minds occupied in pleasant and interesting ways', this institution soon gained a high reputation, both among government inspectors and the public at large. It was even reported that by the end of its first year 10% of the patients had been returned to the outside community with their sanity restored.

A second enlightened early municipal enterprise was the building of the town's first public baths in Kent Street. Even before the passing of the 1846 Act allowing municipalities to own baths and wash-houses, over £6,000 had been collected by a privately organized Baths Association. This spur proved sufficient to persuade the corporation to erect a swimming baths, with attached laundry facilities. According to Showell, the latter 'turned out to be not wanted'. But the baths, which were opened in 1851, were crowded from the beginning, and there were frequently long queues waiting for admission.

In sharp contrast to progressive municipalities like Liverpool and Manchester, however, none of Parliament's other adoptive measures were followed up in early Victorian Birmingham. At the time when the Kent Street venture was evoking so much enthusiasm, the council passed a resolution which stated that a 'public park or open space suitable and convenient for walking, amusement and recreation would be of great benefit to the inhabitants'. But nothing was done to implement this resolution. Nor was anything done at this stage to provide the town with such other government encouraged amenities as a museum, art gallery, or even a public library.

Considering the municipal corporation's relative inactivity in the many fields where it already had the power to act, it seems ironic that this body should have been so utterly determined to take over the work of the Street Commissioners. Yet as early as 1844 Town Meetings of ratepayers were already voting in favour of sweeping away 'the Babel of confusion in Birmingham local government'.

In terms of administrative structure, a 'Babel of confusion' it certainly was. Apart from the Borough Council, the Guardians of the Poor and the Birmingham Street Commission, there were two further Street Commissions — for Deritend and Bordesley, and for Duddeston-cum Nechells — plus three sets of Highway Surveyors: for Deritend, Bordesley, and Edgbaston. So, as Rawlinson observed, the town had 'eight distinct and separate government powers'; and he went on:

Kent Street Baths, built 1849-51 by D. R. Hill in 'a thin brick Gothic' style.

These establishments act in opposition to each other. The Commissioners of Birmingham expend large sums of money to keep the sewage of the town out of the River Rea, and the surveyors of Edgbaston make a sewer to turn their refuse into that river.

Another problem with the old patchwork system of local government was the extremely restricted authority which any given public agency possessed. This, too, was noted by the perceptive Rawlinson:

The Commissioners of Birmingham have made sewers, but have no power to construct private drains, or to compel parties to construct them, although large sums of money have to be expended to remove and cleanse accumulations of foul, dangerous, and highly offensive matters, which might be more cheaply passed into sewers.

Nor were the two small Street Commissions anything like so efficient as that for Birmingham. The commitment and skill of Pigott Smith were beyond question. But in 1845 his counterpart for Duddeston had told a Parliamentary Committee, amidst roars of laughter, that 'he never could see that there was any art in laying down sewers', that 'he never had no instruction', that 'he knew nothing of the use of a spirit level', and that he 'took levels [for sewers and roads] by three sticks: crow-sticks'.

Aware of the many problems, from the early 1840s, the Birmingham Street Commission had repeatedly pressed to have its powers increased and its district enlarged so as to include the whole borough — if not the 'natural drainage district'. But in the eyes of the local radicals, whatever its merits, this body represented an upper middle class clique, and as such a permanent affront to the democratic principles which Birmingham had so long championed. Apart from the Street Commissioners' lack of accountability, their enemies also constantly attacked them for extravagance, arguing that the rates they imposed, and the debts they ran up, were needlessly high. Once the democratically elected borough council took over, ratepayers were assured, the town would be governed both more efficiently and at a much lower cost.

With the ever increasing nationwide concern about public health, however, it was the sanitary condition of the town that eventually provided the strongest argument for amalgamation. Realizing this, immediately on the passing of the Public Health Act of 1848, the council petitioned the General Board of Health to arrange for an inspection of the borough. The inspector it appointed was Robert Rawlinson, whose report of the following year has already been extensively quoted. And, as the general tenor of his comments will have suggested, he came down strongly in favour of the transfer of all local government powers to the municipal corporation.

The Birmingham Street Commissioners at first resisted, but eventually bowed to the inevitable, and even co-operated in the drafting of the 1851 Improvement Act. This transferred the responsibilities of all local government bodies within the borough—apart from the Board of Guardians—to the municipal corporation, which thereby became the sole authority for roads, street improvements, lighting, public buildings, markets and fairs, etc. The same act also empowered the corporation to purchase the Birmingham Waterworks Company, though not the two gas undertakings. Most important of all, it gave the corporation the powers of a local Board of Health, and in so doing charged it with the positive duty of completing the sewerage and drainage scheme, and of improving sanitary conditions throughout the town.

On the face of it then, the Birmingham Borough Council, having at last reached the position achieved by Leeds in 1842, Manchester in 1846 and Liverpool in 1847, now had the opportunity of becoming one of Britain's major reforming municipalities. Unfortunately the same electoral and financial constraints which had inhibited its activities before 1851 continued to do so afterwards. The town had been promised greater efficiency *and* greater economy. Yet there was never the slightest chance that the new municipal corporation could provide both. Instead, for the next twenty years, council politics became a perpetual struggle between those who championed the first and those who championed the second.

Things began well enough when the new council took over in January 1852. Having wisely appointed Pigott Smith as the first Borough Surveyor, a loan of £100,000 was quickly allocated for the continuation of his drainage scheme. Within twelve months a further 8½ miles of main sewers were completed or under construction. On 1 August 1853 'a numerous party . . . assembled' at Nechells Green, 'to inspect the progress of the works connected with the outlet of the new sewerage of this Borough', and to celebrate 'the great system of sewerage that had been inaugurated that day'. Meanwhile, work on street improvement had also been proceeding apace.

But from the spring of that same year, Joseph Allday, the son of a Digbeth butcher, was organizing a municipal revolt at the hands of what a local newspaper called 'the unprogressive tradesmen class . . . not accustomed to . . . spending large sums of money'. From that time onwards the radical Birmingham Council became divided between an 'economist' and an 'extravagant' party.

The latter pressed hard for the purchase of the Birmingham Waterworks Company, as authorized by the 1851 Act. But in 1854, backed by a Ratepayers' Protection Society, the economists defeated this proposal, so putting off the municipalization of water for two full decades. The following year Allday's men—again with the ratepayers behind them—blocked proposals for increased borrowing and higher rates to finance the continuation of street improvement and the sewerage scheme. The Public Works and Finance Committees resigned *en bloc* in protest. But this only opened the way for the economists to replace them, with Allday assuming the chairmanship of both committees.

During the next four years remarkable economies were forthcoming. The annual deficits incurred by the council between 1852 and 1856 add up to almost £90,000, which was roughly equivalent to a whole year's municipal rate. The period 1857-9, by contrast, produced three annual surpluses totalling over £52,000.

However, the social cost of this 'negative parsimony' was no less unmistakable. Despite the council's responsibilities for public health, and the fact that Liverpool, for instance, already had a full-time Medical Officer, Birmingham decided in 1855 that even the services of a part-time equivalent were no longer needed, his duties being transferred to the Inspector of Nuisances. In the same year Pigott Smith estimated it was necessary to spend £8,000 per annum on the roads and footpaths of the borough for the next twenty years. He was authorized to order 500 square yards of 'Yorkshire flagging'. The 'state of the Borough Funds' also prevented any of the 1,200 street lamps then required from being provided. And when 500 new lamps were sanctioned two years later, that still left the town with 45 miles of unlit streets.

But the most serious consequence of Allday's programme of ruthless retrenchment was the virtual abandonment of the sewerage scheme. One wonders whether Rawlinson had second thoughts about his 1849 recommendations when he was again charged with inspecting the sanitary state of the town nine years later. The same offensive open sewers, and courts overflowing with nightsoil were still to be seen everywhere. Furthermore, by 1858 there was an additional difficulty. Most of the sewage which was being piped out of the town was simply shot untreated into the River Tame, and the resulting pollution was so repulsive and dangerous that, pending the construction of the necessary filtration plant, a legal injunction had been obtained which prevented the corporation from making any further connections to its main sewers.

Throughout this unhappy period there was constant friction within the council, and also between the economist politicians and municipal officials. The Borough Surveyor was accused, not only of being too friendly with the opposition and 'repeatedly at variance with the Public Works Committee', but also of conduct 'inimical to the interests of the Borough'. Robert Stephenson had called Pigott Smith 'one of the first surveyors of the day'. But in 1857 he was replaced by his deputy, W.S. Till, who was expected to do the same job on half the salary.

The economists suffered a setback in the elections of November 1859. Even 'the mighty and omniscient Joe Allday' lost his seat as an alderman and withdrew from politics. The brief interlude which followed enabled the extravagant party to force through the 1861 Improvement Act. As well as sanctioning the borrowing of £50,000 for street improvement and £150,000 for renewal of work on the drainage scheme, this statute provided that all new houses were in future to be equipped with proper drains.

The same intermission brought the building of two new public baths — in Woodcock Street and Northwood Street — the appointment of a borough analyst to test food and drink, the adoption of a public libraries scheme (see page 135), and the purchase of 102 acres of land at Witton for the first borough cemetery.

Moreover, although by 1862 the economists were regaining control, at least one of their leading members had a much less socially harmful philosophy than that which had dominated the 1850s. A partner in the famous scales firm, Thomas Avery, like Allday, was against 'imposing heavy burdens upon the present generation of ratepayers'. Nevertheless, he believed that the way to secure economies was not through the sheer neglect of the public interest, but by good management and the careful evaluation of priorities.

Quite rightly, the main priority in the short term was adjudged to be the drainage scheme. The work of laying street sewers was therefore resumed as a matter of urgency, with builders and developers now being required to meet half the cost. By the end of 1864 the council could inform the Home Office that Birmingham had 'constructed on the most approved principles of modern science a complete and efficient system of main and contributory sewers in all the populous parts of the Borough', as well as tackling the outfall problem by spending £25,000 in the purchase of land and the construction of purification works.

Less happily, however, the corporation's report went on to state that an area of 7 acres was already covered to a depth of 4 feet with the sludge that came out of the Saltley filter beds. The only way its advisers could then see of coping with this

Although 'full to repletion', as late as 1852, 'upwards of 3,500 interments' took place in the town's four main churchyards. The 12 acre General Cemetery at Key Hill (below) and the 11 acre Church of England Cemetery, Warstone Lane (right) were established by private shareholders in 1836 and 1848 respectively. Both were 'tastefully laid out in walks interspersed with lawns and shrubberies'. Rawlinson, however, had condemned burial grounds 'situated within the heart of the town', and it was in response to this advice that the first municipal cemetery, opened in 1863, was sited 3 miles away, at Witton (above).

problem was to acquire further land over which such 'wet mud ... impossible to resolve until it had lain for several months' could be distributed. The council accordingly pressed the government for legislation which would enable local authorities to create and run sewage farms outside their own boundaries. Moreover, when this legislation was passed in 1865, an area of 140 acres just north of the Saltley outflow was at once purchased for that purpose.

Elsewhere economy was more in evidence. The library scheme was fortunately continued, and in 1864, after much shilly-shallying, £19,000 was found for the purchase of Aston Park. On the other hand, a Medical Officer of Health was still considered unnecessary; and although the 1861 Improvement Act had given the council the right to municipalize gas and to institute public tramways, the economists steadfastly refused to have anything to do with either extravagance.

Thomas Avery, 1813-1914.

As late as 1869, too, the council was still opposed to the purchase of the waterworks company. Significantly, however, by that time, Thomas Avery himself was arguing in favour of municipalization, even supporting his new-found cause by publishing a pamphlet on 'Polluted Well Waters'. This emphasized the appalling extent to which wells used by at least 150,000 inhabitants remained contaminated. With the contents of so many middens seeping into the subsoil, the solid matter in most wells had been shown to vary from 100 to 500 grains per gallon, as compared with a pure standard of 13 grains. From this Avery was driven to conclude that only a publicly managed water supply, conducted irrespective of profit, could possibly meet the needs of the whole population, and especially of the artisan class. And in strange language for an economist, he added:

> Wealth can always take care of itself, but poverty cannot; and surely it is the duty of a wise local government to endeavour to surround the humbler classes of the population with its benevolent and protecting care.

Avery himself was a Congregationalist; and for several years now leading Birmingham nonconformist ministers had been enunciating a new 'civic gospel'. Clearly, their message was beginning to get through.

And so, no doubt, was another message, less eloquent but no less politically potent. In 1869, following an amendment to the 1867 Reform Act, the right to vote in municipal elections was extended to all householders—including those who lived in the courts, with their contaminated wells.

The days when small manufacturers, traders and shopkeepers could control local politics, and the municipal development of the town, were over. The time had come for Birmingham to think again of 'the union of classes', and to recover some sense of its moral mission.

Provisioning the Town

At the beginning of the nineteenth century Birmingham's food requirements could still just about be handled through its traditional open air markets. Those for corn and vegetables continued to be held in the Bull Ring, as they had been for centuries. Horses, cattle, sheep and pigs were offered for sale in High Street, Dale End, New Street and Ann Street (Colmore Row).

Down to 1851 responsibility for all matters relating to markets and fairs rested with the Street Commissioners, who were also responsible for preventing the town seizing up from the thrombosis of men, vehicles and animals which constantly threatened its streets. It was no doubt mainly with the last danger in mind that as early as the 1810s the Street Commissioners acquired the site of the old Birmingham manor house, and having filled in its moat, laid out an open cattle market of almost 3 acres. Once this 'New Beast Market' or 'Smithfield Market', as it came to be called after its London counterpart, had been opened in 1817, it was an offence to 'expose to Sale any Cattle, Horses, Sheep and Pigs, Hay or Straw, in any other Part of the said Town' — except, that is, during the 'two Public Fairs', when horses could still be sold 'in a Place called the Horse Fair, as usual'.

By the late 1820s, with the stalls of meat, vegetable and other sellers straggling ever further beyond their traditional bounds, the next priority of the Street Commissioners was to get the bulk of the Bull Ring's retail marketing off the streets. This led to the erection of the Market Hall, opened in 1835, and at a total cost of about £100,000, claimed to be 'the finest building of the kind in the kingdom'. Behind its 'lofty Doric entrance in High Street', 600 stalls could be 'accommodated in

The Bull Ring – from a sketch by David Cox.

the body of the hall, and space left for four thousand persons to perambulate'.

At least in the judgement of one private company, though, even these arrangements did not provide sufficient market facilities for Birmingham's rapidly advancing population. So in 1837 Messrs E. & C. Robins erected, 'at their own expense', a New Market Hall in Prospect Row, at the far end of Coleshill Street. This private retail emporium, with its interior 'divided into compartments for the sale of provisions', was still flourishing in 1852. But although the building survived at least until 1905, when it is marked as 'Old Market Hall' on the second edition of the 25 inch Ordnance Survey map, according to Dent, 'it was only used as a market for a few years'. Probably the reason for this failure had more to do with location than anything else. Three-quarters of a mile away from the Bull Ring, it could hardly have attracted town-centre shoppers. And one must assume that the trade emanating from the predominantly poor Ashted/Duddeston part of the town in which it was situated was not enough to sustain it either.

The only other private venture in market building was a great deal more successful. Well into Victoria's reign, despite the fact that 'with the increase of population, the trade in grain became of great importance', Birmingham's corn market remained on the pavements of the Bull Ring. But in the mid-1840s, encouraged by the Street Commissioners, a joint stock company was formed for the erection and operation of a corn exchange. Birmingham must have been one of the very last major towns in the country to acquire such a virtually obligatory institution. Nor does much risk-taking seem to have been involved in the project, for within 7 years of the Birmingham Corn Exchange's opening in 1847, 'trade had so much increased as to render it necessary to afford more accommodation'. This long forgotten building was sited on a piece of ground roughly in the centre of the present-day Marks and Spencer's, with access from Carrs Lane and High Street, via Corn Exchange Passage. Designed in the Classical style, it had

Left: The Market Hall, as depicted in an engraving made soon after its erection. Above: The interior of the Market Hall in the early 1900s.

a great wagon-vaulted glass roof, 'with counters and desks on each side for the accommodation of dealers'. The corn exchange transacted its own business on Tuesdays and Thursdays, with the latter being the 'principal day', when it was 'crowded with farmers and dealers from the town and country'. By 1874, too, and probably long before, a Grocers' Market was being held in the same building on Wednesdays, when the attendance of leading firms from London, Liverpool, Manchester and Bristol made it 'one of the most influential in the provinces'.

Just before their demise the Street Commissioners managed to carry through two other improvements in the town's marketing arrangements. The first was the erection of the St. Martin's Market in Jamaica Row, which was opened in 1851 as a wholesale butchers' market for carcass meat. The second was a major reorganization of the Market Hall. Among other things, this brought the fish market in from Dale End, by providing 'eighteen fish stalls . . . with movable marble slabs 4 feet wide, and each fitted with a water tap, and an independent drain'.

For all their sterling service in other directions, the record of the Street Commissioners in this sector of their responsibilities was far from exemplary. Liverpool, Manchester and Leeds had much better marketing facilities by 1831 than the Street Commission left Birmingham with twenty years later. At Leeds, for instance, huge sums of both public and private money had been spent on the erection of a corn exchange, a butchers' market, a fish market and three general retail markets — all before 1830.

The St. Martin's Meat Market, Jamaica Row – from a photograph taken in 1891.

Yet if the Street Commissioners did not do enough, even less was done once the town council had taken over from them. In fact, the corporation's only significant improvement prior to the 1880s was the erection of a Wholesale Fish Market. The site for this, at the corner of High Street and Bell Street, was bought by the corporation in 1861, it having 'found that the supply of fish was much restricted by the inadequate accommodation, and that the public was consequently deprived of obtaining, at a cheap rate, a necessary article of food'. After the deprivation had been allowed to continue for a further eight years, this market was eventually opened in 1869. And predictably, it 'proved so valuable by rapidly increasing the fish supply to the town', that a 'strong case' was soon being made out for its extension — a case which was of course as strongly ignored.

Overall then, the operation of Birmingham's central markets, even in high Victorian times, remained so obdurately and ludicrously archaic as scarcely to be believable. Right down to the opening of the Smithfield Vegetable Market in 1884, 'the standing places of wholesale vegetable dealers' — for a town of over 300,000 people — 'were in High Street, opposite the Market Hall, in Worcester Street, and in Spiceal Street (all in the open air) and in the vaults beneath the Market Hall'.

The procedures of the meat trade were even more astonishing. Because of its distance from the ports, Birmingham continued to rely almost exclusively on the bringing in of live animals long after other towns were able to avail themselves of the American and Australian dead meat trade. In 1865 a proposal was made to acquire Duddeston Hall and grounds 'for a cattle, hay, and horse market'. Bunce tells us:

> The property, well adapted for the purpose, comprised about nineteen acres of land, the main sewer of the town ran through it, two railways bounded it, the streets adjoining it were perfectly formed and drained, and there was upon it a mansion house suited for a market tavern and office. This property could be bought for £10,000, and the surplus land not required for the market might have been sold for the whole of the money.

But there was 'fierce opposition to the project . . . the Council came to an even division, and the Mayor, not considering it proper that so important a question should be carried by his own voice, gave his vote against it'.

Throughout the 1870s over a quarter of a million cattle, sheep and pigs were passing through Smithfield Market each year. And these animals were not merely driven into the centre of the town; having been bought at the Tuesday, Thursday or Saturday market, they then had to be taken away by the butchers for slaughter on their own premises. There were constant complaints about 'the inconvenience and danger of cattle being driven through the crowded streets', and 'the annoyance of having slaughter-houses located . . . in the midst of a densely peopled district'. Yet 'no further proposal to remove the cattle market was made until 1883'—and then it was turned down.

The bulk of the Victorian town's food supply was doubtless produced in the West Midland region. As early as 1813 'large flats of cucumbers, onions, and asparagus; also potatoes and turnips' were being grown in the Vale of Evesham 'for the supply of neighbouring markets, and the town of Birmingham'. Such provisions would have been transported by road and canal; but even more, as time went on, by railway. Curzon Street, in particular, eventually became largely devoted to the handling of corn, livestock, meat, fish, fruit and vegetables.

Though there must have been countless barrow-boys trundling their hand-carts through the streets, within the town itself much of the movement of food—as of raw materials and finished products—would have been done on horse-drawn wagons and carts. In 1873 horse duty was paid on 6,275 animals, while in the following year the Greater Birmingham area had 76 carriers, together with 164 'smiths, blacksmiths and farriers', many of whom would have made the biggest part of their living from shoeing horses.

Although, then as now, lots of Birmingham people must

Blacksmith's shop, Parliament Stree, Small Heath (now demolished, The wall inscription reads: 'SHOER GENERAL / SMITHS / Specialists IRON WORK OF/ Every DES CRIPTION.

Above: A purpose-built corner shop, dating from c.1870. This once stood at the junction of Herbert Road and Glovers Road, Small Heath. Below: One of Birmingham's few surviving Victorian shop fronts – A. R. Wood & Co., Loveday Street. Comparison with early photographs suggests that this could well date back to the 1870s or '80s.

have hunted for bargains in 'the Bull Ring shopping centre', the finger-tips of the food distribution network, as it were, consisted of the local shopkeepers who were to be found in almost every street of the town. Some idea of the growth in their numbers may be gained by comparing figures derived from the 1835 *Pigot's Directory* with similar reckonings made from the 1874 *Kelly's*. According to the first, in 1835 there were 90 'bakers and flour dealers', 275 butchers, 165 'grocers and tea dealers', 29 'fruiterers and greengrocers', 17 fishmongers and 450 (general) shopkeepers. By 1874 the corresponding figures were approximately 510 bakers, 440 butchers, 600 'grocers and tea dealers', 600 'fruiterers and greengrocers', 86 fishmongers and 2,000 shopkeepers.

The 1835 figures total 1,026, and those for 1874 4,236. This apparent fourfold increase is undoubtedly an over-estimate: because, whereas *Pigot's* takes in only Aston Manor and Handsworth, *Kelly's* also includes shopkeepers in Smethwick, Harborne, Yardley, King's Norton, and other surrounding parishes. Nevertheless, over the same period, Birmingham's population little more than doubled. So, despite the primitive marketing infra-structure, it looks as though the town as a whole may have been considerably better supplied with food in the 1870s than in the 1830s.

We have already come across evidence for 'rapidly increasing' fish consumption, and the fact that the number of fruiterers and greengrocers goes up no less than twentyfold tempts one to think in terms of a democratization of fresh fruit and vegetables. Moreover, although butchers show a mere 60% increase, the 33,152 beasts, 12,839 calves, 141,627 sheep and 64,455 pigs that were offered for sale at Smithfield in 1874 point to a weekly meat consumption of over 2lbs. for every man, woman and child in the town – with the greater part of this being beef. 'Birmingham is a beef-loving community', wrote a local journalist a few years later. Compared with pre-industrial days, it certainly seems to have been a well fed one.

Charity, Church and Chapel

Even after the local government reorganization of 1851, the Poor Law remained outside the control of the municipal corporation. Moreover, its operation was greatly complicated by the fact that it involved, not only three parishes, but three separate Poor Law Unions. Showell tells us:

> The parish of Birmingham works under a special local Act, while Edgbaston forms part of King's Norton Union, and the Aston portion of the town belongs to the Aston Union, necessitating three different rates and three sets of collectors, &c. If a poor man in Moseley Road needs assistance he must see the relieving officer at the Parish Offices in the centre of the town; if he lives on one side of Highgate Lane he must find the relieving officer at King's Heath; but if he happens to be on the other side he will have to go to Gravelly Hill or Erdington.

Apart from the administrative anomalies resulting from this situation, there were considerable differences between the poor rates of the three Unions. In 1856 the cost of maintaining the poor belonging to Birmingham worked out at 5s. 2½d. per head of population, as against Edgbaston's 3s. 5d., and Aston's 1s. 1¾d. The main reason for this was that Birmingham parish, being entirely urban, contained 73% of the borough's population. But despite the municipal meanness, Birmingham also had the reputation for being a comparatively generous poor law authority. In any case, a government enquiry showed that its 1856 poor law expenditure was rather above the average for the 'fifty principal towns' of the country — and this despite the fact that there must have been less destitution here than in many other big urban centres. Aston, by contrast, claimed as late as 1873 to have a lower *per capita* expenditure on the poor law than any other union in England.

The Birmingham Board of Guardians consisted of 106 members down to 1873, when the number was reduced to 60. Elections could be as keenly contested as those for the borough council, and as a rule produced 'the usual local result' of a strong Liberal majority. The town's original workhouse had been built in Lichfield Street in 1733 to hold 600 poor persons. If only because of the constantly growing population, it was soon 'found necessary to house a much greater number'. Yet, although under discussion from the foundation of the Board of Guardians in 1783, the erection of a replacement building had to wait a further 70 years. Opened in 1852, the workhouse at Winson Green provided accommodation for 3,000 inmates, with several additions being made later 'in the shape of new wards, enlarged schools, and extended provision for the sick, epileptic and insane'. In 1878 Cottage Homes and Schools were established at Marston Green 'for the rearing of children left in the care of the Guardians'. The number of persons receiving 'in and out relief' naturally fluctuated with economic conditions. Thus, during 1876, at the back end of a period of unprecedented prosperity, the tally of Birmingham paupers

ranged from 7,058 to 7,687. With the slump that followed, the number 'on the books' in 1881 varied from 7,183 to 11,064. However, even this last figure represented under 4.5% of the total population—and many of these were receiving relief in respect of old age.

Thinking of England generally, Lord Briggs has called the period 1783-1867 'The Age of Improvement'. As we have seen, so far as municipal government in Birmingham is concerned, its last thirty years might more reasonably be regarded as 'The Age of Neglect'. Fortunately this municipal laggardness in the face of unprecedented environmental and social problems was offset—at least to some extent—by the tireless activities of an ever increasing number of charitable and voluntary organizations, and a good deal of individual philanthropy.

Joseph Sturge and Josiah Mason stand out as Victorian Birmingham's archetypal philanthropists: the first because of his 'practical benevolence towards men in general', the second for the munificent way he re-cycled the profits of his great industrial enterprises for the communal good.

The Quaker corn merchant and radical reformer, Joseph Sturge, 'had by nature a strong sympathy with all who were in need'. Apart from campaigning for the abolition of slavery through his weekly paper *The Philanthropist,* and for the enfranchisement of the working classes through his Complete Suffrage Union, Sturge became deeply involved in the Birmingham Temperance Society, and—when the town was desperately short of open spaces—provided several acres of land to be used as playing fields for children. In 1845 his interest in adult education led him to establish the invaluable Severn Street First-Day School (see page 131), and later to play a prominent role in the formation of the Midland Institute. It was Sturge, too, who started off the Reformatory School movement in Birmingham, using three cottages in Ryland Road, while 'one of the last works of his benevolent life' was to found a Reformatory House at Stoke Prior, near Bromsgrove. John Bright said of this modest, intensely religious man on his death in 1859, 'there was about him a ripeness and goodness which is rarely seen'; the *Daily Post* that 'the extent of his private charities and good deeds was known only to himself'. But perhaps the tribute Sturge himself would most have appreciated came from a Birmingham working man: 'Why, he wasn't a bit proud; he used to make himself just one of *we*'.

Joseph Sturge does not seem to have been excessively wealthy. As one of the town's leading pen makers and a partner of the Elkingtons, on the other hand, Josiah Mason clearly amassed a vast fortune. There was nothing particularly unusual about his first benefaction, which consisted of an almshouse for 20 women and a home for about 30 girls in Station Road, Erdington, both opened in 1858.

However, Mason tells us that when he informed the then

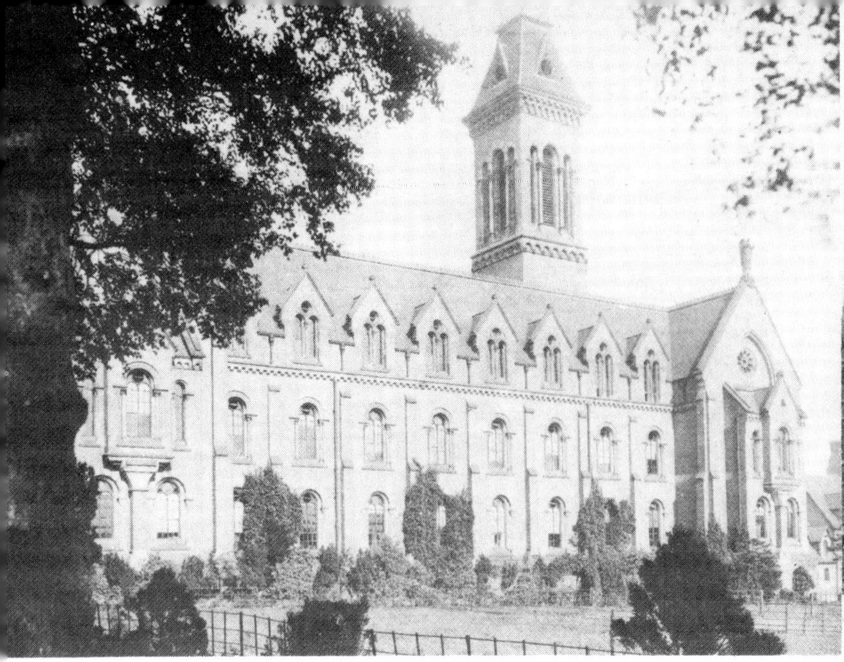
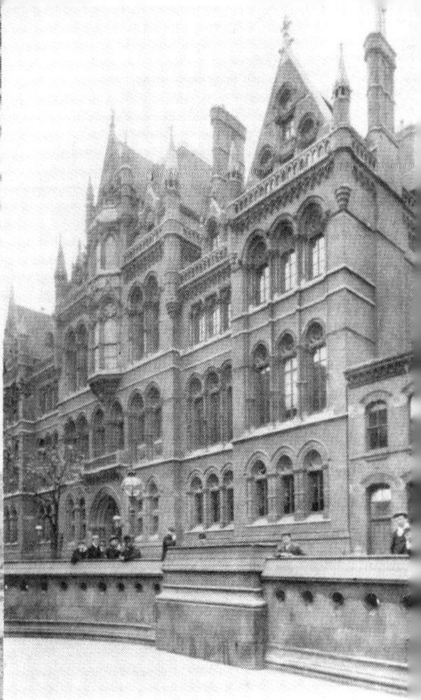

Rector of Birmingham, Dr. Miller, of his intention to follow this by establishing an orphanage on the nearby Chester Road for upwards of 200 children, and mentioned the sum of £100,000, the latter looked him up and down 'as if I were scarcely to be considered in my senses'. Others were equally staggered. Indeed, when Miller in his turn reported this figure to an advisory committee on the project, one of the gentlemen present interrupted with, 'I presume you mean £1,000?'; and the philanthropist himself had to be asked to corroborate the two extra noughts.

Left: Mason's Orphanage, 1908. (Warwickshire Photographic Survey, Birmingham Reference Library). Right: Mason College, as photographed soon after it had become 'The University' in 1900.

In the event, Mason's generosity far exceeded his promise. As well as spending £60,000 on the 'stately building', by the time he handed over his orphanage to a body of trustees in 1869, he had added endowments worth £200,000. Nor was that all. The following year Mason embarked upon spending almost as much again, this time on the foundation of Mason College, which was opened in 1880, and was eventually to provide the nucleus of Birmingham University.

It helps to grasp what all this meant in terms of the currency of the time—and therefore the reason for everyone's incredulity—when we reflect that Mason's total philanthropic outlay must have been in excess of the produce of four years' municipal rate. It is hardly surprising that he was rewarded with a knighthood; or that, once 'the worthy knight' was no longer 'alive to veto the project', 'a figure of him' was erected outside his college in Edmund Street.

No other Birmingham manufacturer came anywhere near to rivalling Mason in charitable prolificacy. William Chance and Robert Winfield were both noted as public benefactors, spending 'thousands in the erection of schools', among other

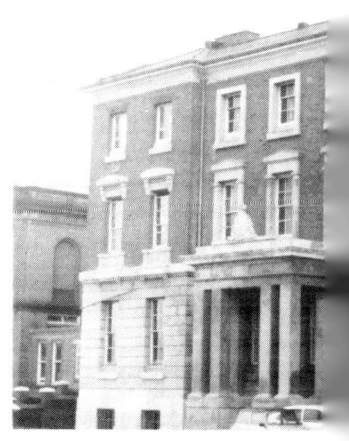

William Sands Cox, 1802-75.

Queen's Hospital, Bath Row. This was designed by Bateman and Drury, and still has the Warneford arms above its portico. With Martin & Chamberlain's 1873 addition, just visible on the left, it eventually became the Birmingham Accident Hospital.

things. But Joseph Gillott, although a millionaire and 'a great patron of artists' whose pictures realized £170,000 at his death, bequeathed a mere £3,000 to local charities.

All the same, the case of G. F. Muntz suggests that charity was habitual enough among the wealthy for it to have been actively expected of them. As a leader of the Political Union and then a Birmingham M.P., Showell tells us that Muntz was for many years 'the idol of his fellow-townsmen'. Yet this did not prevent him from being widely censured for 'having given little' during his life, and on his death 'leaving not one farthing to charity'.

Apart from industrialists, the town frequently had occasion to be grateful to its big landowners. The Calthorpes helped to provide the Deaf and Dumb Asylum (1814), the Botanical Gardens (1832), the General Institution for the Blind (1851) and Calthorpe Park (1857), not to mention three of Edgbaston's nineteenth-century Anglican churches. The fourth Lord Calthorpe had the reputation of taking part in 'all the major Birmingham charitable and voluntary societies' of the mid-Victorian period, while Edgbaston itself could be described by a local poet as 'patron of the charities of life', with 'buildings dedicate to charity and education'. In his very different manor of Saltley, C. B. Adderley, later Lord Norton, was instrumental in endowing the community with Saltley College (1852), Saltley Reformatory (1853), Adderley Park (1856) and Adderley Park Free Library (1864).

Just as salutary as the gifts of the big spenders, however, were the many charitable foundations which depended on the generosity of large numbers of middle class and even artisan townsfolk. Although usually inspired by the passionate commitment of one or two individuals, most of the town's hospitals had to rely, both for their foundation and subsequent upkeep, on widely based community support of this kind.

Queen's Hospital, for example, was a pipe-dream of the eminent local surgeon W. S. Cox, who, having established Queen's College for the training of medical students in 1828, then had the idea of erecting a sister institution. This was conceived partly as a training hospital. But it was also to serve 'the sick and lame poor' of the town, being open 'for the reception of contagious fevers, as a dispensary for out and home patients', and for 'poor lying-in married women, who are attended in their homes, under the direction of the professors of midwifery at Queen's College'.

Among the initial contributions to this institution was not only £1,000 from the Rev. Dr. Warneford, whose coat of arms was accordingly placed above the main entrance, but also 'the munificent sum of £905 raised by a penny subscription instituted by the artisans of the town'. Once the hospital had opened its doors in 1846, 'subscribers of one guinea' had 'the privilege to recommend one in-patient, one home-patient, and one out-patient, and so on in proportion'. As with other of the so-called 'associated' charities of this period, management was by a committee, which — in the case of Queen's — was elected annually 'by subscribers of two guineas and upwards'.

Like Queen's Hospital, many medical and other local charities were essentially secular in their origin and organization. But since religion provided the main motivation for good works in Victorian times, the number of benevolent institutions, big and small, which were inspired and run by the various Christian denominations must have been absolutely countless. The very top priority among the churches, though, had to be the salvation of souls, and in a rapidly expanding community that meant a constant drive on the part of committed Christians to erect and pay for new places of worship. As in other industrial towns, therefore, the first thirty years of Queen Victoria's reign brought what in retrospect looks like a veritable orgy of church building: and this despite the fact that progress never kept up with requirements — or at least with requirements as these were assessed by church leaders at the time.

The Birmingham Church Building Society was founded in 1836 with the aim of erecting 10 new churches in the poorer districts. In the event, this fund-raising organization was able to build only 5, these being shared between the town itself, Duddeston, New Town Row and Bordesley. By 1865 another 10 Anglican churches had been erected in Birmingham, Edgbaston and Aston, together with a further 9 in the outlying parts of what was ultimately to become Greater Birmingham. The peak of church construction, however, came between 1865 and 1869, when 10 new edifices were financed by the Birmingham Church Extension Society in half as many years.

Architecturally, Birmingham's church builders, as well as making the town — in Pevsner's words — 'a key centre' of the Gothic Revival, ensured that it 'remained true to the Gothic style' for the rest of the century. Apart from Pugin's brick and slate, yet amazingly dramatic, St. Chad's Roman Catholic Cathedral (consecrated 1841), R. C. Carpenter's recently

Contrasts in early Victorian Gothic. Left: R. C. Carpenter's St. Andrew's Bordesley, built 1844-6. Right: S. S. Teulon's St. John the Evangelist Ladywood, built 1852-4.

restored St. Andrew's Bordesley (1846) was much admired at the time for its restraint and historical correctness. By contrast, S. S. Teulon's St. James's Edgbaston (1852) and St. John's Ladywood (1854) go every bit as far in the direction of quirky and picturesque originality. J. A. Chatwin, the versatile local architect who designed St. Augustine's Edgbaston (1868), for instance, as well as rebuilding the parish churches of both Birmingham and Aston, was rather more conventional, and therefore earned the reputation of being 'thorough but uninspired'.

By the 1860s the Gothic style was spreading from church to chapel architecture; and indeed, through the work of men like D. R. Hill and J. H. Chamberlain, to public, industrial, commercial and domestic buildings. Except for cheap housing, the 'dull uniformity' of Georgian classicism was totally banished. Nevertheless, in all but the ecclesiastical field, Gothic extravagance now had to compete with a wide range of equally ornate Classical styles — and mixtures of styles — that derived ultimately from the Renaissance and the Baroque. Most Victorian architects were happy to cross and re-cross stylistic frontiers, but it was undoubtely Yeoville Thomason who emerged as the foremost local exponent of nineteenth-century Classical idioms.

Both the Catholic and Jewish communities were smaller in Birmingham than in many other large nineteenth-century towns, though the former grew steadily, if only because of the steadily growing Irish population. Having had 2 Roman Catholic churches in 1835, therefore, by 1874 Birmingham had 8, with others at Handsworth, Erdington, Oscott and Sutton Coldfield. In 1851 the Jewish community is thought to have numbered about 730, and its synagogue was then in Severn Street. Five years later, though, this was replaced by Thomason's 'splendid Byzantine edifice' in Blucher Street.

The progress of nonconformity is difficult to trace in detail. Apart from the multiplicity of sects, congregations would often meet in houses or other non-ecclesiastical buildings. Even chapels could change denominations or pass out of religious use altogether. The chapel-like building which still stands on the corner of Bath Street and Loveday Street, in the Gun Quarter, was originally built by the Wesleyans in 1839. *Kelly's Directory* of 1874 lists it as a United Methodist chapel. But some time after 1884, this denomination also relinquished it, and according to the 1906 *Kelly's*, it had by then become part of the 'Abingdon Works Co. Lim., gun, rifle & pistol makers'.

As the town grew, the major nonconformist sects seem to have propagated their kind almost in the manner of a biological species. Thus the Particular Baptist chapel in Cannon Street (founded 1738) opened daughter chapels at Newhall Street (1814) and Heneage Street (1841). Then in the next generation, as it were, Newhall Street opened The People's Chapel, Great

Above: The Hebrew Synagogue, Blucher Street. This was erected in 1856, to a design of Yeoville Thomason, later the architect of the Council House. Below: The front of the former Methodist Chapel in Bath Street, built by the Wesleyans in 1839.

King Street (1848); and Heneage Street two daughter chapels, at Bradford Street (1848) and Yates Street (1859). Meanwhile, similar lines of descent were emanating from the General Baptist church in Lombard Street, for instance, and the Congregational chapel in Carrs Lane.

Such a process naturally ensured vigorous growth. In 1830 the town had possessed 21 nonconformist chapels, as against 12 Anglican churches. By 1851 the municipal borough could boast 54 chapels, as against 25 Anglican churches. The corresponding figures had risen to 90, as against 46, by 1872 — with perhaps an additional 23 nonconformist places of worship elsewhere in the Greater Birmingham area.

According to the Religious Census of 1851, churches and chapels within the municipal borough then provided seating accommodation for 61,554 people, which represented 26.4% of its total population of 232,841. By 1872 the equivalent percentage had increased to 29.5%, with 101,253 sittings for a population of 343,787. So during the 1850s and 1860s the provision of places of worship was at least keeping up with the growth in numbers.

But what proportion of the population actually went to church? The 1851 census gives adult attendance figures for morning, afternoon and evening services on Mothering Sunday of that year. The fact that a considerable number of people must have gone to more than one service makes it impossible to arrive at an exact total for church-goers. But a recent general survey estimates the Birmingham figure at 36% of the population. This was marginally better than Sheffield's 32% or Manchester's 34%, yet well below the 45% and 47% attributed to Leeds and Liverpool respectively, and scarcely half the nationwide estimate for small towns and rural areas, at 71%.

It would be difficult to argue, however, that Birmingham's relatively poor showing was due to shortage of accommodation. For, overall, on the Sunday of the census the town's existing churches and chapels were no more than two-thirds full at their busiest service.

The figures for the various denominations show that, despite Birmingham's reputation as a strong centre of nonconformity, and the fact that it had over twice as many chapels as churches, only 29,162 of the 61,554 main service attenders — or 47.4% — were chapel-goers.

With 7,814 worshippers, Wesleyans formed the largest nonconformist denomination. The addition of New Connexion Methodists (1,388), United Methodists (870), Primitive Methodists (656), and Welsh Calvinistic Methodists (32) produces a total of 10,760. By this yardstick, then, Methodism, in one or other of its forms, accounted for over a third (36.9%) of all nonconformists, and about a sixth (17.5%) of all church attenders. Against this, 7,317 people attended Baptist main services, while Congregationalists mustered 6,657, Unitarians 3,084, Quakers 774 and Presbyterians 700.

The town's four Roman Catholic churches provided 1,549 sittings, with 3,383 people attending mass on the Sunday in question. But all this left the Church of England a very clear 'top of the poll'. In fact, with 30,843 worshippers turning up at its most popular services, it looks as though in 1851 something like 5 out of every 10 Birmingham church-goers would have been Anglican.

All denominations were undoubtedly at their least effective among the working classes. But again, it is by no means certain that this was due to a serious lack of provision. In any case, the maps of Victorian Birmingham show that many places of worship had been deliberately sited in working class districts. Such an area was at Hockley, in the triangle of predominantly back-to-back territory between Summer Lane in the east, Constitution Hill/Great Hampton Street/Hockley Hill in the west, and New John Street in the north. Within this triangle by 1874 there were three Anglican churches — St. George's Church, Upper Tower Street; St. George's Chapel of Ease, Hospital Street; and St. Nicolas's, Lower Tower Street. To these the nonconformist denominations had added the Swedenborgian New Jerusalem Church in Summer Lane, the Baptist People's Chapel in Great King Street; a New Connexion Methodist chapel in Unitt Street; and a Wesleyan chapel, Primitive Methodist chapel, and Presbyterian church in New John Street.

By the middle of the century, too, although better-off people continued to pay pew rents, most of the places of worship in working class areas offered a high proportion of free seats. In 1874 this applied to 600 of the 800 seats at the Church of Immanuel, Broad Street; 1,600 of the 2,200 seats at St. Thomas's, Bath Row; and all 600 of the seats at St. Nicolas's, Lower Tower Street.

Nor were the slum areas, where the poorest of the poor lived, entirely neglected. As early as 1837 Cannon Street Baptists and Carrs Lane Congregationalists founded slum mission rooms at Hill Street and Allison Street respectively. At first such institutions were little more than preaching stations. But with Quakers and Unitarians leading the way, the emphasis gradually shifted more in the direction of social and community work. By 1854 the latter's Lawrence Street mission had a day school for girls, a newsroom and library, a savings club, a Band of Hope, even a cricket team. In the same year Dr. Miller founded a working men's association at St. Martin's with a similar range of activities, while in 1860 the Wesleyans opened their Bloomsbury Institution as a centre for educational, social, charitable and temperance work. Many similar working class and slum missions, with their characteristic 'Halls', followed.

Because of their concentration in the now redeveloped inner districts, relatively few mission halls have survived. This is the large, but late, 'Institute' in Jenkins Street, Small Heath.

If the 1851 Religious Census is to be trusted, Birmingham was one of the very few big industrial towns in which Anglicanism was numerically as strong as dissent. Its dominant role in elementary education was no doubt a major reason for this (see page 124). But the Church of England also showed a remarkable commitment to those at the lower end of the social scale. Rejecting the idea of 'ragged churches', it led the way in making large numbers of free pews available. Incumbents like G. R. Bull of St. Thomas's, J. C. Barrett of St. Mary's, and the Hon. Grantham Yorke of St. Philip's, worked tirelessly among the poor. 'We must go among them', urged Dr. Miller in 1855, using words that might have been accommodated in George Dawson's 'civic gospel', 'we must improve their dwellings, we must provide the means, not only of mental self improvement, but of physical recreation'.

Yet if the Church of England struggled hard to hold its own among the 'masses', by and large, it was nonconformity that exercised the greatest sway over the town's leading citizens. Most people in the upper echelons of local society were practising Christians, and it was predominantly through them that religion effectively influenced charitable work and welfare services, along with many other aspects of secular life.

In Birmingham such people had the choice between two establishments, as it were. On the one hand, there were the leading Churchmen, who were generally Tory in politics. Apart from parsons, this group included prominent doctors, lawyers, bankers and schoolmasters; some merchants and manufacturers; and also prestigious landed families like the Adderleys and the Calthorpes. On the other hand, there were the leading dissenters, the majority of whom were big factory owners and businessmen, with Whig or Liberal — though rarely radical — political leanings.

These two contrasting *élites* had deep historical roots in Birmingham, and there was a long tradition of them co-operating in public affairs, for the good of the town. During the early Victorian period they also tended to draw together in the face of the more extreme forms of working class radicalism. Education persisted as a perennial bone of contention. But this aside, once the Church Rate issue had been settled in the early 1830s, there was comparatively little bad feeling between the leading Anglicans and dissenters of the town. Even their respective clergy were generally on friendly personal terms, favoured dialogue rather than bigotry, and constantly championed the principles of freedom of conscience and toleration.

But if the Church and dissent showed a good deal of mutual respect, there was never any doubt that it was the latter which provided the town with its most forceful and effective secular leaders. And within nonconformity, there was never any doubt that the big battalions of Methodism counted for

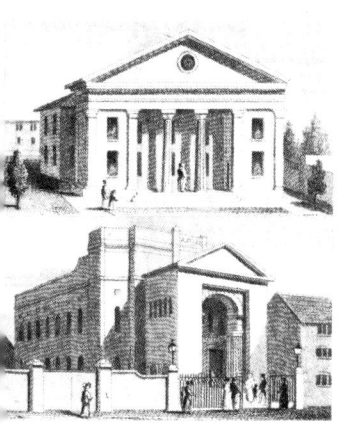

Top: Mount Zion Chapel, Graham Street, opened 1824. Above: Carrs Lane Chapel, rebuilt 1820.

much less from this point of view than the numerically smaller Baptist and Congregational communions—and above all, the tiny Unitarian and Quaker sects.

If only because of their practice of inter-marrying, these last gave the town, not outstanding individuals merely, but whole dynasties of civic leaders: with such renowned names as Beale, Chamberlain, Kenrick, Martineau, Phipson and Ryland among the Unitarians, and Barrow, Cadbury, Lloyd and Sturge among the Quakers.

Such families mostly lived in Church-of-England Edgbaston, where ironically not a single nonconformist chapel was to be found. But it was to Graham Street, Carrs Lane, Bull Street, Edward Street and Broad Street that they proceeded on Sundays. In consequence, as we shall see, the most influential places of worship in the Victorian town were the Mount Zion Chapel, Graham Street, opened in 1824 as a Presbyterian church, but used by Baptists from 1827 onwards; the 'mother chapel' of Birmingham Congregationalists in Carrs Lane, rebuilt in 1820; the Quakers' Bull Street Meeting House, rebuilt 1856-7; the Unitarian Church of the Messiah in Broad Street, opened 1862; and George Dawson's Church of the Saviour, Edward Street, opened 1847.

The Religious Census figures for the rural parishes of the Greater Birmingham area are not to hand. But in these places church attendance would no doubt have been much closer to England's rural average of 71% than to the 36% of nearby Birmingham. Certainly, the religious life of early and mid-Victorian Harborne, as depicted by Tom Presterne, seems a world away from the teeming industrial town, with its proletariat that was apparently so indifferent to Marx's 'opium of the people'.

At Harborne in 1845 the Rev. John Garbett took over the parish from a 'High Church vicar', whose 'intolerance of nonconformists', 'ritual services' and 'surpliced choir' had made him extremely unpopular. The newcomer 'was welcomed by all the people'. Surplices were banished, the organ and choir were removed back to the west gallery, 'and a healthy religious tone was soon established'.

A few years later, the Church Rate issue caused a 'great turmoil', with 'a huge bus-load of voters on the Nonconformist side' being brought from Smethwick (then still a part of Harborne parish) to vote for their man in the election of Churchwardens. But 'the Nonconformist was defeated', and 'we settled down fairly amicably afterwards under the influence of this sensible old vicar'. When the Rev. John Garbett came through the village, 'men would stand aside and make their bow, and the women their curtsey'.

The Struggle for Literacy

One of the ways the Victorians tried to come to grips with the problems of rampant industrialization and urbanization was by the constant setting up of investigatory committees and the carrying out of statistical enquiries. Many of these were government sponsored national surveys. But the collection of factual information on various worrying aspects of contemporary life could also be initiated locally. The earliest important Birmingham survey of this kind was undertaken in 1838 by a local Statistical Society for the Improvement of Education.

The Blue Coat School, established i 1724 and 'greatly enlarged and im proved' in 1794. Although the origina building has gone, the school itself sti flourishes at Harborne.

According to the resulting report, rather under 1 in 5 of the town's 45,000 children aged 5-15 were then attending day schools; and over two-thirds of these came from middle class or skilled artisan families who could afford to 'educate' their children privately. The 155 'dame schools' of the town were said to have 2,263 children on their rolls. What good they did them was another matter. Some of the mistresses openly admitted to the investigators that they disliked teaching and only kept their school as a way of earning a little money. So the majority of these short-lived ventures were probably more effective at minding children than teaching them. Nor do the 103 'Common Day Schools' sound much better. Their 2,860 pupils apparently got plenty of caning but little oral instruction, spending most of their time practising writing, and learning by rote. Arguably, therefore, the only children who were receiving anything like a decent private education came from among the 822 who attended the 36 schools that were described as 'Superior'. And with an average of 23 pupils each, many of these must have been so small and ephemeral as to be no more than relatively satisfactory.

Turning now to the still extremely embryonic public sector, the 1838 municipal borough had the King Edward Grammar School, plus 21 endowed elementary schools and 6 (separate) infant schools, which catered for about 2,800 pupils between them. The schools under Anglican patronage, apart from King Edward's, included the Blue Coat Charity School, on the north-eastern side of St. Philip's churchyard; the National schools in Pinfold Street, at Ashsted and Bordesley; and day schools in connection with several Anglican churches. Among non-Anglican institutions were St. Peter's Catholic School; the boys' and the girls' Lancastrian schools; the Protestant Dissenting Charity School for 'poor Female Children'; the New Jerusalem Free School in Summer Lane, and the Wesleyan School in Union Street.

In general, the 1838 investigators were favourably impressed by the standard of teaching and the educational facilities offered by these endowed institutions. However, although called 'free', a good few of them charged fees of from 1d. to 4d. per week, which must have made them largely

inaccessible to the town's poorer families. The 24 Evening schools, which taught the three Rs along with some general knowledge to about 560 pupils, were even more expensive, costing from 4d. to 1s. per week.

Finally, as a somewhat desperate 'long-stop' to its educational system, early Victorian Birmingham had about 56 Sunday schools, roughly half of which taught reading only, and the other half reading and writing. Perhaps as many as 10,000 children attended these invaluable institutions. But three-quarters of the youngsters in question received no other form of education. And according to the 1838 survey, 23,000 out of the town's 45,000 children aged 5-15 attended no school whatever, and therefore presumably grew up totally illiterate.

From the nationwide 1851 Census of Schools we learn that 35.5% of Birmingham's children aged 5-14 were then enrolled at a day school. This compares with Wolverhampton's 30% and Manchester's 32%, on the one hand, but on the other, with Leeds's 48%, and an average for the 71 'principal towns' in England and Wales of 52%. It is also interesting that whereas under a third of Birmingham's 1838 scholars were in public and endowed elementary schools, the equivalent 1851 figure works out at almost 48%. This was no doubt partly due to an expansion of the public sector between the two dates.

At the same time, with the constantly increasing pressures of industrialization, the town itself must have presented an ever less inviting environment to the promoters and patrons of private schooling. So perhaps it is hardly surprising that by the mid-Victorian period the number of private schools inside the borough had roughly halved; or that this decline was compensated by a substantial increase in the surrounding districts. Among over 250 'Schools — Private' listed in the 1874 *Kelly's Directory*, we find 7 at Harborne, for instance, 17 at Handsworth, and no less than 38 in the conveniently situated Aston Manor.

King Edward's Grammar School, New Street, in the early 1900s.

Birmingham's most prestigious school of course, then as for centuries past, was what the 1874 *Kelly's* is still calling the 'FREE GRAMMAR SCHOOL, Founded by King Edward VI'. Moreoever, this institution's pre-eminence had been secured into the future by the way it had been completely re-structured and re-housed, following two parliamentary acts of the 1830s. Down to this time its curriculum had continued to be restricted mainly to the teaching of Latin and Greek. But now the school's scope was broadened by the development of a 'Modern' side, in which boys could study English, Modern Languages, Mathematics, Science and Drawing. Meanwhile, with the income from its property constantly increasing, the Governors were able to enlarge the school's New Street site, and to completely rebuild it to the Tudor Gothic design of Sir Charles Barry.

King Edward's more commodious accommodation in

turn enabled the number of pupils to be increased from barely 100 to upwards of 500. To the chagrin of nonconformists, boys could still only be admitted on the nomination of a Governor, all of whom had to be members of the Church of England. Nevertheless, at a time when nationally so many old grammar schools were continuing to run to seed, and when good institutions for the education of middle class children were so few in number, the reformed and up-dated King Edward's became an absolutely major educational boon to the town. In fact, by the mid-nineteenth century the two headmasters who had successively supervised the re-modelling — Dr. Jeurn and Dr. Prince Lee — had established traditions of academic excellence which gave this institution a recognized place among the great schools of the country.

Dr. James Prince Lee, Chief Master of King Edward's, 1838-48.

In the early 1840s, too, the same foundation was able to open four branch schools, which in the short term provided nearly 800 much needed extra elementary places in different parts of the town, and which by the 1880s were being developed into branch grammar schools.

Only one boys' private school could in any way compete with the academic standards of King Edward's. This was the Birmingham & Edgbaston Proprietary School, which, for understandable reasons, was established in 1838 by the local nonconformist *élite*, primarily for the education of their own sons. Financed on a share-holding basis, with proprietors able to nominate one pupil in respect of each £20 share, its aim was to combine 'the advantages of a classical and commercial education'. Accordingly in 1874 the 'Head Master' was assisted by a 'Second & Classical Master', a 'French Master', a 'German Master', a 'Lecturer on Chemistry', a 'Drawing Master', a 'Dancing Master' and Sergeant Major Robottom who was 'Drill Master'. Most of the Proprietary School's clientele must have come from Edgbaston, and it therefore made good sense that the 'handsome Elizabethan structure' which was built to house the school in 1841 should have been situated at Five Ways, on the Hagley Road.

Eight or nine other boys' schools in the Greater Birmingham area probably had some academic pretensions — and certainly they had headmasters with formal academic qualifications. Among these were the Handsworth Bridge Trust Middle Class School (later Handsworth Grammar School), opened 1862, and the old established King's Norton Grammar School and 'Bishop Vesey Free Grammar School', Sutton Coldfield. More ephemeral private schools with qualified headmasters included the Camp Hill Collegiate School and two academies at Acock's Green taught by Reverend gentlemen, the one with B.A., the other with B.A., LL.B.

The average private school, though, was probably not much better half way through Victoria's reign than at the beginning. About 170 of the 250 listed in the 1874 *Kelly's* were kept by spinsters or married women exclusively for girls, as against about 50 identifiable boys' 'academies'. Some of these schools were accommodated in purpose built—or at least purpose adapted—premises, like the building in Monument Road which in 1874 served as William Nichol's "boys' boarding school", and which, once one is armed with this information, remains recognizable as such even today.

Other middle class private schools were accommodated in distinguished buildings, like the Misses Grimley's "ladies' boarding school" at Stratford House, Camp Hill, or the Misses Howell's "ladies' school" at Metchley Abbey. Tom Presterne tells us that the three Howell sisters were 'highly educated', and their pupils Wesleyans 'of the higher classes who paid high fees'. But like their predecessors of a generation before, many of these educational ventures—however pretentious in their nomenclature—must have been both extremely small and extremely domestic. We know that Victoria Road, Aston Park, was mainly lined with medium sized terraced houses that were built under the Freehold Land Society. Yet in 1874 it boasted no less than six private schools, including Mrs. Emma Jane Phipps's "seminary" in Clent Villas, Miss Sarah Sheppard's "seminary" in Rock Place, and Miss Ann Perry's "ladies' school" in Providence Buildings.

So far as public elementary education is concerned, the first half of Victoria's reign was a period of substantial progress. Between 1839 and 1870 at least 130 new schools were founded in the Greater Birmingham area. Some of these were factory schools, others institutional schools like Josiah Mason's Orphanage School (1868) or the 'new Workhouse schools for boys' at Winson Green (1869). Then there were the free-standing schools established by individual benefactors. A number of the town's 'ragged schools' came into this category. So did more general schools like that founded at Saltley in 1858 by Joseph Wright, a railway carriage maker, 'for the children of his workmen and of the village'; or the one erected by James Horsfall beside his wire works at Hay Mills in 1863. Attached

Below: The former William Nichol's 'boys' boarding school", Monument Road. Right: The School Room, Hay Mills, built by James Horsfall, May 1863.

to 'the glass and chemical works of Messrs. Chance Brothers', too, was 'a pile of buildings for educational purposes' which, among other things, provided 'excellent schools ... for the children of persons in their employ, and of the other inhabitants generally in the vicinity'.

Despite these industrially, institutionally or individually backed ventures, however, the vast majority of early Victorian elementary schools owed their existence to the missionizing zeal and educational enthusiasm of the churches. Aided by state grants and church endowments, as well as voluntary subscriptions, the Anglicans led the way, opening schools at a considerably faster rate during this period than they were opening churches. Between 1839 and 1870 about 52 'National', 'Church', or other Anglican schools were founded in the borough itself, with a further 23 in the surrounding Greater Birmingham area. For reasons of economy, too, many of the resulting buildings embraced a boys', girls' and infant school — so that if these were reckoned separately the total of new Church of England schools would be substantially greater.

Relatively speaking, the Roman Catholics may have done virtually as well, for they established 11 new schools in the Greater Birmingham area between 1839 and 1870. But the nonconformist denominations apparently found it harder to compete. Lacking the endowed wealth of the Church, and obviously spending large sums on the erection and upkeep of new chapels, they were initially still further handicapped by their reluctance to accept educational grants from the state, and the state inspections that went with them. Certainly, whatever the reasons, only 8 Wesleyan schools were opened during these years, with the other sects establishing about 22 'British' schools between them. In 1846 it was reckoned that, as against the 1,921 children attending nonconformist schools in the borough, 5,837 — or three times as many — were attending those of the Church of England. It seems unlikely that the

Two early National schools. Above: All Saints Schools, All Saints Street, Hockley, erected in 1843. Right: St. Mark's, Helena Street, erected 1849. In its first year All Saints was accommodating 616 boys, girls and infants in three separate classrooms, or 'schools'.

The Lancastrian or British School, Severn Street, established 1809. This early nineteenth-century print shows the monitorial system in operation.

nonconformists would have improved on this proportion thereafter. Perhaps the leading role in bringing up the young which dissent thereby conceded to Anglicanism was one of the main reasons such a relatively high proportion of Birmingham adults were members of the Church of England.

The overall increase in the number of elementary schools of various kinds was accompanied by no less important improvements in the quality of the education they provided. At the time of Victoria's accession such schools had depended heavily on the ingenious but obviously limited monitorial system of instruction. But with the establishment of teacher training colleges — like Birmingham's own Saltley College, founded 1852 — more and more properly qualified teachers could be recruited; and this in turn encouraged a gradual extension of the curriculum, beyond the three Rs, to include grammar, history, geography, and even a certain amount of science. No doubt it also augured well for educational standards that by 1868 as many as 63 elementary schools in the town had come under regular state inspection.

Another way in which the early Victorian period brought undoubted progress was in making education available to the very poorest members of the community. National and British schools — if only because of their need to charge fees — might just as well not have existed so far as the 'submerged classes' were concerned. But by the 1840s schools were being established in the slum areas which, as well as being free, invariably 'doubled' as mission stations, distributing food and clothing, and generally befriending the poor.

One of Birmingham's early ragged schools was founded by William Chance in Windmill Street in 1845, with accommo dation for 280 children. Three years later 'the same benevolent gentleman' provided another similar institution in Digby Street. Meanwhile, in 1846 St. Philip's Ragged School was

The Worcester, Lichfield & Hereford Training College, more generally known as St. Peter's College, Saltley. Built 1847-52 by Benjamin Ferrey 'in a simple Tudor style', this now forms part of Aston University.

started in Lichfield Street, using a hired workshop. Soon this had also attracted over 200 children, who were 'watched over carefully, their faults patiently and kindly corrected . . .', while 'every other day they received a substantial meal'. In 1850 the St. Philip's school moved to a specially designed building in Gem Street, where, as the Birmingham Free Industrial School, it aimed to teach 'children of destitute parents', not merely 'reading, writing, arithmetic and Christian knowledge', but 'trades and industrial occupations'.

St. Martin's founded a ragged school in Well Lane in 1848, and this was eventually followed by others in Penn Street (1858), Slaney Street (1858), Vale Street (1862), Queen Street (before 1869) and Staniforth Street (1869). By this time, too, there was the Girls' Industrial School at Sparkbrook, together with 'reformatory schools' for boys and girls respectively at Saltley and Smethwick.

In 1861, when appealing on behalf of the United Hill Street and Inkleys Schools, which claimed descent from a ragged school founded in Swallow Street about forty years before, its committee argued that 'a personal visit' to the homes of 'the wretched, ragged, half-starved children':

> . . . would satisfy the most sceptical that in order to avert the evils of poverty, drunkenness, and dirt, and in many cases of gross immorality and crime, they must come forward and, without waiting for aid from Government, exercise their private charity and, by properly educating these unfortunate children, rescue them from utter ruin and from being pests to themselves and to society.

With this extension of schooling to the slum population, the mid-Victorian educational system became almost as precise a reflection of the town's distinctive class structure as was its housing and topography. Again, with King Edward's and Metchley Abbey on the one hand, and the ragged schools on the other, there was virtually total exclusiveness at either end of the social scale. Yet, as with housing, in between these extremes, a great deal of intermixing took place. For many skilled artisans undoubtedly sent their children to the lesser private schools of the town, while many lower middle class parents had their children educated, alongside those of the working classes, in at any rate the better of its National and British schools.

Until well after 1870 Sunday schools of all denominations continued to make a major contribution to elementary education in Birmingham. *Allens' Pictorial Guide* of 1852 tells us that 'Sunday schools are attached to nearly every place of worship', with '18,000, or 20,000 children . . . constantly in course of receiving the humble but useful portions of elementary knowledge which they are capable of imparting'. By the end of the 1860s it was estimated that no less than 84% of Birmingham's adolescents had attended a Sunday school at one time or another.

Sunday schools were frequently held in existing educational

Two early Sunday Schools. Above: The abandoned and derelict Unitarian Sunday School, Newhall Hill. Below: The now disused and blind-walled, but still well-preserved Sunday School at Yardley village.

and ecclesiastical buildings, but there were also many purpose-built structures, such as the Wesleyan Sunday School on Constitution Hill, the New Connection Methodist Sunday School in Hockley Street, or the Birmingham Free Christian Society's Sunday School in Lower Fazeley Street (see page 12). Opened in 1865 in 'one of the poorest districts', this last organization provided elementary education for hundreds of boys and girls, with the instruction being undertaken 'chiefly by working men of ordinary means'.

In 1868-9 the newly founded Birmingham Education Society carried out a second full-scale survey of the educational facilities of the town. This found that, out of a sample of 37,122 children aged 5-15, 14,464 were attending a day school at the time of the enquiry. So, whereas in 1838 under 20% of children within this age range were engaged in full-time education, by 1868 the equivalent proportion had doubled, to 39%. Moreover, despite the enormous population increase which had taken place between the two surveys, the number of children completely without any form of schooling had fallen from 23,000 to about 13,000. Unfortunately, such satisfaction as these facts may have brought contemporaries was far out-weighed by other considerations.

One of the report's most worrying disclosures was that Birmingham's existing public elementary schools — like its 1851 places of worship — were no more than two-thirds full. They were also mainly teaching very young children. For as against the 64% of school attenders who were aged 3-9, a mere 11% were 11-13. Furthermore, among a representative cross-section of 16,595 children aged 10-15, barely 1 in 4 was a scholar.

Taken together, these findings meant that a great deal more than 39% of the town's children spent some time at day school. But it also meant that for far too many such children the duration of their school stay was 'altogether insufficient for the purpose of education'. In fact, the average length of attendance worked out at 1 year 9 months for boys and 2 years 3 months for girls. The consequences were as disastrous as they were inevitable. Given an adequate commitment to schooling, most children aged 10-15 might be expected to be able to read and write. Yet of the 16,595 children within this age range, no less than 50% proved unable to write, and 36% could not read either.

But why, even when children went to school, was their school life so often and so severely truncated? It was not merely a matter of them starting work at a tender age. For although 37% of 10-15 year-old children were already in employment, almost 38% were found to be 'neither at school nor at work'. Some of the latter may have been needed at home to look after younger brothers and sisters while the mother went to work. But pretty certainly there was also a good deal of parental indifference if not hostility to education: and this may have been true not only in the slums, but to a certain extent among relatively prosperous workers as well. The compilers of the 1868 report drew attention to the 'large numbers of parents' who were 'able to send their children to school and yet . . . either from apathy or from selfish considerations fail to do so'.

Nevertheless, they also had 'no doubt that poverty is the cause of absence of a large number of children from school'. And this last contention is amply borne out by their detailed figures for different parts of the borough. St Mary's Ward, which was one of the very poorest, was in fact better provided with schools than any other. Yet with 2,620 places, it could muster only 1,262 scholars, which meant that a mere 48% of its school capacity was being utilized. At Edgbaston, on the other hand, where the spectre of poverty must have been relatively unknown, and where parents also presumably had a better appreciation of the value and importance of education, 89% of the public elementary school places were occupied at the time of the survey.

Despite the improvements that had occurred since 1838, therefore, the writers of the 1868-9 reports were extremely gloomy. Far too few youngsters, they concluded, were getting anything like an adequate education. Moreover, in their view, it was impossible to 'overstate the serious consequences that must ensue to society from the fact of . . . nearly half the children in Birmingham growing up in ignorance and idleness'.

From Mechanics' to Midland Institute

The early history of adult education in Birmingham is a history of false starts. The Birmingham Mechanics' Institute, which was established in 1826, had as its aim 'the Promotion of Knowledge among the Working Classes' by 'the cheap instruction of the members in the principles of the arts they practise, and in various branches of science'. The Committee report of 1829 claimed a membership of 1,550, counting juniors, and went on to describe how its classes 'in arithmetic, the mathematics, and ornamental and architectural drawing' had been 'numerously attended, with great advantage to the pupils'. There were also weekly lectures, which included courses in chemistry, mechanics and literary subjects. Inconvenienced by 'the Library and Class-rooms being in a different part of the town from that in which the Lecture-room is situated', the committee in this same year launched an appeal to raise £2,000 for the erection of a suitable building. Ten years later though, only £500 had been collected, and there was no alternative but to settle for the adaptation of an existing premises in Newhall Street. Meanwhile, and more ominously, the Institute's membership had badly declined from its initial level. There were a mere 350 full members in 1835, and although this figure had recovered to 487 by 1840 only 240 were men 'receiving weekly wages, and young persons under age'. Declining membership in turn meant inadequate subscriptions. And after a desperate attempt to boost recruitment by the staging of two expensive public exhibitions, in 1842 the Institute finally 'had to succumb to debt', with its headquarters passing into the hands of creditors.

Such was the tenacity of those who were committed to the adult education movement that the Polytechnic Institution was founded in the very next year, with much the same aims as the Mechanics' Institute. Through the generosity of Joseph Sturge, it even took over the latter's library of 3,000 volumes. But although the Polytechnic had built up a membership of 825 by 1846, like its predecessor, it soon ran into serious financial difficulties, and in 1848 received notice to quit its Steelhouse Lane premises. Other similar educational ventures, like the Athenaeum and the People's Hall of Science proved no less ill-fated. Indeed, even the old established and predominantly middle class Philosophical Institution was compelled to close its doors in 1849. While this last institution was in its death throes, however, Arthur Ryland and other leading members considered the possibility of bringing together their own body, the Polytechnic, the Society of Arts, and several similar organizations into a single comprehensive institution. And this seminal idea was eventually to lead to the formation of the infinitely sturdier Midland Institute.

But why was adult education so inordinately slow to develop in early nineteenth-century Birmingham? One problem as far as the working man himself was concerned must have been its relatively high cost. The annual subscription 'to admit a Member' to the Mechanics' Institute started off at 12 shillings, which was roughly half an average weekly wage at the time. Not surprisingly, when this was put up to 16s., consumer resistance was such that the order had to be quickly rescinded. Yet the Polytechnic Institution expected its 'ordinary' members to find a subscription of £1 per annum.

Showell suggested that the failure of the Mechanics' Institute was 'possibly through lack of assistance ... from manufacturers and large employers', who in general 'preferred strong men to wise ones, and rather set their backs against the opening of the doors of knowledge to their work people'. Upper middle class leaders of both Tory and Liberal persuasion gave active support to the adult education movement. Richard Spooner and Thomas Attwood were president and treasurer of the Mechanics' Institute respectively; William Scholefield became actively involved with the Polytechnic and the People's Hall. Nevertheless, the inability of the Mechanics' Institute to raise £2,000 for a suitable building over a ten year period hardly suggests a great deal of support from the wealthy inhabitants of the town. Neither does the fact that when the group of working men who built the People's Hall issued 2,000 £1 shares, 1,400 were never taken up, and 'the entire sum raised from the donations and shares of the wealthy, was only one hundred and fifty pounds'.

The political dissensions of the period could hardly have helped. Of the late 1830s, Lord Briggs says 'there were signs even in Birmingham that working class education might be regarded as politically dangerous'. In any case, the involvement of thousands of artisans, first with the Political Union and then with the Chartist movement, was bound to turn attention away from educational pursuits to a certain extent.

But the main reason all the early Victorian agencies of adult education failed to gather adequate working class support was probably deeper and more fundamental than any of the generally proffered explanations. Way back in 1825 'the institution for the Instruction of Mechanics' had been specifically conceived as a means of 'continuing the Education they receive at the Infant Sunday and Public Schools'. But how many 'mechanics' had received such an education? Even in 1854 the Artizans' Committee which was involved in setting up the Midland Institute was at pains to point out that:

> ... Though a very great impulse has of late been given to primary Schools ... it must not be overlooked that the Adult Operative of today had not such advantages to fall back upon, their boyhood was passed at a time when education was not valued or considered so important as it is now ... and the opportunities for securing instruction ... in reading, writing and arithmetic, by no means so plentiful, or efficient as they are now, it is not therefore to be wondered at that many have grown up to manhood necessarily ignorant of the first principles of ordinary education.

By the mid-1850s, however, this 'literacy barrier' was at last in process of being eroded away. The Artizans' Committee report itself acknowledges that 'there may be but few of the Junior population at present who cannot procure elementary education, (*should their parents desire it*)'. And just as importantly, from the mid-1840s onwards — though hardly before — strenuous efforts were being made to provide disadvantaged working men with 'sufficient Elementary Education to enable them to profit by the higher kind of instruction'.

Adult Sunday schools had existed in embryonic form at least since 1818, when Dr. Johnstone, a local physician, held a number of adult classes on Sunday evenings in his home at Edgbaston Hall. A few years later similar classes were offered by the vicar of Christ Church, New Street. But it was not until Joseph Sturge set up his first adult class in Severn Street that the adult school movement really began to count for something.

The First-Day School was born in 1845 when Sturge, realizing that existing Sunday schools made little provision for older scholars, persuaded 'some younger members of the Society of Friends' to start teaching 'a class of lads over fourteen' at the Severn Street British School. Before long 'grown men of various ages also sought instruction'. An 'adult division' was accordingly formed, with a separate 'Women's School' being established at the Girls' British School, Ann Street in 1848. By 1850 there were 282 men and 145 women scholars. A decade later the corresponding figures had risen to 654 and 300, while some 40 or 50 members of the Bull Street Meeting House were serving as teachers. Among these last were William White, Alfred Southall and George Cadbury, all of whom worked in the schools for over 50 years.

Astonishingly, after the first few months, classes were always held between 7.30 and 9.30 on Sunday mornings, being preceded by a 7 o'clock teachers' breakfast which Sturge himself invariably attended. As the movement gathered momentum, evening schools and lending libraries were developed, together with a wide range of social activities, from tea parties and day excursions to saving funds and temperance meetings. But the principal emphasis always remained on the teaching of reading and writing, coupled of course with the awakening of religious consciousness. One of the earliest testimonies to the First-Day Schools' success on both counts began as follows:

DEAR SIR, – When I come to Severn Street School, at the beginning of the new year two years ago, I could not any more have wrote a letter than have flyed. But I am getting proud now of my performance, for when my wife was gone to Nottingham to take care of her mother, I was able to write and tell her how me and the children was getting on, and I thought, sir, you would like to see that Severn Street had done some good. I never thought a bit about religion till I went to school two years ago, and now, thank God, I know a little what it means . . .

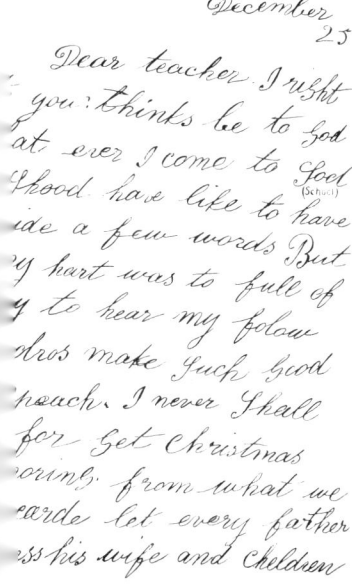

Right: The original classroom of the First-Day School, Severn Street, c.1895. Below: Facsimile of the first page of a letter written by a pupil of Severn Street, c.1870. Above: A prize label of the Severn Street First Day Adult School, 1881. The prize was 'The Throne of David', by J. H. Ingraham, in 'The Home Treasure Library'.

December 25

Dear teacher I right you thinks be to God at ever I come to Sool (School) I hood have like to have ide a few words But y hart was to full of y to hear my folow dros make Such good neach. I never Shall for Get Christmas orning from what we earde let every father ss his wife and children

Similar 'Early Morning Schools' were subsequently organized by many Birmingham churches and chapels, with Charles Vince conducting one at Mount Zion Chapel, for instance, and George Dawson at the Church of the Saviour. Other organizations provided adult evening classes, like the 'Congregational Society for the support of evening schools', which in 1848 reported that its 'adult classes had been well attended, and an additional room opened for the young men'. Moreover, by 1870 branches of the First-Day Schools were being established in other districts. The first of these utilized the People's Chapel, Great King Street, but later the newly opened Board schools provided convenient teaching centres. As a result of this outward expansion, and of the way in which some who had learned to read and write were prepared to stay on as pupil-teachers, by 1880 the number of men and women scholars had soared to 2,397 and 684 respectively. Bearing in mind the enormous back-log of unlettered adults which had been left behind by the inadequate educational provisions of the early Victorian town, this Quaker inspired adult school movement represents one of the most remarkable voluntary undertakings of the period.

Arthur Ryland, 1807-77.

Time and again in nineteenth-century Birmingham, it was 'the close association between middle and working classes' that really brought success, and this was certainly the case in adult education. The Mechanics' Institute had elicited the patronage of upper middle class leaders, but had no thought of instructing the middle classes. And indeed, at that time such people would have belonged to the Philosophical Institution, or similar middle class associations. The Polytechnic, with its 'honorary' and 'ordinary' membership, tried to bring together the middle and working classes. But the moment, or else the particular amenities it offered — including baths and a coffee house — were misjudged, and sufficient support failed to materialize from either quarter.

The scheme for the Midland Institute, which seems mainly to have been crystallized by 'Arthur Ryland and several friends' during 1852, was not only more timely but also more down to earth. The Philosophical Institution and several working men's organizations alike having failed, in essence the idea was to create a single institution which would serve as both a general scientific and literary association, such as might be expected to appeal to the middle classes, and an 'industrial institute', providing adult education for the working classes. It was hoped that such a dual-purpose organization might draw upon 'the energy of those who would support either', and at the same time 'economize buildings, attendance, management and expenses of lectures'.

Charles Dickens, who in 1852 raised £300 for the proposed Institute by giving readings of *The Christmas Carol* in the Town Hall, fully appreciated both its educational and social implications. On one of the evenings he told the audience:

> Erect in Birmingham a great educational institution to which all orders of men can contribute, in which all orders of men may meet, wherein all orders of Birmingham men are faithfully represented, and you will erect a Temple of Concord which will be a noble example to the whole of England.

The plan to establish the Birmingham and Midland Institute was formally adopted at a large public meeting in January 1853, and a committee was elected for that purpose 'on the understanding that they would not start unless they got £4,000'. In November of the same year another public meeting resolved that, 'the artizans of the town ... being specially interested in the success of the undertaking', an Artizans' Committee should be formed 'to co-operate with' the main committee.

With the enthusiastic help of many individuals and voluntary organizations, the £4,000, and more, was quickly raised. Almost unanimously, the Town Council agreed to donate the site, which was situated immediately west of the Town Hall. In 1854 an Act of Incorporation gave the new body its constitution, and in the following year Prince Albert laid the foundation stone of the building. Teaching and other educative work actually began in 1854 in the old rooms of the Philosophical Institution, moving to the new premises in 1857.

Of the Institute's two sections, the General Department

The Birmingham and Midland Institute. The original Italianate building (1855-7), with its attached Corinthian columns, was by E. M. Barry. However, J. H. Chamberlain was responsible for the bold Gothic Paradise Street façade of 1881, which can be seen on the left of the photograph.

set out to provide 'lectures and meetings for discussions in the higher branches of knowledge', together with libraries, reading and news rooms, scientific and fine art collections. The Industrial Department organized classes 'for elementary and progressive instruction in mathematics and practical science, and such other subjects as may seem fit to the Council of the Institute'. Among these last in the early days, were 'Penny Scientific Lectures', started at the request of the artisans themselves, an English Literature class taught by George Dawson and Samuel Timmins, and a wide range of others covering 'arithmetic . . . English history, logic, language and thought'.

With class fees kept down to 9s. per year, by 1862 the Industrial Department had 717 students. Of these 8% were manufacturers or their sons, 31% 'earned their living by manual work', about 16% were women, and the remainder mainly clerks and shopmen. In a town which still lacked any systematic provision for technological education, part of the aim of the Industrial Department was to design courses that would help to supplement the apprenticeship and other training schemes of local manufacturers. There is some evidence of success in this direction. Writing of Elkington's in the late 1860s, for instance, Elihu Burritt tells us that:

> . . . fifty or sixty of the young men attend evening classes in the Midland Institute, and take such lessons in design and in the application of science to the different branches of the manufacture as shall fit them for its highest grades of art.

Queen's College. The existing building dates back to 1843, but it was refronted in 1904.

Such direct and practical vocational relevance may partly explain the fact that by 1868 artisans were accounting for 45% of the Industrial Department's students. In any case, this was regarded by Dickens as 'a most cheering sign' of the Institute's 'vigorous vitality': for he considered artisans 'the class within my experience the least reached in similar institutions, and whose name is oftenest and most constantly taken in vain'.

Birmingham University, and even Mason College, belong to the late Victorian period. But 'higher education', in its strictest sense, was not totally unavailable in the early Victorian town. Founded in 1828, largely through the generosity and enthusiasm of William Sands Cox, Queen's College was initially open to medical students only. But from 1846, we learn from *Allens' Pictorial Guide*, 'it was authorized by a warrant . . . to issue certificates to candidates for degrees in the University of London, and is now open to all classes of students desirous of obtaining degrees in arts, law, or medicine'. Situated in Paradise Street, facing the Town Hall — and for over a hundred years the Midland Institute — this still extant building then had 'accommodation for seventy resident students'. We are also told in *Allens'* that 'measures have lately been adopted for establishing an engineering department'. Unfortunately, problems arose, leading to 'internal discord and costly litigation'. So in 1874

The attractive Chester Road lodge of St. Mary's College, Oscott.

Spring Hill Congregational College. This foundation started in a private mansion. The college at Wake Green was built in 1855-6, the architect being Joseph James, who used the Decorated style, with 'a wealth of crockets, ballflower ornament and window tracery'. The Congregational college moved to Oxford in 1885, but the building is now used by Moseley School.

the only departments were in Theology, Medicine and Arts.

Two other local colleges became affiliated to London University soon after its own foundation. Occupying 'a noble establishment' built in 1835-8, St. Mary's College, Oscott, prepared students debarred from the older universities for London degrees. So did Spring Hill College, Wake Green (1838), which had facilities for educating 32 students as Congregational ministers.

The professional and middle classes were already reasonably well supplied with sources of reading matter when Victoria came to the throne. According to *Pigot's Directory*, the 1835 town had 35 'Booksellers and Stationers', plus 12 commercial circulating libraries. Then, for the use of lawyers, there was the Birmingham Law Society's Library, which Arthur Ryland had founded in 1831; and for the use of the clergy, the St. Philip's Theological Library, founded 1733. Finally the Old and New Subscription Libraries, established in 1779 and 1796 respectively, made a wide range of general literature available to middle class inhabitants who found it worthwhile to become members. In 1860 these, until then, rival bodies amalgamated to form the Birmingham Library which remains a major local institution even today, and indeed one of the foremost private subscription libraries in the country.

Nor was the provision of books for the working classes entirely neglected in early Victorian Birmingham. Apart from the libraries built up by the Mechanics' Institute and other similar institutions, adult and day schools invariably had them. *Allens' Guide* mentions that the 'Congregational society for the support of evening schools' had 'a library consisting of 1,250 volumes, and a reading and news room'; and St. Mary's School in Bath Street 'a well supplied reading room and library'. As early as 1838, too, 35 of the town's 56 Sunday schools 'were enlightened enough to provide lending libraries'. Yet all these voluntary facilities were by no means so adequate as to excuse Birmingham for allowing 25 other public authorities to open free public libraries before eventually doing so itself.

The first attempt on the part of enlightened members of the town council to establish such institutions came within two years of the passing of the 1850 Free Libraries Act. But this statute laid down that a library scheme had to be approved by a two-thirds majority in a town poll. Supporters of the Free Libraries movement, like George Dawson, Samuel Timmins and J. A. Langford, organized a thorough canvass of burgesses. Yet only 897 out of the 7,000 on the electoral roll bothered to partake, and the votes in favour fell 25 short of the required proportion. Thereafter, the economy party's vice-like grip on municipal affairs was enough to ensure that the issue remained in abeyance until 1859. In January of the following year, however, a meeting of burgesses voted in favour of adopting the Free Libraries Act by a large majority, and within a few months a comprehensive scheme had been approved by the town council.

This First Library Scheme proposed the erection of a Central Reference Library, which would incorporate Reading and News Rooms, together with a Museum and Art Gallery. There were also to be four District Lending Libraries and News Rooms, these being spaced out to serve the northern, southern, eastern, and the central and western parts of the town. In the event, though, it was decided to accommodate the latter on the ground floor of the Central Reference Library building, which was destined to be erected immediately adjacent to the Midland Institute.

The mayor and council opened Birmingham's first Free Public Library on 22 April 1861. This was the Constitution Hill (northern) District Library, which could be easily and rapidly made available because it was accommodated in a rented premises, while its initial stock of '6,500 volumes of standard literature' represented a bulk purchase from the New Subscription Library, following the amalgamation to which we have already referred.

The Library Committee report for 1861 tells us that on the day the Constitution Hill Library was opened, 'Crowds of persons presented themselves for tickets, and so great was the excitement that for several weeks applicants had to wait upwards of an hour before their turn arrived to be attended to'. By the end of 1861, 108,000 issues had been made to 5,422 members of the public; and although 2,373 volumes were added to the collection during the first eight months, the demand for books was such that 'they have never been on the shelves since they were purchased, excepting for the half-yearly examination'.

What became known as the Adderley Park Library was presented to the town as an additional district library by C. B. Adderley in 1864. This was followed by the opening of the corporation's own Central (and western) Lending Library in 1865, the Central Reference Library and the Deritend (southern) Library in 1866, and the Gosta Green (eastern) Library in 1868.

Those who had devoted so much time and energy to the Free Libraries movement now had some reason to be gratified. The whole of the town's first library scheme had been put into operation within eight years. Nor was this achievement merely a matter of buildings. The reference library had by then already assembled 20,136 volumes, while the five lending libraries shared 28,872 between them, and made 302,805 loans during the scheme's first full year of operation. J. D. Mullins, Birmingham's first Chief Librarian, claimed:

These Free Libraries seem to reach all classes with their elevating and gladdening influence. There are not only books for the student and worker, by which they may be helped in the business life; but there are books for the weary, books of standard music, books for little children, and

The interior of the second Reference Library, built by J. H. Chamberlain after fire had destroyed the first in 1879. This magnificent room was L-shaped and particularly notable for its iron galleries and clerestory lighting.

books for the blind.

Yet it is an interesting comment on what must still have been a predominantly illiterate town that the hunger for books seems to have been almost entirely confined to the younger half of the population. A survey made of 1,883 Constitution Hill ticket holders in 1863 showed that a mere 8% were over 40, as against 78% aged 12-30. The same survey also revealed that about 14% of the total readership were school children, 6% shop assistants, 18% clerks and office boys, and 34% artisans working in the jewellery, gun and button trades — or in other words, the trades which predominated in the Constitution Hill district.

No further libraries were built by Birmingham until the 1890s. But Aston Manor opened a Free Public Library in 1877. Situated on the corner of Witton Road and Aston Road, this was initially equipped with 4,050 volumes, and R. K. Dent served as its first Chief Librarian.

Rational Recreations and Popular Amusements

A contemporary periodical called *Leisure Hours* wrote of the mid-nineteenth-century Birmingham artisan:

> If he be a reading man, and studiously inclined, he has the means of educating himself at his command, by the aid of public institutions open to his class. In winter he may employ the long leisure of his evenings in private study, or in attendance at the rational recreations, which are open to meet his peculiar tastes and exigences; and in the summer he may get away from the smoky associations of the workshop and the forge, by a ramble among the green fields and villages.

However, after quoting this passage in the Appendix of his poem *Birmingham*, Harry H. Horton comments:

> He *may*, it is true, do all this, but he may also be allured by attractions of another and counteracting tendency ...

Clearly, there were two opposing leisure traditions in Victorian Birmingham: the 'rational recreations', and a 'counteracting' tradition, which was of course the tradition embodied in the vernacular or popular sports and pastimes. Both these traditions can be traced back into the eighteenth century and beyond, and both are still with us today. Yet only in Victorian times were they seen as being so completely antipathetic to each other. Indeed, it could be argued that this sharp dichotomy in the way Victorian people spent their leisure hours was of more significance than any distinction of wealth, status or class. For it represented that quintessential Victorian social divide: between, on the one hand, the uncouth, the rough, the feckless, and on the other, the respectable.

At the behest of the latter, the popular leisure tradition was kept under intense pressure throughout the Victorian period. Following national legislation in 1835, the brutal sports had been all but eliminated by the opening of the Queen's reign. The last recorded example of bull baiting in the Birmingham area took place in 1838. Cock fighting and dog fighting were less easy to totally expunge. As late as 1868 a Birmingham publican was fined £5 for 'unlawfully keeping open his house . . . for the purpose of fighting cocks', and according to tradition this practice continued at the White Lion in Digbeth at least until the 1870s. Greater success was had with 'men fights'. Birmingham is said to have been 'the head-quarters of provincial pugilism' in the first half of the nineteenth century. But by 1850 the police had completely stopped this 'sport of high and low life blackguards'—not out of concern for the participants, but because of the mass rowdyism that was invariably associated with it.

The long running struggle against St. Monday, the patron saint of the old popular pastimes, has already been described (page 70). Almost equally frowned upon by the respectable were the town's three traditional wakes. This seems ironic in a way, for they were all respectable enough in origin. The Deritend Wake commemorated the erection of St. John's Chapel there in 1381, the Chapel Wake the completion of St. Bartholomew's Chapel in 1750, and the Bell Wake the hanging of ten bells in St. Philip's steeple in 1751. By 1852, however, according to *Allens' Guide,* these festivals 'were only recognized and attended by the lower classes, and persons of bad character and depraved habits', and were consequently 'scenes of drunkenness and tumult'. A few years later another source tells us that they were once occasions 'of the grossest cruelty, absurdity and debauchery', but at 'the present day are celebrated chiefly by drinking and sight-seeing'.

Nor were Birmingham's two ancient fairs immune from the strictures of 'industrialists and moralists'. Unlike the wakes, these events look innocent enough in the guide books:

> The Whitsun Fair, happening at a season of general holiday, is most important. The Michaelmas fair is remarkable for an abundant supply of onions, and from this circumstance is known as the Onion Fair.

All the same, these three-day junketings were soon being condemned as 'a hindrance to trade, and a cause of annoyance to sober and quiet people'. Accordingly, from 1861 the town council limited the once far-flung Onion Fair to the Bull Ring, Smithfield and the upper part of Digbeth. Then in 1875, after a fierce council debate, this most popular of all annual events was banished from the borough altogether, leaving the showmen with no better alternative than to set up their 'swing boats . . . shooting galleries, instruments for the trial of physical strength and the like' a mile away, on the Old Pleck, near Aston church. It is hardly any wonder that Showell is noting ten years later that 'the "fun of the fair" is altogether different now to what it used to be'.

As the old popular amusements were systematically repressed then, what alternative pastimes were on offer, and how satisfactory did they prove? One of the 'rational recreations' or 'innocent pleasures' was almost as traditional as the wakes and fairs themselves—and almost as strongly threatened.

In his 1849 report on the town, Robert Rawlinson was particularly impressed by its allotment gardens, of which there were 250 at Edgbaston, and many others 'in Bordesley, along the Rea valley, and in the direction of Handsworth and Moseley'. The majority of these plots, which ranged in size from a sixteenth to a quarter of an acre, were let to 'workmen, who took great pride in their patches of garden ground'. They 'fenced them carefully, grew vegetables for the family use, made them gay with old-fashioned flowers, and besides working in them at all spare hours, occasionally made them the scenes of little family festivals—the rustic arbour constructed on almost every allotment serving as a place for tea-drinking'. But by 1878, according to Bunce, apart from some at Edgbaston, these 'guinea gardens' had 'almost all been swept away by the extension of the town'. However, because of its more gradual urban development, large numbers of allotments survived in Aston Manor throughout the Victorian period, with a local paper reporting in 1904 that 'many a public house loafer' was converted into 'a sober, industrious citizen' by having come into possession of one.

The Birmingham artisan's love of gardening no doubt formed part of a deeply seated nostalgia for the old rural way of life—a nostalgia which the upper middle classes could readily gratify in their idyllic suburban villas. But until the last decades of Victoria's reign, when so many workers began moving out to the relatively open developments of what became known as the Middle Ring, their contact with the soil was either non-existent, or else all too often confined to a plot of a few square feet in a sunless back-to-back court.

Public parks and gardens were one obvious way of compensating for the resulting sense of loss and deprivation. The famous Vauxhall Gardens succumbed to the mammon of progress in 1850. But five years before, the Birmingham Botanical Gardens—although founded in 1832 exclusively for the private enjoyment of its wealthy subscribers—was thrown open one day a week to the 'working classes', at a penny per head. Monday was chosen for this purpose, that being considered the 'day their habits lead them more than any other to seek for amusements'. The response was remarkable. *The Morning Chronicle* reported in 1851 that the gardens 'were literally swarming with a well-dressed, happy and decorous body of the working classes'; and that 'all appeared to be

A Birmingham back-to-back, with its diminutive garden.

luxuriating in the glories presented'. Two years later the annual tally of Monday 'perambulators' came to no less than 49,509, with the same paper commenting wryly that 'if the summer had not come to an end the lawn certainly should'.

The early history of public parks in Birmingham was not only laggardly, like that of so many other basic amenities, it depended far less on municipal enterprise than on private philanthropy and voluntary effort. During the 1850s the town council toyed with the purchase of 250 acres in Sutton Park, and then of Aston Hall and Park—only to abandon both projects. In 1856, however, C. B. Adderley prevailed upon the municipality to take over his 10 acre Adderley Park on a lease of 999 years and a nominal rent of 5 shillings per annum (if demanded). Lord Calthorpe followed suit in 1857 by virtually giving the council the 31 acre Calthorpe Park, with the proviso 'that the working classes shall have free admittance at all hours of the day during the six working days'.

Meanwhile, when the council jibbed at making a realistic offer for Aston Park, 43 acres of this were purchased for £35,000 by what might almost be called a philanthropic company, and in 1858 opened as a place of public amusement by Queen Victoria. The intention of the company was to recoup the investments of its shareholders out of the profits of entertainments and refreshments, and then to transfer the park to the corporation. Many setbacks were encountered, but in 1864—after the Queen herself had interceded with the council—this transfer was finally effected, at a cost to the ratepayers of £19,000. However, that was the end of public park making until the Chamberlain epoch. And a combined total of 91 acres could hardly be regarded as extravagant for a population of over 300,000 largely street-bound inhabitants.

Fortunately, if only because of its appalling congestion, the extent of the town's built-up area was still relatively limited, so that 'a ramble among the green fields and villages' remained feasible. Dent tells us that even after Vauxhall Gardens 'had

Left: The Birmingham Botanical Gardens, Westbourne Road. Although the original 'elliptical conservatory' has vanished, the range of hothouses seen across the lawn corresponds closely with that shown in an illustration of c.1890. The gardens, extending to over 14 acres, were initially laid out by J. C. Loudon. Above: The Angel Inn, Stratford Road, Sparkbrook. This is cited by Dent as one of the 'suburban taverns' which boasted a tea garden in the early and mid-Victorian period.

been cut up into building lots':

> There were few, indeed, of the suburban taverns which did not boast a tea
> garden where a few arbours, a few flowers and shrubs, and a supply of tea
> and other (stronger) liquids afforded sufficient attraction to the artisan and
> his family on the rare occasions on which they could leave the close court
> and the ill-ventilated workshop for such rural delights as the suburban tea
> garden afforded.

From quite early in Victoria's reign there was another potential way for Birmingham people to get a breath of fresh air and a few hours of outdoor recreation. Railway excursions from Birmingham began in the summer of 1841 with a cheap day offer to visit the metropolis. But in the early days, although there were some commercially organized trips, many of them seem to have been initiated by the better paid working men, through their friendly societies. In 1846 twenty-two such excursions have been traced, all but six of them taking place on a Monday. It is said to have been the Great Exhibition of 1851 which really popularized the railway outing, with over 100,000 people in the Birmingham area availing themselves of various excursions during that one year. By 1866, according to Samuel Timmins:

> ... the numerous railways which converge on Birmingham, have afforded
> ready and cheap facilities for the mass of the working-classes to enjoy a
> holiday, breathe the fresh air of mountains, and the coast of
> Wales — advantages unknown, even to the mass of the middle-classes sixty
> years ago.

At the end of the next decade Dent reported that:

> ... on all holidays and throughout the summer months, the 'iron horse' has
> carried out into the pure country air, or away to the seaside, thousands of
> the toiling artisans of Birmingham . . . There are few Birmingham artisans
> nowadays who have not paid more than one visit to the seaside, or who
> have not climbed the hills of Wales, or explored the little world of the
> metropolis.

All the same, with the cheap day to London, for instance, costing 19s., and the wages of semi-skilled and unskilled workers improving little, if at all, until the 1870s, it seems virtually certain that there would have been a time lag of 20 or 30 years between skilled craftsmen and the 'mass of the working classes' tasting such pleasures — except perhaps on a work's outing, or on a trip to Sutton Park, which, with the opening of the Sutton Coldfield Railway in 1862, became 'a popular rendezvous for the working people of Birmingham'.

Encouraging progress was gradually being made in the sphere of physical recreation and organized sports. Thanks to the Allday economists, the Kent Street Baths continued to provide the town's only indoor swimming facilities throughout the decade they dominated. In 1860 and 1862, however, further baths were opened at Woodcock Street and Northwood Street respectively; and like Kent Street, these are stated in a Baths Committee report to have been 'largely frequented by the working classes'. Moreover, although the annual number of admissions had never exceeded 100,000 during the 1850s, in

1865 the equivalent figure stood at 236,229, and by 1880 the total of male and female swims in the town's three public baths had topped 300,000.

We read of a public meeting of local inhabitants 'friendly to ... providing ground for the encouragement of cricket, rackets and other games' in 1834. An Athenic Institute was founded in 1842, with its members playing 'cricket, quoits, and other health inspiring sports in their own field at the outskirts of town' during the summer months, and following this with gymnastics and 'mutual improvement classes' in the winter. Such an organization, though, must have been beyond the means of all but the better paid artisans. The members of what was, in effect, an early informal sports club belonged to the same comparatively restricted socio-economic group. About 1850 the employer of 120 steel toy makers introduced them to cricket and archery, and before long a local paper was reporting:

> ... the men possess bats, wickets and balls, bows and arrows and targets in common; in summer ... [they] turn out to play two or three times a week, and often sacrifice a Monday afternoon to the exercise of these sports, which, at all events, is better than drinking away the Monday.

Athletics and football seem to have been slower in gathering momentum than cricket; and again, they were probably relatively *élitest* pastimes initially. We first hear of the Birmingham Athletic Club in 1865, when it was meeting at Bingley Hall. The following year it opened a Gymnasium in King Alfred's Place, and two years later mounted Birmingham's first 'athletics festival'.

The history of football cannot be traced so far back here as in Derby or Nottingham, for instance, and may not have counted for much prior to the mid-1860s. Twenty years later, on the other hand, Showell is claiming that 'there are hundreds of clubs in the town and district'. Among these, of course, were the Aston Villa club, which was founded in 1874 by youths belonging to Aston Villa Wesleyan Chapel, and the Small Heath Alliance, founded in 1875, which ultimately became Birmingham City F. C. Saturday afternoon football matches were being advertised in local papers by this time, with visiting teams already coming from as far away as Sheffield. Nevertheless, like cricket, football did not mature into a spectator sport with a really substantial following until the 1890s.

In the first two-thirds of Victoria's reign, therefore, these 'modern' sports, although no doubt respectable enough, could hardly be described as popular. And in fact the only major pastime which came anywhere near to being both at this time was the theatre. Nonconformist hounding and censure had ensured — and continued to ensure — the respectability of the local entertainments industry. At the same time, the fact that it could not survive without attracting large regular audiences meant that it had to appeal to as wide a social spectrum as possible.

The Theatre Royal, New Street, from a print of 1829.

The long-forgotten façade of the Prince of Wales Theatre, Broad Street. Built in 1856, although reconstructed at least twice since, this is the oldest architectural remnant of Birmingham's theatrical history.

The only theatre to run right through the nineteenth-century was New Street's Theatre Royal, and even this had to struggle hard for its existence during the early years of the Victorian epoch. After its rebuilding in 1820, 'Shakespeare's tragic glories', operas, and contemporary dramas played by 'metropolitan stars' proved increasingly incapable of filling its 2,500 seats. As a result, during the 1830s and 1840s, successive managers found themselves obliged, not only to twice lower admission prices, but also to provide 'for less critical tastes' by engaging 'Ducrow's famous stud of horses', 'Van Amburgh's lions and tigers', and in 1841 introducing the Victorian-style pantomime into Birmingham. This policy of democratization must have had some success, if only among more prosperous workers, for at six pence a time, according to the *Birmingham Journal* of 1846, every Monday brought the Theatre Royal 'a heaped-up gallery'.

The history of Birmingham's second most prestigious theatre followed a remarkably similar course. What became the Prince of Wales was opened in Broad Street in 1856 as a 'Music Hall' which concentrated exclusively on presenting oratories and other high class music. Six years later, however, it changed its name to the Royal Musical Hall Operetta House, at the same time moving its offerings 'down market', as it were, with the 'performance of vaudevilles, operettas, and light pieces generally'. Finally, after capitalizing on the royal wedding of 1863 by assuming its ultimate name, the Prince of Wales ended up with a programme of 'diversified dramatic entertainments' that was more or less the same as the Theatre Royal's. Thereafter it became 'one of the most prosperous and successful theatres in the provinces'.

The fact that the top theatres had no alternative but to address themselves to the working classes was doubtless due to the presence among their betters of many strict nonconformists for whom 'all pertaining to the theatre was a snare set by the Evil One'. However, Victorian Birmingham seems to have been no more able to sustain exclusively low-brow places of entertainment than exclusively high-brow ones.

The erection in Bradford Street in 1838 of what its proprietor called the Amphitheatre was intended to provide the town with a permanent circus. But the populace failed to turn up in sufficient numbers; and, not for the first time in Birmingham, by 1848 a place of entertainment had been transformed into a place of worship, as the Circus (Baptist) Chapel. A second attempt to do much the same thing began in 1853 when a Mr. John Tonks opened 'Tonks's Colosseum' at Bingley Hall, fitting the building up as an amphitheatre capable of holding 4,500 persons and engaging a resident equestrian company. When things started to go wrong here, Tonks tried to stave off disaster by moving 'up market'. But popular dramas like Lord Lytton's *The Lady of Lyons*, intermixed with the inevitable Shakespeare, proved of no avail, and the whole enterprise soon foundered.

A similar fate befell a theatre which was opened as the New Theatre in Moor Street in 1851. The principal fare here consisted of popular melodramas, like *Pauline; or, the Children of the Night, The Pirate of the Gulph,* and *Nick of the Woods.* But they were either not popular enough, or alternatively there were too few working class people who could afford to attend them. Either way, despite changing its name three times, this theatre had expired altogether within five years.

The only low-brow places of entertainment to really get off the ground in mid-Victorian Birmingham were the music halls, of which there are reported to have been 9 here in 1868, as against 8 in Manchester, 10 in Leeds and Sheffield and at least 300 in London. Generally linked with pubs, these are widely regarded as having been the almost exclusive preserve of the working classes; and indeed this is clearly how Dent regarded them when discussing 'Birmingham at Play . . . 1826 to 1850'.

> A lower class of entertainment was, however, gradually beginning to assert its claims to public patronage, in the 'free and easy' of certain public-houses, which proved to be the forerunners of the modern establishments which have debased the name of concert hall . . . One of these was held at a public-house in Coleshill Street, known as the 'Old Rodney', in connection with which, somewhere about the beginning of the fifties a large hall was built, and a curious mixture of music and acrobatism known as variety entertainment was set up in what came to be known as Holder's Concert Hall.

Yet an advertisement for the Rodney Inn Concert Hall in the 1852 *Allens' Guide* incorporates the following assurances:

> . . . nothing shall be wanting or expense spared to make this establishment the most complete place of instructive and rational amusement in Birmingham. The manner in which the room is conducted prevents the most fastidious from being offended . . .

Was the aim here merely to disarm prudish criticism; or, having pledged decorum, hopefully to boost attendance by attracting some of the more gullible of the town's *élite?* In any case, it looks as though Birmingham's theatrical managements, apart from cultivating respectability, also came to realize that, as in political affairs or adult education, so in the amusements industry, the best chance of success came from thinking in terms of the 'union of classes'.

An intriguing photograph in the Benjamin Stone Collection provides a graphic 'What's on?' record of the local entertainment scene as it was between November 1868 and January 1869. The Prince of Wales Theatre promised 'Great Excitement!' and 'Thunders of Applause!!' in 'UNDER THE GAS LIGHT', together with 'Express Train Sensation!', followed by 'The Pilot!' At the Theatre Royal the famous actor SOTHERN had recently appeared in 'A Hero of Romance', and another Theatre Royal poster confidently announced that 'The Great Comedian Mr. J. L. TOOLE IS COMING'. Two more visiting music hall artists who would no doubt have

Top: Bingley Hall, erected in 1850 by Messrs. Branson & Gwyther. Covering nearly 1½ acres and capable of holding 20-25,000 people, Showell says it was 'principally used for Exhibitions and Cattle Shows; with occasional "monster meetings" . . . to save sinners and convert Conservatives'. Above: Holder's Music Hall, pre-1857. The photographer was 'a Scotsman, John Johnstone, who opened Birmingham's second photographic studio in 1851'. (Birmingham Reference Library).

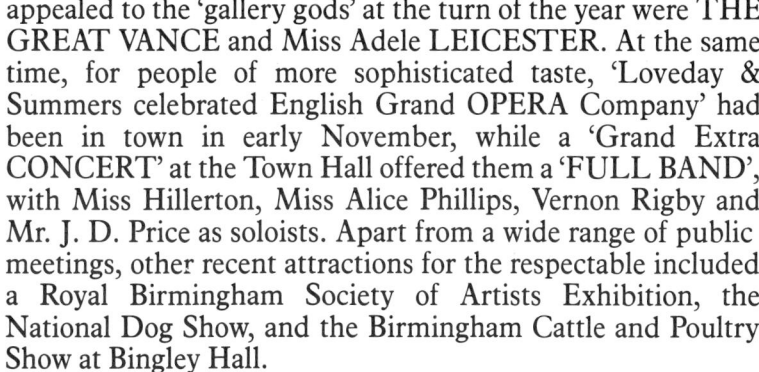

appealed to the 'gallery gods' at the turn of the year were THE GREAT VANCE and Miss Adele LEICESTER. At the same time, for people of more sophisticated taste, 'Loveday & Summers celebrated English Grand OPERA Company' had been in town in early November, while a 'Grand Extra CONCERT' at the Town Hall offered them a 'FULL BAND', with Miss Hillerton, Miss Alice Phillips, Vernon Rigby and Mr. J. D. Price as soloists. Apart from a wide range of public meetings, other recent attractions for the respectable included a Royal Birmingham Society of Artists Exhibition, the National Dog Show, and the Birmingham Cattle and Poultry Show at Bingley Hall.

When it came to combining respectability with a wide range of entertainments, easily the most ambitious venture was the so-called 'Aston Lower Grounds'. This was developed by Mr. Henry George Quilter on 32 acres of what had formerly been the northernmost portion of Aston Park. The 1874 *Kelly's*

heffield's Private Bill Posting Station, 868-9. This was a local advertisement rvice, which five years later was in the ands of Mrs. Mary Ann Sheffield, 'bill oster', of Upper Priory. (Sir Benjamin tone Collection, Birmingham Public ibraries).

Directory tells us:

This gentleman has, at great expense, formed a beautiful pleasure garden for the population of Birmingham and visitors from all parts of the country; it contains archery and cricket grounds, also two beautiful lakes covering five acres, for boating.

Writing five years later, Dent adds to the picture:

In connection with the beautiful pleasure grounds . . . a handsome block of buildings . . . have been erected . . . comprising a large and complete Aquarium, with a series of Fine Art Galleries over it . . . a Great Hall 220 feet long, by 90 feet wide . . . [with] a handsome stage, suitable either for modern comedy or for elaborate spectacular pieces . . . During the present year (1879), theatrical performances have been given by the late Mr. Craven Robertson's comedy company . . . Mr. Durand's English Opera Company, and others . . . Among the works performed by the Holte Choral Society have been Rossini's 'Stabat Mater', Mendelssohn's 'Loreley', the 'Messiah' . . . A series of ballad concerts have also been given.

Here was Victorian Birmingham's ideal leisure centre: a place of wide popular appeal, and yet with innocent pleasures and rational recreation *par excellence.*

A long succession of local writers bear testimony to the ever more respectable character of leisure pursuits as the nineteenth century advanced — or at least to the successful elimination of many of the unrespectable ones. Even by the early 1850s Horton was convinced that:

Those who can recollect (as I do) when almost every day our thoroughfares were blocked up by a savage crowd collected to witness a pugilistic encounter, and every Sunday morning the neighbourhood of Vaughton's Hole was infested by a congregation of ruffians assembled to fight their bulldogs, will allow that a better state of things has come to pass, and that we may with confidence look forward to still brighter days.

Fifteen years later Timmins confirmed Horton's optimism by declaring that, 'The habits of the people, generally, have changed greatly for the better during the last thirty years'. For all that, however, as in the eighteenth century, so throughout the nineteenth century, by far the most popular working class recreation was drinking — and in this area 'improvement' was by no means easy to accomplish.

In 1835 the town had 497 public houses; by 1852 the number had gone up to 596, and by 1880 to 670. Far from all

Left: The Lower Grounds, Aston, from a photograph taken in the 1880s. Above: The Holte Hotel, all that survives of H. G. Quilter's entertainments empire today. Situated at the junction of Witton Lane and Trinity Road, this marks the southern end of his territory. Aston Villa Football Ground, immediately to the north, now occupies much of the rest of it.

Right: Four public houses which still occupy the same building and carry the same sign as in early Victorian times. Reading from the top, The Crown Inn Broad Street, and The Wellington Bristol Street, both listed in Pigot Directory of 1835; The Fountain Wrentham Street, and The Peacock Darwin Street, not found in Pigot, but listed in the 1874 Kelly's Directory.

these licensed premises were lacking in respectability. The figures include the town's many 'family and commercial' hotels, headed in 1874 by the Queen's and the Midland, facing each other across Stephenson Place. And there were also respectable inns and taverns, some of which became well known for particular leisure activities or were patronized by particular interest groups. The Hope and Anchor Inn, Navigation Street, served as the base for the Sunday Evening Debating Society from the mid-1850s to the mid-1880s. Described by one of its members as 'the best Sunday School for politics that had ever been established in our Town', at its weekly gathering between 20 and 40 local radicals discussed current politics, moral and religious issues for 2½ hours in front of audiences that often exceeded 150. The Woodman in Easy Row was renowned as the meeting place of actors, musicians, writers and politicians. Indeed, in the 1850s and '60s its parlour served as the favourite haunt — and to all intents and purposes, the policy making chamber — of the economist councillors who then controlled the affairs of the town.

Lower down the social scale, Rawlinson reported in 1849 that of the 213 'clubs and friendly societies', which he estimated to have 30,000 members, all but 54 met in public houses. However, while not denying the social usefulness of these associations, Rawlinson also argued that it was 'false economy to take a shilling to a public house, to give a club threepence to take care of it, and to spend another threepence over the arrangement'.

In any case, the majority of the town's pubs, with or without their friendly society, were at best convivial social centres in which the conviviality was accompanied by a good deal of hard drinking. Furthermore, in early Victorian times the threat which drink posed to respectability was enormously increased by the sudden advent of 'gin palaces', with their tremendous size, their prominent corner positions, their richly ornamented façades, plate glass windows, gilded lettering and brilliant lights. Horton gave vent to the contemporary horror as follows:

> I cannot find words sufficiently strong to express my horror and disgust, at the sight of those countless gin-palaces which are rising at every corner of our streets . . . Look at that gorgeous den of iniquity, called the Crystal Palace, in Edgbaston Street, crowded every night, Sundays not excepted. Do we deserve the blessing of heaven upon our efforts to evangelize the world, when we allow such publicly brutalizing associations to exist . . . There was nothing of the kind in our fathers' times, though they were fond enough of the social glass . . .

Nor was the story of drink merely a matter of gin palaces and pubs. Numerically, and probably socially more important were the beer houses. Some of these were off-licences, but the vast majority were permitted to serve drink for consumption both on and off the premises. Legally speaking, what distinguished beer houses from pubs was simply the fact that they could not serve spirits. But they were also much more modest establishments, often being run by an artisan's wife or mother, in an artisan's home, and as such able to dispense their generally home-brewed ale extremely cheaply. Prosperous artisans might do their drinking in gin palaces and music halls, but for the average semi-skilled denizen of a Birmingham back-to-back a nearby beer shop would have been a much more regular port of call. So it was really the beer house which provided the main working class drinking institution in Victorian Birmingham. There is clear statistical evidence of this. For whereas the number of pubs increased by only a third between 1835 and 1880 — as against a more than doubling of the population — the number of beer houses went up by 360%, from 420 to 1,514.

The strong concentration of beer houses in working class districts offers further confirmation of their mainly proletarian appeal. As against the 9 places of worship which were to be found in the triangle of predominantly back-to-back territory at Hockley (see page 117), the 1874 *Kelly's Directory* lists 32 pubs and 79 beer retailers. The predominantly middle class area of Aston Park (bounded by Witton Road in the west, Witton Lane in the north, Park Road in the east and Park Lane in the south) had 15 pubs and 14 beer retailers. We have no population figures for these districts, but it should be possible to make some comparison of their respective drinking habits by reference to the number of food shops to be found in each (see page 109). In the Hockley sample area there were 222 food outlets, and at Aston Park 75. On this basis, Aston Park was more generously provided with public houses, having 1 pub for every 5.0 food shops, as against Hockley's ratio of 1:6.9. But beer retailers were twice as thick on the ground in Hockley than at Aston, the former having 1 beer house to every 2.8 food shops, compared with Aston's 1:5.4. Taking pubs and beer houses together, this gave Hockley exactly 1 drink outlet to every 2 food shops, in comparison with Aston's ratio of 1:2.6.

At a superficial level, it hardly looks as though drink created a major social problem in Victorian Birmingham. 1,213 inhabitants of the borough were charged with being drunk and disorderly in 1859, 2,033 in 1869, and 2,187 in 1879. Even the total number of court cases in which drunkenness was involved averaged only about 5,000 during the 1870s — or in other words, 1 for every 70 or 80 members of the population. However, in the eyes of the social improvers the trouble with drink was not that it landed a few thousand people in court, but that it incarcerated tens of thousands of them beyond the threshold of self-reliance and respectability.

Nor was this exclusively a poverty or a class issue. Though rare in the middle classes, alcoholism was not confined to any one socio-economic group. Rawlinson noted that it was often the workmen who earned the highest wages who were drunken and improvident. In Timmins we read that whereas jewellers tended to be 'staid, quiet, respectable', many gun workers were 'a good deal like sailors', with 'a recklessness which is fatal to good economy'. Skilled artisans or not, among such people 'high wages confer little benefit, the money is frequently wasted, and bad habits encouraged'. Yet other men in the same trade 'are known to have saved money' and 'will be found enrolled in one or other of the freehold land societies of this town, and living in houses of their own'.

Understandably, workmen in the hot and heavy industries were particularly prone to drink. In the brass and wire trades, the 'out-door run' to fill jugs and cans for the workshop provided nearby pubs and beer houses with constant daytime business. A mid-century manager at Webster and Horsfall recalls, 'As the day shift started at 6 a.m. the public houses opened earlier and they stayed open all day to the conclusion of the evening shift'. Interestingly, to this man — and presumably to the Hay Mills management in general — there was nothing the least unusual or disturbing about this. On the contrary, we are told:

> The staple diet of the older men appeared to be beer. They consumed immense quantities and thrived on it. Unlike most of their masters and managers, nearly all of them lived to a good age and sixty years service was common.

When the Atlantic Cable was being made, 'barrels of beer were rolled into the Mill and distributed free to keep the men at work'. Even in normal times 'it was considered important that the men should be supplied', while Monday absenteeism was apparently regarded as perfectly reasonable:

> Pay day was Saturday but as licensed houses were restricted on Sundays, a great many kept St. Monday.

But of course other employers — even in the hot and heavy industries — took a very different view. Richard Tangye would not allow drink on the premises of the Cornwall Works. And as early as the 1840s we hear of J. Bourn, a prominent brass founder, who 'has always been very careful in preventing drunkenness'. It was also reported of this or another brass foundry in the same decade that 'if one of the workmen absents himself from work for drunkenness, he returns to the manufactory amidst the ridicule and hootings of his comrades'.

Even in general working class parlance, St. Monday was often referred to as 'Shackling day' or 'Fuddling day', and a local broadside sold by the street hawkers of mid-Victorian Birmingham gives voice to what many a long-suffering wife must have thought about it.

> St. Monday brings more ills about, for when the money's spent,
> The children's clothes go up the spout, which causes discontent;
> And when at night he staggers home, he knows not what to say;
> A fool is more a man than he upon a fuddling day.
> *Chorus*
> For it's drink, drink, smoke, smoke, drink, drink away,
> There is no pleasure in the house upon a fuddling day.

The shortening of drinking hours helped to reduce the availability of alcohol as the Victorian period advanced. Showell says that prior to 1864 'tipplers could be indulged from the earliest hour on Monday to the latest on Saturday night'. But the Early Closing Act came into operation here in 1864, when the rule was 'to close at one and open at four a.m.' 'The eleven o'clock closing hour' was introduced in 1872.

The fight against drink, though, was pre-eminently the work of the temperance movement. The Birmingham Temperance Society was founded in 1830, being one of the earliest in the country; and this organization was later joined by the Birmingham Band of Hope which encouraged people to sign 'the total abstinence pledge', and from 1855 by a Prohibitionist body known as the United Kingdom Alliance. Most nonconformist and many Anglican churches became involved in one branch or another of the movement, holding regular temperance meetings in connection with their churches, adult schools and mission halls, organizing 'teetotal processions with flags and banners flying', and above all striving to exert 'private influence'. The movement also fostered specific campaigns, such as that 'for the promotion of Total Abstinence in the Police Force', and supported the establishment of Temperance Hotels and Coffee Rooms. Birmingham had 5 of the former by 1874, and 14 of the latter.

Nor was the temperance movement working in isolation. On the contrary, in so far as the battle against drink was also the battle for respectability, it formed part of a truly formidable alliance which included the whole of the educational movement, the mission to re-christianize the masses, and the many charitable organizations which, alongside their efforts to relieve destitution and suffering, invariably purveyed 'the message of self-improvement'.

From one point of view, such an overbearing social concensus may be seen as little more than a thinly disguised conspiracy to inflict middle class values on an entirely misunderstood and misrepresented popular culture. And certainly the beleaguered participants in that culture could be forgiven for thinking so: as did the group of slum dwellers who greeted a mid-nineteenth-century town missionary with 'ruffianly sarcasm', complaining that 'ten or twelve times a day we have religion crammed down our throats as if it were a drum stick'.

But, away from the slums at least, many members of the working classes were just as committed to the ideals of self-reliance and respectability as the middle classes themselves. Of 'educated workers' it was said in 1843, 'they do not engage in low amusements and drinking'. Moreover, such people were perfectly capable of launching their own self-generated reforming crusades, as happened, for instance, when in 1846 a group of local artisans sponsored the admittedly short-lived People's Hall, and announced as their objective 'the educational, moral and political improvement of the people'.

Yet, although it was never drawn on a straight-forward class basis, the demarcation line between the rough and the respectable was a disturbingly stark phenomenon. For in a society which, despite the gradual growth of rational amusements, remained for many years relatively starved of recreation, the working man in effect had to choose between two sharply contrasted life styles. On the one hand, there was the life of the beer house, the pub and the music hall; on the other, the life of the temperance society, the adult school and the chapel. Many who had experienced the former ultimately chose the latter. Asked 'what good he had got from Severn Street', one young man replied:

> Well, I have attained that for which I was seeking — I am glad to say the drink has no charm for me now; and I can see some difference between myself and my old friends, for where they waste their money I have kept mine, or spent it in a way that will bring hours of quiet enjoyment ... I might make mention of another good I have obtained ... the habit of plain and sensible speaking, and not the coarse, filthy, and bad language so common among such a large number of people. I could go on to mention ... the good of saving ... the good of helping others ... the good of always trying to improve one's house, one's body, and last, but not least, one's soul.

Working class families who chose respectability thereby secured for themselves a good chance of going up in the world, until ultimately perhaps they were not only keeping a respectable house, but a respectable house in a respectable street. And for all the reassuring comments of the Hay Mills manager, those who were content with the alternative at least ran the risk of descending, rather than climbing, the socio-economic ladder. Edward G. Davis in his *Passages from my Life* (1887) describes how the prosperity of his family was undermined by the drinking habits of his father, and how in consequence they were constantly having to move from home to home. Eventually, he tells us, 'We moved from Holt Street ... and went to a house in Lister Street. There it began to dawn on me that I belonged to what is known as "the poor class of society"'.

All too many must have taken the same course as Edward Davis's father. For in Britain as a whole, the alcohol consumption per head of population rose to an all time peak about 1875 — and there is little reason to suppose that Birmingham provided much in the way of an exception.

One of the main causes of this unprecedented resort to drink can hardly be far to seek. Despite the Botanical Gardens, the seaside excursions, a few belated public baths, parks and libraries, so far as all but the most prosperous workers were concerned, there must undoubtedly have been a 'leisure gap' in Birmingham during the mid-Victorian period. Because of the sheer weight of numbers, the lack of education, the municipal inertia, rational amusements had simply not been developed fast enough or extensively enough to offer the bulk of working class people any really suitable alternatives to the beer house, the pub and the music hall. The Hay Mills manager put it with admirable succinctness, so far as his own workers were concerned:

> Cock fighting, rat pits and prize fighting provided their recreation until these activities were made illegal, after which there was nothing to take their place . . . Their club was the Public House . . .

Horton railed against the 'Gin Palaces, Music Saloons, &c.', regarding them as 'nurseries of vice, disease and crime', 'the most detestable and loathsome spots on the page of our present civilization'. He urged 'those who are in a position to . . . influence the moral and social condition of the people, to put down such evils . . .' But there were others who felt that the terrible hold which drink had on so many lives was a symptom rather than a cause, and therefore that a much more radical solution was required than merely shutting down the gin palaces. Thus in 1870 — admittedly before all the social advances of that remarkable decade — a sympathizer with the principles of the 'civic gospel' addressed the middle class readers of *The Town Crier* as follows:

> . . . like you, the working Man wants . . . relaxation, and fun and amusement . . . You have your lawn and your croquet ground, the tree under which you can sit in the evenings, your libraries, your billiard tables, your thousand-and-one means of escape from the troubles of daily life. He has — what? The dreary, dusty, ill-drained, dirty, pestilential street. The noise of his drunken neighbour in his ears, the crying of neglected children. His croquet ground is a backyard shared by a dozen neighbours, and surrounded by a crowd of houses. The country is too far off to tempt him, and impossible to reach even if it did tempt him. There are no playgrounds for his children, no parks for himself. The rights of that sacred institution, the landlord . . . keep the Working Man imprisoned in the towns, from the end of one long year to that of another long year. Yet he is like ourselves. We must have pleasure. He must have pleasure also. And we are hypocrites enough to whine, and howl, and storm, and rage, because he turns naturally to the only means of pleasure which are left to him.

George Dawson and the Civic Gospel

Three men did more than any others in developing Victorian Birmingham's special qualities as a political community and in advertising them across the nation. Two were outstanding political leaders, Thomas Attwood and Joseph Chamberlain. The other was George Dawson, the nonconformist minister and lecturer whose charismatic presence dominated the three decades between them.

George Dawson was born in London in 1821, the son of a devout Baptist who kept a private school there. With a grounding of ten years' 'systematic education' in his father's academy, a Glasgow M.A. in Humanities, but uninhibited by any specifically ecclesiastical training, Dawson began his ministry as pastor of a small Baptist church at Rickmansworth in 1843. The following year, this 'athletic young man of twenty-three, with long, black, curly hair and clothes of a most unclerical cut', sought and obtained the pastorship of the Mount Zion Chapel, Graham Street.

Dawson's impact on Birmingham was as dramatic and immediate as it was to prove profound and long-lasting. When he arrived at Mount Zion there were about forty regular attenders. But 'as his name was noised abroad', Wright Wilson, his contemporary biographer tells us, 'every available inch of room in pew, aisle, and staircase was covered'. Foremost among the newcomers were many of the towns leading Unitarians. Apart from the almost mesmeric attraction of the man himself, these people were drawn by Dawson's obvious contempt for 'sectarian narrowness and prejudice'; by the fact that he seemed to take 'all life as his province', and even thus early, to be striving 'to get religion out of the pale of the chapel'.

Portrait of George Dawson as a young man.

Unfortunately, many of the views of this unconventional divine were 'such as the Baptist denomination has not been accustomed to recognize'. After a mere sixteen months, therefore, Dawson found himself with no alternative but to announce his resignation. But those who had been bowled over by his teaching were not prepared to be denied. Inviting Dawson to become the minister of a new non-denominational congregation, they immediately set about erecting the Church of the Saviour as its place of worship. Here Dawson was destined to go on teaching them for another thirty years. Among the founder members of this chapel, which opened its doors in 1847, were such future public servants and civic dignitaries as William Harris, J.A. Langford, Robert Martineau, Arthur Ryland, Samuel Timmins and Robert Wright.

Joseph Chamberlain spoke of Dawson as 'one who, perhaps more than any other, had set his mark upon modern

Birmingham'; and certainly this was the man who, more than any other, crystallized that 'new way of thinking about the nature and function of municipal government' which became known as the 'civic gospel'.

Dawson lived at precisely the right time to embark upon such an enterprise. For in Britain as a whole, the middle decades of the nineteenth century were 'socially happier and more harmonious' than the difficult, strife-torn decades which preceded and followed them. The late 1830s and the 1840s were deeply affected by Chartism, while the 1880s were to bring the revival of mass radicalism in its socialist form. But in between came the thirty years of comparative prosperity and social calm which has been called 'The Age of Equipoise'.

Moreover, Dawson not only lived at the right time, in coming to Birmingham, he chanced upon the right place. It is sometimes forgotten that during the nineteenth century the British people had before them two quite distinct ways of pursuing political reform and socio-economic advancement — the way based on class conflict, and its opposite, based on class co-operation. Since the days of Attwood, Birmingham had been the principal testing ground and sounding board for the latter alternative.

This fact must have been of crucial importance to Dawson. So much so, that it could be argued that his teachings, as well as growing out of the thought of such writers as Burke, Carlyle and Ruskin which so strongly influenced the intellectual climate of that particular time, also grew directly out of the 'moral mission' of Thomas Attwood's Birmingham.

In his 'Letter to the Middle Classes', written in 1848, at the climax of the Chartist epoch, with France in the midst of its third revolution, Dawson proclaimed:

The exterior and interior of the Church of the Saviour, Edward Street, built 1846-7 by Bateman and Drury.

> Physical force we will not have, we love it not. How shall we prevent revolution and violence? By the only sure plan — reform. . . . Organize in every locality — petition (if you will) — 'pronounce'. . . . Try in what points you can unite with the working men. In every town meet at once to adopt all peaceful and constitutional measures to prevent the present Parliament from going to grass, until some true reforms have been carried.

These words could easily have issued from the mouth of Thomas Attwood himself. And the fact that the people of Birmingham had listened to and accepted talk of a moral mission and the union of classes so often before must have meant that Dawson was in some measure preaching to the converted.

Yet whereas Attwood concentrated exclusively on economic and political reform, Dawson's approach was primarily that of a moral and spiritual teacher. A political alliance for economic ends was not enough for Dawson. Rather the 'union of classes' which he sought was based on the Christian idea that 'we are all truly of one kindred and one brotherhood'. It was the full acceptance of this fact that for him offered the people of Birmingham and Britian 'a new plan

for forming ourselves together . . . capable of bringing about a better union of classes'.

Dawson was an intuitive, highly emotional thinker, rather than a man given to careful systematic reasoning, a 'feel-osopher' rather than a philosopher. It is not easy, therefore, to trace the volatile, almost bouncing, progress of his thought. As far as one can tell, though, the 'new plan' was at first centred in his mind on the church itself:

> . . . a great want of our time is *Unity*, and the present age seeks a Church that shall teach the great doctrine of Brotherhood and Equality . . . swallowing up all vain distinctions.

However, partly perhaps because of the comparative impotence of religion in a nineteenth-century urban context, Dawson soon found himself transferring what he saw as the role and values of the church to the municipal corporation. Until the town itself, along with the nation, became for him the modern expression of God's will, and as such 'the largest and widest Church ever established'. This visionary, if somewhat imprecise, line of speculation culminated in Dawson's famous speech at the opening of the Birmingham Reference Library in 1864, when he declared:

> . . . that a great town exists to discharge towards the people of that town the duties that a great nation exists to discharge towards the people of that nation – that a town exists here by the grace of God, that a great town is a solemn organism through which should flow, and in which should be shaped, all the highest, loftiest and truest ends of man's intellectual and moral nature.

This remarkable 1864 address came to be widely accepted as the charter of the municipal reformers. But Dawson's mission involved far more than rarefied mystical rhetoric. The visionary, with his head high above the clouds, also had his feet on the ground. Before all else, therefore, his call – just as much as Attwood's – was a call to action. Pitching into the working classes, he would say:

> . . . I may be a dreamer . . . but if each man will become a sober and intelligent man, there exists no power and no wrong practice that can withstand us. . . . The reason you have not been listened to more is that your voice has often come forth from the smoky atmosphere of a pot-house, and uttered in words low-minded and coarse. . . . The reason that class legislation has been so long dominant . . . is that the people have been too much bemuddled with drink to interfere. . . . Take your affairs into your own hands; look to your amusements . . .

When it came to choosing, Dawson's ultimate commitment was always to the working classes – 'With him, Labour was first, Capital second, because Capital was the fruit of Labour'. At the same time, Dawson warned the working man not to make the mistake of 'the bellows-blower of the organ, who spoke of the sublime symphony as the production of "we"'.

The great activator's message to the leading families of the town was no less blunt and down-to-earth. To them he preached 'the gospel of public duty'. 'It was of vital importance to Birmingham', he told them, 'to secure the services on the

Town Council of men who were not only able, but gifted with something above ordinary talent and wisdom, and who were known to be men of uprightness'.

Dawson could be extremely impatient in his drive to recruit such people into the public service, constantly upbraiding those who thought they had 'a patent to sit at home at ease and do nothing'. But he and his followers also tried to teach by example. Between 1847 and 1867 no less than 17 members of the Church of the Saviour became members of the town council, six of them being elected mayor. Indeed, throughout the long, bleak 'economy' period, it was Arthur Ryland, Robert Wright, William Harris and other Dawson men who provided the backbone of the 'extravagant' party that constantly pressed for the adoption of more enlightened municipal policies. As a minister of religion, Dawson himself was ineligible to stand for the council. But there was never any danger of such a strongly committed man becoming 'one of those who, contented with preaching reforms, refuse to take part in the labour by which they are carried out'. Apart from constantly lecturing to working men, not only in Birmingham, but throughout the country, he actively involved himself in the movements for universal suffrage, public baths, temperance, early closing, the reformation of juvenile offenders, and popular education. In 1847 he was instrumental in founding the Freehold Land Society, which he served as a vice president. In 1856 he became a regular lecturer at the Midland Institute, in 1857 campaigned in support of Bright's canditure for Parliament, and in 1858 took on the chairmanship of the committee formed to secure Aston Hall and Park 'to the use of the public for ever'. Having been a passionate advocate of the Free Libraries Act for a full decade, when this was finally adopted in 1860, he worked countless hours with Timmins on the actual acquisition of books, as well as donating part of his own Shakespearean collection to one of his favourite projects, the building up of a unique Shakespeare Library for the municipality. During the late 1840s and the 1850s he even found time to successively edit two local radical papers.

Attwood's union of classes had in large measure been an alliance of the lower middle and the upper working classes, of small manufacturers, traders and shopkeepers with skilled artisans. In a sense, moreover, it was this far too limited sector of local society which—following the demise of the paternalistic Street Commissioners—had been mainly responsible for the decades of municipal mediocrity and inertia. Dawson saw the necessity of revitalizing what had long been a moribund alliance by bringing the social extremes back into the picture more—the big businessmen and professional people of Edgbaston, on the one hand, and the mass of the common people who lived in the back-to-backs and even the slums, on the other.

Samuel Timmins.

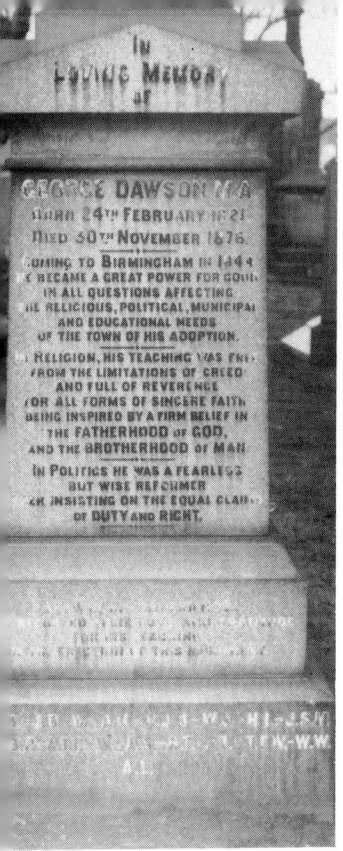

The upper classes had to be persuaded, not only to take a more active part in municipal affairs, but to show a sincere personal interest in those less fortunate than themselves.

> I make it my duty to visit the working men of Birmingham. . . .
> If the thousands of professed Christians that were able to do it would pay a visit per week to the homes of misery and poverty, a wonderful change would come over the land.

Philanthropy, charity and missionizing were not enough:

> We must go as men, and not as gentlemen . . . with no fuss of condescension . . . as man with man, brother with brother, and sinner with sinner.

But how, in practical terms, were the working classes to be brought into the 'new plan'? A second reform bill would obviously help; and for this reason Dawson was totally convinced of the *'expediency'*, as well as the 'justice' of 'a large extension of the franchise'. But perhaps even more urgent than that was 'the educational improvement of the people':

> Look at the marriage register . . . and you will see the vast number of parties who cannot sign their names. . . . Ignorance must be met by education. If a man, ignorant himself, had little children, and was too poor to pay for their education, they must be educated at the public expense.

Alongside this must go really radical social and environmental improvement:

> If the streets were dirty and ill-paved, unsewered, and badly lighted; if people herded together in common lodging-houses, where common decency was not common, and where water was scarce and dear, then sanitary committees and inspectors must be appointed to see that matters were mended.

For a long time Dawson's 'civic gospel' seemed only to speak to the two sects which had always set the most store on the doing of good works. Apart from his own church members, it was therefore the Unitarians and Quakers who served as leaven. In 1869 the Unitarian Church of the Messiah appointed H. W. Crosskey, a close friend and follower of Dawson, as its minister. Joseph Chamberlain, of the same church, entered the town council in the same year, and was soon followed by his two brothers, Arthur and Richard.

'I loathe the most hateful cant', cried Dawson '. . . which says that Christian men may not meddle with politics'. 'Christian men' of the Baptist, Methodist, Congregationalist and other evangelical denominations, however, were highly suspicious of Dawson's 'latitudinarian' teachings, with their emphasis on conduct rather than faith, social activism rather than private piety. And indeed it was understandable enough that his idealization of the municipal corporation should appear to people of the Mount Zion ilk as theologically dangerous. For in their eyes such a concept confused the ways of God with the ways of man, the kingdom of heaven with the kingdom of the world, the eternal city with Victorian Birmingham.

It was the achievement of Dr. R. W. Dale, minister of Carr's Lane Congregational Church, to reinterpret Dawson's

Above left: The George Dawson statue, Edmund Street. Above: The Dawson obelisk in Key Hill Cemetery. Below: Where Dawson preached the 'civic gospel'. A fragment of the south, 'preaching' end of the Church of the Saviour has somehow eluded the bulldozer. The rest of the site now serves the community as a waste-ground car park – empty of course on Sundays.

message in such a way that it became acceptable even to many of these evangelical dissenters. Dale had trained for the ministry at Spring Hill College, and throughout his sojourn there he went to hear Dawson at the Church of the Saviour on every available occasion. But although greatly attracted to Dawson as a man and a preacher, it was only slowly that he came to terms with the main thrust of his ideas, and he was never able to accept the claim that municipal authorities should be seen as the modern equivalent of churches. Nevertheless, by 1867 Dale was telling his wealthy Carrs Lane congregation that prosperous men

> . . . ought to work on the Committees of Hospitals. They ought to be Aldermen and Town Councillors. They ought to give their time as well as their money to whatever improvements are intended to develop the intelligence of the community. They ought to be reformers of local abuses. They ought to see to it that the towns and parishes in which they live are well drained, well lighted, and well paved; that there are good schools for every class of the population; that there are harmless public amusements; that all parochial and municipal affairs are conducted honourably and equitably.

Dr. R. W. Dale, 1829-95.

And although the municipality for him had to remain part of the secular world, Dale went as far as declaring on another occasion that he believed his Quaker friend, Alderman White, 'was trying to get the will of God done on earth as it is done in heaven just as much when he was fighting St. Mary's Ward, just as much when he was speaking in the Town Council, as when he was teaching his Bible Class on the Sunday morning'. So politics presumably, as well religion, *could* be holy.

The 'conversion' of Dale had considerable influence on other evangelical ministers in the town, and they in turn influenced their own congregations. As a result, from 1874 Congregationlist and Methodist—though never Baptist—laymen began to join the ranks of the active municipal reformers.

From 1869, too, the mass of the common people had become burgesses, with over 42,000 householders having a say in local and parliamentary elections. The time had come when the municipal reforms of which Dawson had dreamed for decades could at last be implemented.

Joseph Chamberlain, the elder statesman.

Left: George Dixon. Below: Jesse Collings.

Joseph Chamberlain and the Municipal Revolution

If George Dawson, with his vision of a new social order, was the Rousseau of the municipal revolution, Joseph Chamberlain was more like its Napoleon. 'Brummagem Joe' was born in London in 1836, the son of a prosperous businessman with strong Unitarian convictions. After a private school education, he entered the family business in 1852, being despatched to Birmingham two years later when his father and uncle launched the firm of Nettlefold and Chamberlain for the production of screws by a newly invented American method. Although only 18, Chamberlain at once took charge of the commercial and financial sides of the business, and within ten years had established it both as 'a prime example of modern monopoly capitalism' and a 'model of Victorian paternalism'. At this stage Chamberlain was not involved in politics, restricting his community service mainly to teaching in the Church of the Messiah's Sunday and evening schools. But in 1865, four years after marrying into the local Kenrick family, he joined the Liberal Association and 'began to interest himself in the public life of the town'.

There seems to have been an inevitability about the career of Joseph Chamberlain, which almost calls to mind a natural phenomenon. And certainly during his early middle age this pocket-sized, dapper, autocratic, intensely dynamic and ambitious man was to work even greater wonders for the town and people of Birmingham than he had worked in his youth for Nettlefold and Chamberlain.

It could hardly have been more fitting that the politician who was to become the idol of the ordinary Brummie should have been elected on to the town council in the 1869 elections, which were the first to be held under the new extended franchise. Once there, as if by divine right, he quickly became the leader of 'a small party of four of those who were then known as Municipal Reformers'. Furthermore, Thomas Avery and several other council members who favoured 'economy through efficiency' found themselves increasingly in sympathy with this group.

However, in a sense, the municipal revolution began outside the town council, in what Dawson and the reformers saw as the absolutely crucial field of elementary education. It was Jesse Collings, a member of Dawson's own congregation, who in 1867 persuaded the then mayor, George Dixon, to establish the Birmingham Education Society, of which Chamberlain at once became a leading committee member. Apart from carrying out an enquiry into the town's schools (page 127) and establishing a public fund which provided school fees for over 6,000 poor children, the Birmingham

Education Society went on in 1869 to found the National Education League. This organization aimed to unite 'all those, throughout the country, who desired to promote a really national system of education'; a system 'which shall secure the education of every child in England and Wales'. If only because of the rivalry of the more conservative, Manchester-based National Education Union, the League's influence was far from universal. Nevertheless, with Chamberlain as its main driving force, and Dixon — by then a Birmingham M.P. — presenting its views in Parliament, it was the Birmingham-based League which served as the pace-setter in what was unquestionably one of the nineteenth century's most crucial social reform movements.

The resulting Forster Education Act of 1870 instituted local School Boards, which were given the role of ensuring that there were enough school places for all children within their district. Existing 'voluntary' schools would be retained, but new 'Board schools' were to be provided wherever necessary, with their erection and running costs being defrayed from a combination of Treasury grants and locally collected rates.

The group of nonconformist and Liberal reformers who had organized the National League naturally hoped to seize control of the Birmingham School Board. But in fact the first election to that body produced an Anglican/Conservative majority. Important issues were at stake. For it was part of the reformers' doctrine that local authorities should secure full control over education, and indeed over all other matters of vital public concern. Even more strongly, they believed that rate-supported education, instead of indoctrinating children with a particular religious creed, as had been the case under the old voluntary system, ought to be non-denominational, or 'secular'. This meant, in effect, that they 'wanted the Bible read in schools without explanation or comment'. The Churchmen, on the other hand, having down to that point always dominated the field of education, were naturally determined to do all they could to preserve the 'Scriptural teaching' of their own independent foundations.

Chamberlain, as might be expected, was one of the five nonconformists who had been successful in the first School Board elections. So in the early 1870s he found himself the leader of a small group of reformers, both on that body and on the town council. However, the only way to ensure the triumph of rate-supported, secular education in Birmingham was for the Liberal reformers to gain majority control of the School Board. And the only way to ensure a truly radical programme of municipal reform was to gain majority control of the town council.

It was William Harris, another member of the Church of the Saviour, who is said to have invented the ingenious form of political organization known as the 'caucus', which — along

with so much else that was happening in Birmingham at this time—was ultimately to be imitated right across the nation. This system was first adopted by the local Liberal Association after the 1867 reform bill, with parliamentary elections in mind. The need for it arose from the fact that, although in future Birmingham was to be represented by three M.Ps., each elector continued to have only two votes. Had the vast majority of Liberals cast their votes for the two most popular party candidates, this might easily have let in a Conservative. Harris's aim was to prevent such a calamity.

The resulting caucus system was based on permanent Ward committees, each electing representatives to a General Committee, which was in turn 'steered' by a small Executive Committee of party leaders. The job of the ward committees was to build up grass roots support, while the strategy for fighting an election campaign was worked out in the central committees. Finally, and crucially, back in the wards, individual party members were then expected to vote 'as they were told'.

This procedure worked perfectly in the 1868 general election. All three Liberal candidates—Bright, Muntz and Dixon—were safely returned, with less than a thousand votes between them. Clearly, what was required in the early 1870s was to adapt the same system to the municipal and School Board elections. However, in order to secure a working majority on the council, the reforming Liberals had to take on and defeat, not only the Tories, but also the many old 'economy' radicals who were still resolutely opposed to new and extravagant municipal policies.

Left: Alderman James Brinsley. Below: Joseph Chamberlain, during the municipal phase of his career.

The reformers' trump card was Joseph Chamberlain, whom they accordingly nominated for mayor. So the municipal election of November 1873 was fought in all wards as a straight Chamberlain v. Brinsley election, Brinsley being the mayoral nominee of the old economist party—who also, for obvious reasons, attracted Tory support. Such a direct gladiatorial contest between the suave, nonconformist business magnate, on the one hand, and on the other, an uncouth local grocer whose influence was 'based on the good fellowship of the public house', perfectly epitomized the momentous choice that then confronted the electors of Birmingham.

Their decision was unequivocal. The reformers achieved a landslide victory. And a month later this success was repeated in the School Board elections, with the 'Liberal eight' securing control of educational policy, and Chamberlain becoming School Board chairman, as well as mayor.

It is important to appreciate, however, that it was not just the nonconformist *élite* of the town who had brought about this remarkable opportunity. For the fact that the denizens of the back-to-back courts and the slums now had the vote must have been no less vital. In 1838 a mere 272 burgesses had been entitled to take part in the election of the three councillors who represented St. Mary's Ward, and 152 burgesses in the election of the three councillors for Ladywood. Nor would the electoral rolls have seen much of an advance in the number of burgesses until after the second reform bill. But by 1871 St. Mary's Ward had 2,151 burgesses with the right to vote, and Ladywood 5,943.

In the past the landlords, shopkeepers, small manufacturers and garret masters who had dominated such wards inevitably tended to support 'weaker and less effective members'. But now, as Dr. Dale pointed out, 'the mob' could be counted upon to 'prefer a gentleman to a blackguard in the long run'. And in any case, there were always plenty of educated, respectable artisans to help the gentlemen. When William White first stood for municipal office in 1873, for instance, his pupils and ex-pupils from Severn Street School automatically turned out to support him:

> Mr. Michael Maher's seat in St. Mary's Ward might indeed have been deemed impregnable. . . . 'Who is Mr. William White?' the St. Mary's burgesses might have asked not unreasonaby, and from every quarter of the town there came into the ward an army of unpaid canvassers, each eager to do a little to repay his benefactor, by testifying who he was and what he had done.

Chamberlain himself, of course, fully understood the significance of this major shift in the electoral centre of gravity. 'The working classes', he wrote, 'who cannot contribute pecuniarily... are now the majority in most borough constituencies, and no candidate and no policy has a chance of success unless their good-will and active support can be secured'. John Mason, the Chartist shoemaker and lecturer, had said way back in 1849, 'The strength of democracy consists in reconciling the various classes of society . . .' Now at last, such a reconciliation had been made genuinely possible.

Victorian Birmingham had never had such a mayor as Joseph Chamberlain; and the impact of his mayorality seems to have been increased more like thirtyfold than threefold by the fact that he served for almost three years. Previous mayors, even including Avery, had tended to become passive agents of municipal policy, modelling their conduct on that of an impartial presiding officer, and thereby inhibiting themselves from exerting much in the way of either personal or party initiative. It was even rare for them to take a leading part in debates.

The new man's approach, by contrast, was almost despotic. Success in industry had made him shrewd, tough, aggressive and supremely self-confident. Far from being a mere presiding officer, Chamberlain was determined to run Birmingham as he had run his business. He would lead the council in the direction he thought it should go. And as well as initiating policies, he would provide the drive and creative energy which was necessary to see that they were carried out. E. P. Hennock tells us:

> He began his year of office by rebuking members for unpunctuality, and the speed with which he despatched business was a new experience for the Council. Occasionally he used this briskness and the increasing personal ascendancy which he acquired in order to out-manoeuvre the slower members of the Council, and people 'found themselves giving their votes at the very moment they had intended to make a speech or move an amendment'.

Describing how he pushed through the 1876 building bye laws which effectively eliminated the erection of back-to-back houses, Chamberlain himself wrote to Jesse Collings:

> I took the matter in hand myself, explained the position of affairs to the council and begged them to pass the Bye-laws without discussion of the details. This they did like trumps as they are, and the whole set was printed and approved before the opposition had time to turn round . . . Deykin says the resolution was carried by a majority of 47, 46 of whom voted against their consciences. I don't care about their consciences — we have got the bye-laws and mean to work them.

The Chamberlain administration inherited two major municipal improvement programmes which had been started in the early 1870s, when the reformers were still a minority on the council, but which they were subsequently able to drive forward with a new sense of urgency. Almost inevitably, the most pressing and costly of these related to that perennial Victorian problem, the sewering of the borough.

In 1871 a Sewage Enquiry Committee, under Thomas Avery's chairmanship, established that although only 3,884 properties had water closets, all but 5,500 of the town's 20,000 middens were by then draining into the sewers. With horror, it also reported that taken together these middens occupied about 13½ acres, being 'the greater part uncovered and polluting the atmosphere, while the soakage fouled the earth and contaminated the wells'. However, the condition of the town itself was far from being the only cause of concern. On the contrary, by this time Birmingham's most desperate sewage problem 'started at the place where more fortunately situated towns ceased to think about it'. Liverpool could tip its outfall into an open estuary, and Manchester into several large rivers. Birmingham had only the spindly River Tame at Saltley.

Under legal pressure, the corporation had constructed a filtration works there in 1858, enlarged this in 1860, and acquired its first sewage farm in 1865. Yet as the population grew and more and more water closets and middens were connected to the system, the quantities of sewage arriving at the outfall increased every year and even the best available technical knowledge was at a loss to know what to do with it. Meanwhile, the 140 acre sewage farm at Saltley was soon reduced to a 'sodden morass' and the council again found itself confronted by serious legal problems.

The town's foremost opponent in this respect was one of its foremost philanthropic benefactors, C. B. (by now Sir

Virtually the only 'monuments' the 'Victorian archaeologist' interested in sanitation can find above ground are the late nineteenth-century street urinals. Apart from the odd post box and pillar clock, these are also virtually the only items of Victorian street furniture to survive. The urinal above is in Vyse Street, while the post box still stands beside the portico of the Curzon Street railway station.

Charles) Adderley. From 1858 onwards he had been persistently protesting about the state of the River Tame which ran past his country seat at Hams Hall, and which even thus far down stream 'had a pestilential stench making people ill'. Despite the council's repeated efforts to improve the situation, by 1870 Adderley was threatening to renew legal sanctions. And to add to the corporation's troubles, in the same year the residents of Gravelly Hill, having complained vainly for six years, had also lost patience. Nor were they merely threatening. Incensed at 'the deposit of solid sewage matter' in the proximity of their homes, these people had obtained a Chancery injunction which — as in 1858 — 'virtually forbade any further connection . . . with the town sewers' until the problem of the pestiferous sludge had been eradicated.

Urged on by the reformers, the Avery committee investigated every conceivable way then known to sanitary science for dealing with this 'almost unimaginable difficulty'. Its 1871 report of nearly 300 pages advocated a multi-stranded solution which included the purchase of an 800 acre sewage farm, the creation of a 'Joint Drainage Commission', and, in order to immediately cut down pollution at Saltley and at the same time rid the town of open middens, the introduction of a pan system for the collection of excreta. Despite the fact that the cost of implementing this report was estimated at £324,800, its recommendations were accepted in full both by the unreformed council and the ratepayers. However, due to the opposition of Adderley and other local landowners, the necessary parliamentary bill was defeated at Westminster.

Worse was to follow. By the end of 1872 a threat of sequestration was hanging over the town council, which meant that unless it acted quickly Chancery might take the entire matter out of its hands. Yet, with the failure of its legislation, the council was left with the power to implement only one aspect of its original comprehensive plan. So, for the time being, the fundamental concept of a piped sewerage scheme had in large measure to be abandoned. Instead of being carried to the Saltley outlet through the town's sewers, as much excreta as possible was to be disposed of by the cumbersome means of the 'Rochdale pan system'. Bunce outlined this as follows:

> Beneath each closet seat is placed a metal pan, capable of affording closet accommodation for a week. In the yard is placed a wooden or iron tub for the reception of dry ashes and vegetable and other refuse from the houses. Once a week these receptacles are cleared of their contents. The closet pans are carried away in closed vans, each containing about eighteen of the pans, and holding also about one ton of ashes taken from the ash tubs. The pans in process of removal are covered with close-fitting metal lids, fresh pans being left in their places. The pans are then taken to the Corporation wharf in Montague Street, are emptied, thoroughly cleansed and disinfected, and are then again ready for use.

Although the attempt to exclude excreta from the sewers was later condemned by a government enquiry, the

Chamberlain administration had no alternative but to persist with this system. And in any case, the use of pans rather than open middens, with 'the contents being removed weekly instead of being left for months', was bound to have a beneficial effect on the public health of the town. At the end of 1874 only 3,845 pans were in circulation. But this figure had been increased to 15,992 two years later, which meant that about a third of the town's excreta was being dealt with by the new method, and presumably that a similar proportion of its open middens had been filled in.

Meanwhile, work was going ahead on the extension and improvement of the sewage farm at Saltley, where progress was sufficient for the Court of Chancery to be satisfied in March 1875 that no further nuisance existed. On the passing of the 1875 Public Health Act, too, the way became clear for the council to proceed with the creation of a 'Joint Drainage Commission'. Chamberlain himself presided at the conference with neighbouring local authorities which in March 1876 resolved to set up such a body. The resulting Tame and Rea District Drainage Board began work the following year, with

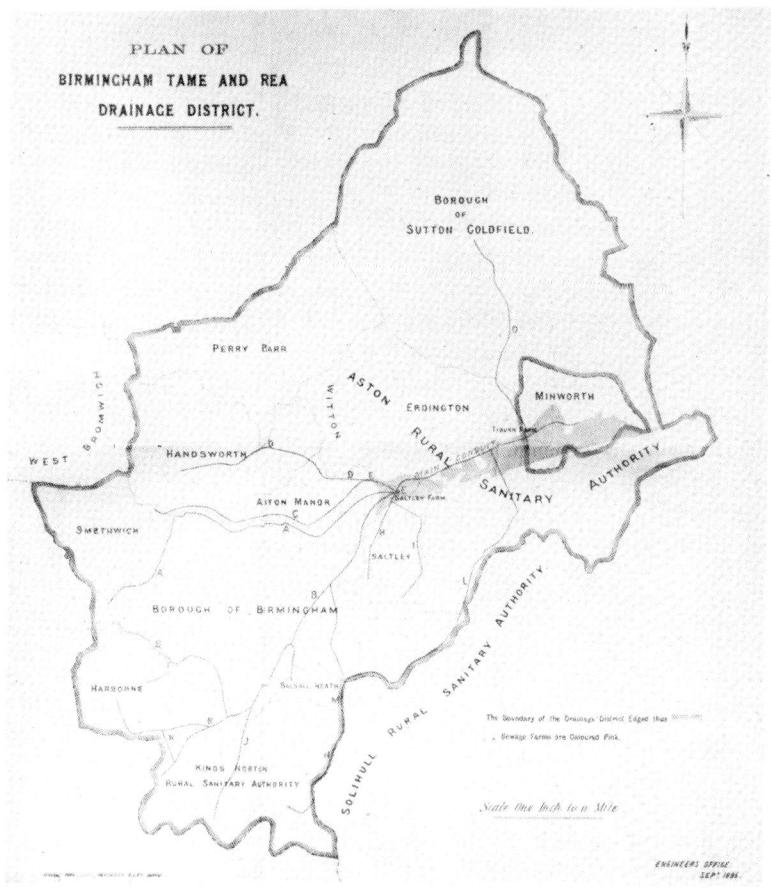

Birmingham Corporation providing 12 members, and one member each from the local boards of Aston Manor, Balsall Heath, Handsworth, Harborne, Saltley and Smethwick, plus the rural districts of Aston, Perry Barr and King's Norton.

With Avery again exercising strong leadership as chairman, by 1884 this board had completely reconstructed the Saltley filtration plant, established a 1,500 sewage farm running from there to Tyburn, and laid an 8 foot conduit which enabled the bulk of Birmingham's piped sewage to be conveyed thither. Thus the corporation's 1871 sewerage plan was back on course. And however belatedly, so was that idealistic vision which Pigott Smith had outlined as long ago as 1857 of 'ultimately and universally' introducing 'the water closet . . . and house drainage by means of tubular pipes' — a vision which for several years even the municipal reformers had found it desperately difficult to hang on to.

DR. ALFRED HILL,
Medical Officer of Health and Analyst to the City.
From a Photograph by H. J. Whitlock, New Street.)
(PLATE 0.)

The second improvement programme which the Chamberlain administration inherited in 1873 might more accurately be described as a blank sheet, with little inscribed on it except the heading, 'Public Health'. Despite appeals from enlightened local opinion since 1864 and the example of many other towns, the old economy council had persistently resisted the appointment of a Medical Officer of Health. By 1872 it could resist no longer. The Public Health Act of that year made the employment of such an officer compulsory, at the same time constituting the municipal corporation an Urban Health Authority. Dr. Hill had served with distinction as part-time Borough Analyst since 1859, and was now invited to add to this role that of Medical Officer. In response to the 1872 Act the council also renamed its 'Borough Inspection Committee' the 'Sanitary Committee'. But otherwise little progress was made until the reformers took over, under Chamberlain's 'sanitary lieutenant', William Cook.

There were plenty of urgent problems, for, as Avery had told the council in the previous year, 'Nature, geography and soil had done a great deal for the health of Birmingham . . . and the governmental authorities of the town had done very little'.

But now a 'sanitary census' of the town was at once instituted. This found that of the borough's 70,561 houses — 'excluding those of the superior class' — 39,000 were back-to-backs, while 24,000 households depended for their water on corrupted wells. The 1871 sewage report had already drawn attention to the fact that Birmingham's comparatively satisfactory overall death rate concealed horrifying figures for its crowded central districts. Statistics collected by the Medical Officer now showed that the proportion of people dying from zymotic, or infectious, diseases was actually higher in Birmingham than anywhere else in the country. And these were the diseases that were regarded as being directly linked to bad environmental conditions — lack of cleanliness, polluted air, impure water — and as such, readily preventable.

Starting in February 1875, a whole series of far-reaching reforms were rapidly implemented. Despite Alderman Brinsley's insistence that such officers were 'unconstitutional and un-English', the Sanitary Committee's inspection staff was increased from 12 to 38. Down to this time their duties had been confined to inspecting milk and food, and dealing with nuisances. But all houses in the borough were now to be classified according to condition, with the worst being visited once a week. Using the Medical Officer's weekly returns of deaths, the inspection staff were also to identify localities which were particularly susceptible to infectious diseases, and then set about eradicating the causes. Meanwhile, a 'Borough Hospital' was established at Winson Green, so that more smallpox and scarlet fever victims could be isolated. Infected houses were to be cleansed and disinfected, and a Disinfecting Station was opened in Bacchus Road for the treatment of clothes and bedding.

In 1876 the Health Committee, as it had by then become, began the compulsory closing of polluted wells, with landlords being required to connect the properties formerly dependent on them to the town water supply. 291 wells were filled in during the first year. Within nine years over 3,000 had been eliminated, and a supply of pure water thereby made available to an estimated 60,000 inhabitants who had not enjoyed it before. Five public mortuaries were established in 1876, when, with the formation of the Joint Drainage Board pending, the Health Committee also took over responsibility for the removal of refuse, excreta pans and nightsoil.

Nuisances remedied or abated by the Health Department's inspectors in 1878 included 6,087 cases 'connected with drains', 3,155 involving 'filthy houses', 3,839 'filthy courts, passages, and back yards', 8,081 'foul ashpits and privies', and 973 'keeping fowls and pigs'. In the same year the town's 1,533 factory chimneys led to the serving of no less than 1,035 notices for the abatement of 'the Smoke Nuisance'. By 1882, however, although the number of chimneys had gone up to 1,671, a mere 101 smoke abatement cases were necessary.

The cumulative effect of the Health Committee's wide-ranging measures was little short of miraculous. During the 5 years 1870-4 the town's death rate had averaged 24.5 per 1,000. By the period 1880-4 it was down to 20.6, a consolidated reduction of 16% in a single decade.

Such reforms were bound to be costly. The early 1870s brought unprecedented prosperity to the country as a whole. In Birmingham itself they were years of 'excited trade and excessive optimism', with not only inflated business profits, but many workers securing higher wages and shorter working hours. After two decades of 'economy', now, if ever, was the time when Birmingham ought to be able to afford a period of

ALDERMAN W. COOK, J.P.
(From a Photograph by H. J. Whitlock, New Street.)

civic reform.

Yet whenever the corporation had embarked upon a programme of big expenditure in the past, the ratepayers had always called a halt. Chamberlain was acutely aware of this danger, and made up his mind to minimize it immediately on taking office. No issue illustrates more clearly his outstanding qualities as a civic leader.

The course he adopted was far from original. By 1870, 49 municipal authorities were running their own gas undertakings, most of them as a result of buying out a private company. The previous year a parliamentary committee had advised Birmingham to do likewise. With one significant exception, the advice had fallen on deaf ears.

At a council meeting held in January 1874 the mayor himself moved the motion, 'That in the opinion of the Council it is desirable that the manufacture, supply, and sale of gas in the Borough should be under the control of the Corporation...' Chamberlain told the council 'that with him the matter was not at all a new question. Almost as soon as he had a seat in the Council he had thought of the possibility of a bargain being made with these private companies'. He also told them that 'he had in November, 1873 [i.e., the very month of taking office], on his own responsibility and without committing the Council, communicated with the Boards of the two Gas Companies', and that already 'a basis had been formed on which future negotiations would proceed'.

The most immediately cogent reason Chamberlain advanced for such a course of action was financial. If the council 'proposed to increase their duties and responsibilities', they had to face the fact that they would be 'met with opposition from ratepayers unwilling to do justice because their means were insufficient'. The cost of 'the work then pressing on the attention of the Council' was 'overwhelming and alarming'. The acquisition of the gas companies would bring to the borough 'the certainty of receiving in a short time considerable sums in the relief of taxation ... and would help to relieve the ratepayers of burdens which were every day becoming more onerous and oppressive'.

But Chamberlain had more profound, more Dawsonite, justifications for the purchase of the gas companies. In the first place,

> ... he held distinctly that all monopolies which are sustained in any way by the State ought to be in the hands of the representatives of the people, by whom they should be administered, and to whom their profits should go.

And secondly, he told the council that

> ... he was inclined to increase the duties and responsibilities of the local authority, in whom he had so great a confidence, and would do everything in his power to constitute these local authorities real parliaments, supreme in their jurisdiction.

Impressed, no doubt, by both the idealism and the utility, the council carried the mayor's resolution by 54 votes to 2.

THE WIZAR[

THE GAS.

'The Wizard of Gas'– a penny 'Dart Cartoon' of 1879.

In 1879 the Gas Committee decided to spend £25,000 'in bringing up the Saltley Plant to its greatest capacity.' Below: Part of the resulting 35 acre gasworks in the 1920s. Right: The gaunt 'Gothic' remains of its retort house today.

Chamberlain handled the negotiations with the companies personally. By December 1874 the draft Gas Bill had been approved by the council. In July 1875 it passed the House of Lords and the Gas Committee was formed, with Chamberlain himself as chairman.

Meanwhile, the wisdom of Chamberlain's policy had been graphically demonstrated. In April 1874 the ratepayers had given the go-ahead for the municipalization of gas by a 2:1 majority. But the month before they had overwhelmingly defeated a proposed rate increase, leaving the council with no alternative but to cut its improvement estimates by £41,000.

An unprecedented loan of £2,000,000 was required to purchase the companies. But against this, the Gas Department made net profits of £421,467 during its first nine years, of which – after loan repayments – £241,965 could be 'appropriated to public purposes'. And over the same period the price of gas to the consumer was steadily brought down – by a cumulative 30.7%.

The corporation had been empowered to take over the Birmingham Waterworks Company since the Improvement Act of 1851, and for a full quarter century had failed to do so. However, having opened the first year of his mayorality by initiating the municipalization of gas, Chamberlain opened the second by doing the same for water. With over a third of the town's population still dependent on contaminated wells, the case was not difficult to argue. 'What do you think of the inhabitants being compelled to drink water which is as bad as sewage before clarification?', Chamberlain asked. In many cases 'the poorer classes were so destitute of water that they were driven to steal it from the Company's taps in their neighbourhoods'.

The purchase of the gasworks had been intended to improve 'the Council's financial resources'; the main reason for purchasing the waterworks was to improve 'the health of the town'. For whereas 'a private company must needs look to profits', the corporation would be able to shoulder the responsibility of providing all householders with 'an abundant supply, irrespective of commercial return'.

Once again, on first putting this matter before the council in December 1874, Chamberlain disarmingly confessed that 'he had for some time previously conducted private negotiations . . .' But the vote in favour was unanimous. And

although the Birmingham Waterworks Company, which had in many ways given excellent service, fought hard to save itself, in August 1875 the corporation's Water Bill received the royal assent. Thereafter, the municipality was as good as its word. Prior to 1875 the private company was supplying about 21,000 houses. By 1884 the Water Committee had laid 145 miles of additional mains and made pure water available to over 47,000 additional households.

Other initiatives of the Chamberlain years included the authorization of a municipal Fire Brigade and the laying of the foundation stone of the Council House in 1874; the widening of Colmore Row and the voting of £1,000 for the planting of trees along the streets in 1875; and in 1876 a 'Resolution to cause a History of the Corporation to be prepared' — by J. T. Bunce. But Chamberlain's third and last major municipal enterprise was the launching of the Birmingham Improvement Scheme.

The Artisans' Dwellings Act of 1875 extended the powers of corporations to acquire, clear and redevelop urban slum areas. Chamberlain had been consulted by the Home Secretary during the preparation of this bill and was determined that Birmingham should be among the first to make use of it. The scheme was characteristically bold — though, as was usually the case with Chamberlain, nothing in it was particularly original, all its essential elements having been culled from Glasgow and elsewhere. Nevertheless, when first outlined to his closest associates as early as 1873, they found it 'so gigantic and its difficulties so great' that it was thought inadvisable at that stage 'to bring it either before the Public Works Committee or the Council'.

As unanimously approved by the council two years later, this scheme involved the wholesale redevelopment of 93 acres of the Birmingham town centre. The cost — coming on top of about £3 million spent on gas and water — was to be £1,600,000. But if the stakes were high, so were the potential rewards. In fact it might almost be said that the aim of this 'sagacious audacity' was nothing less than to achieve the proverbially impossible: make a silk purse out of a sow's ear. The sow's ear was a dreadful area, mainly in St. Mary's Ward, which, in Chamberlain's words, stood in the way of 'a perfect scheme of sanitary reform'. At a council meeting in October 1875 William White gave a compelling account of this worn-out piece of townscape:

> In passing through such streets as Thomas Street, the back of Lichfield Street, and other parts indicated in the plan before the Council, little else is seen but bowing roofs, tottering chimneys, tumble-down and often disused shopping, heaps of bricks, broken windows, and coarse, rough pavements, damp and sloppy. It is not easy to describe or imagine the dreary desolation which acre after acre of the very heart of the town presents to anyone who will take the trouble to visit it. In houses, too, not of the worst class, but in the front streets, and inhabited by respectable and thriving tradesmen, intolerable structural evils abound ... In one case ...

the sitting room window could not be opened, owing to the horrible effluvia from a yawning midden just under it. . . . If I were to repeat a hundred times 'Dirt, damp, delapidation', I should inadequately describe the condition of things.

The silk purse was to be 'a great street, as broad as a Parisian boulevard, from New Street to Aston Road'. Not far short of half a mile long, and 22 yards wide, this would open up the cramped town centre, let in light and air, enormously improve the town's traffic flow, and set an example of dignity worthy of the place. It would also provide a much needed improvement in the town's shopping facilities. 'I have always held that Birmingham ought to be the metropolis of the Midland Counties', said Chamberlain. Yet there is 'no town in the kingdom of such magnitude which has so poor a show of shops'.

But the Improvement Scheme, stemming from the same 'great entrepreneur in the public service' as the gas take-over, was also conceived and presented as a sound and attractive financial speculation. The big shops, offices and hotels would

Before and after the Birmingham Improvement Scheme. Top: The area in question as mapped for Allens' Pictorial Guide of 1852. Bottom: The same area as shown in Murray's Warwickshire, 1899.

substantially increase the rateable value of the area. Moreover, the plan of letting the properties on 75 year leases was 'part of a system which will make this borough the richest in the kingdom sixty or seventy years hence'. 'It is the only occasion for which I ever wish to live beyond the ordinary term of human life', Chamberlain told the council, 'in order to see the result of this improvement, and hear the blessings which will then be showered upon the council of 1875 which had the courage to inaugurate this scheme'. In the face of such far-sighted concern for posterity, it may seem ungrateful to reflect that had these leases been for the more usual 99 years, the whole of Chamberlain's 'great street' might have retained its original Victorian visage long enough to have become properly appreciated.

But perhaps we are lucky to have Corporation Street at all. For, despite the unanimous vote in the council, it involved the most acrimonious controversy outside it. The mere arithmetic of the scheme appalled many of the old economists, giving them 'vague dreams of an incubus of debt involving the town in ultimate ruin'. Meanwhile, Tories condemned the proposals as 'vile and ruinous and pernicious and wicked and against the constitution and the scriptures'.

Nor was the most expensive part of the plan all that easy to justify. The admittedly dreadful St. Mary's slum lay beyond Bull Street, whereas 'the solid mass of houses' between Bull Street and New Street were in perfectly good condition. Chamberlain argued that driving the proposed road through this 'wall' of buildings would make a 'channel of ventilation' which would 'let light and air into the insanitary area'. But far from everybody felt that this claim carried much conviction.

Having officially been initiated by the Medical Officer of Health on purely sanitary grounds, the scheme had to be approved first by the Local Government Board and then by Parliament. When the Local Government inspector held his statutory enquiry in the town, the opposition used every imaginable device to discredit the proposals. But 'Brummagem Joe' took on their 'large array of legal gentlemen, counsel and solicitors' in person — and predictably won the day.

By the time Parliament had finally given its consent in August 1876, Chamberlain himself had resigned as mayor in order to become a Birmingham M.P. But so many able businessmen of his own ilk had been attracted on to the council

'The Local Obstructionists'— another barbed 'Dart' comment, this time on Chamberlain's Improvement Scheme.

THE LOCAL OBSTRUCTIONISTS.

by this time that the Improvement Committee, under William White, was well able to cope. And in any case, Chamberlain continued to serve as an alderman until 1883 and was always on call when the going got rough – as it frequently did.

Construction work was taking place somewhere along Corporation Street for upwards of two decades. Beginning with the pulling down of buildings at the New Street end in August 1878, the thoroughfare itself was completed in 3½ years. With the petering out of the economic boom, lettings did not go as quickly as had been hoped. But by the end of 1884, 65 leases had been agreed and the income from rents had risen to £34,321, and from rates to £20,000. This was against an 'Interest and Repayment on Loans' of £64,821 per annum. Among the sites already disposed of were those for the North Western Arcade, the Grand Theatre, the Cobden Temperance Hotel, and for several big shops. Sites had also been reserved for the County Court and the Assize Court, the later being opened as the Victoria Law Courts in 1889.

Before the end of the '80s a local journalist was already stating that 'Corporation Street has completely eclipsed New Street as the premier street of the city'. Yet the last plot – at the junction of Corporation Street and Steelhouse Lane – was not let until 1900. Down to 1892, moreover, when the break-even point was at last reached, the 'croakers' were 'continually asserting that the Improvement Scheme will turn out a failure'; or alternatively reminding everyone that 'when large reforms are effected the noble work is done at somebody's inconvenience and cost'.

More damagingly, it was repeatedly claimed that among the disadvantaged were the very people whom the scheme had been intended most to benefit. As its name implied, the main object of the 1875 Act had been 'the removing of buildings unsuitable for habitation' and 'the letting of land so obtained for . . . artisans' dwellings'. Accordingly, the Improvement Scheme as sanctioned by Parliament had provided for 'the accommodation of as great a number of persons as may be displaced . . . within the limits of the same area'. This accommodation was never provided.

At the time of the scheme's inception there were 3,054 artisan houses within the affected zone, and an artisan population of 13,538. Far from all were immediately displaced. Of the 1,335 dwellings acquired by the corporation down to 1882, 697 had been improved and remained tenanted. And indeed, as a result of their demolition programme and the accompanying sanitary work, the Improvement Committee could already claim that the death rate in the area had been brought down from 53.3 to 21.3 per 1,000.

However, providing new houses turned out to be a problem. The corporation was not legally empowered to do so itself. And although land had been purchased between

Highbury Hall, Yew Tree Road, Moseley. Joseph Chamberlain had this 'Gothic monstrosity' built by his namesake, J. H. Chamberlain, in 1879-80 – and it was his much-loved Birmingham home for the rest of his life. The library of the house is now kept as a museum to the great man. Above: The south front. Right: The main entrance.

Summer Lane and New Town Row for this purpose, the committee eventually had to report that there were 'so many dwellings of this kind unlet (owing to over-building) as to prevent any further speculative building of them'. In 1883 most of the Summer Lane site was accordingly sold to the School Board.

Under public pressure, the council instituted an enquiry into artisan dwellings in the same year. This reported that the borough then had 2,773 unlet houses which could be rented at 2s. 6d. – 3s. 6d. per week, and a further 2,500 at a rent of 3s. 6d. – 7s. 0d. The enquiry therefore concluded that 'there is adequate accommodation for the artisan and labouring classes within the borough'.

This assertion was regarded with suspicion at the time, but there are signs that it may have been well founded. Birmingham's population increased by 57,000 between 1871 and 1881. Yet during the same period no less than 17,758 new houses were built within the borough. At the contemporary average of 5 per house, these would have accommodated 88,790 people. So it looks as though there *had* been 'over-building' during the 1870s. And although the displaced slum dwellers would hardly have been able to take on new property, they could – and no doubt did – move into houses vacated by their better-off fellows.

In any case, the demolition of the St. Mary's slum ought perhaps to be seen, not on its own, but in conjunction with Chamberlain's virtually simultaneous insistence on banning the building of any further back-to-back houses. Taken together, these two measures were in effect a symbolic 'bottoming-out' so far as the standard of Birmingham working class housing was concerned. The unspeakable slums of the past could no longer be tolerated, and neither could the prospect of overtly replacing them with unspeakable slums for the future.

It was this aspect of the Improvement Scheme that Bunce – admittedly, a confirmed Chamberlainite – most strongly emphasized:

> Slums and rookeries, pestilential morally and physically, have disappeared as if by magic, and have given place to streets and buildings worthy of occupying the centre of a great town, while other portions of the improvement area have been so far benefited and purified that an artisan population may now occupy them without injury to health or the sacrifice of self respect.

Unfortunately, the 'bottoming-out' *was* only symbolic. For although the construction of John Bright Street, the extension of New Street station, etc., took further bites out of the central slums during the 1880s, Greens Village and the Inkleys were not demolished until 1899, while the wretched courts of Bagot Street easily outlasted Queen Victoria.

How much did Chamberlain's whirlwind programme of municipal reform actually cost the ratepayer? Borough rates averaged 8s. 9d. per head of population during the 1860s; in 1872 they stood at 10s. 2¾d., and in 1873 at 11s. 10d. The ratepayers refused to have them increased above this level during Chamberlain's first year of office. Moreover, although Chamberlain managed to bump them up to 13s. 4¾d. per head during his second year, he then astonished everybody by bringing them down again to 11s. 10¼d. 'This . . . is as good as a three years' lease of power' he wrote. 'I had to use my despotic authority a little in arranging the estimates and took the matter out of the hands of the Finance Committee for the purpose, but they are *bona fide* estimates and *will wash.*'

Unfortunately the rates had to be put up to 13s. 9d. per head in 1877, and were never brought down below that mark thereafter. Considering what the inhabitants got for their money, however, such a level was perhaps hardly exorbitant. The profits from gas helped to protect ratepayers to some extent. But the real secret of Chamberlain's success was his willingness to pay for extravagant reforms by extravagant borrowing on the cheap money markets of the 1870s. The total loans raised by the corporation during the first 35 years of its history amounted to under £1 million. Against this, in less than three years, Chamberlain committed the corporation to loans of over five times as much.

Although a deeply earnest nonconformist minister inspired the municipal revolution, then, it was a high-powered business executive who found out how to accomplish it. Chamberlain's method was to think big, to sell his ideas to the council and the public, and then to implement them on borrowed money. In pursuing such a course — and in pursuing it with such panache — he set what proved to be an irresistible example, not only to Birmingham, but to other British cities, and ultimately to the municipalities of the world.

Like most hyper-active men, Chamberlain made plenty of enemies in his own day, and has attracted more than his share of adverse comment since. Modern historians have characterized the Improvement Scheme, for instance, as anything from 'a shameless piece of property speculation' to 'a form of municipal Stalinism'. Yet his unflagging popularity shows that 'Our Joe' commanded the life-long loyalty of countless townsfolk who could not 'contribute pecuniarily', and of many of those who could. As much a Tory democrat out of the Attwood mould as a 'municipal Stalinist', or even a harbinger of municipal socialism perhaps, with him nineteenth-century Birmingham's unique experiment in self-generated populism culminated in its supreme populist.

Two of the town's topographical tributes to Joseph Chamberlain. Above: The Chamberlain Memorial Fountain, Chamberlain Square (see page 184). Right: The 'Chamberlain Clock,' erected in 1903 by 'his constituents, the electors of West Birmingham', at the junction of Frederick Street and Warstone Lane.

'Look! We Have Come Through!'

The new spirit of the Chamberlain epoch affected almost every aspect of local life. Chamberlain had been a member of the School Board since its inception in 1870, along with George Dixon, Dr. Dale, Charles Vince and George Dawson. Following the Liberal victory of 1873, he himself served as chairman for nearly three years, before handing over to George Dixon, who was to distinguish that office for the next twenty.

Even before 1873, and despite 'the controversial fires that then burned so fiercely' over the question of religious upbringing, the School Board had set about tackling the educational problems of the town with exemplary vigour. A rapidly conducted survey estimated the number of children for whom school accommodation was required at 59,710. Including private schools, there was existing accommodation for 37,442, and therefore a shortfall of 22,268 school places.

As early as 1871 a local bye law was passed making school attendance enforceable for all children aged 5-13, and the first school attendance officer was appointed in the following year. The initial clutch of five Board schools were all opened between March and July 1873, providing a combined total of 5,272 places. By the end of the Board's first decade the town had 28 new schools, accommodating 28,787 children. By this time, too, school fees had been reduced to a uniform 1d. per week across the whole town, and there was a team of 17 attendance officers under a superintendent. As a result, 89% of Board school children 'were in average attendance' during 1879, while the other public elementary schools of the town had achieved a similar record. Showell claimed a few years later that the Birmingham School Board had provided 'a set of schools that cannot be equalled by any town in the kingdom, either for number, magnificence of architecture . . . high-class

Only two of the initial clutch of five Birmingham Board schools survive: Steward Street (left), and Garrison Lane (right). Like all the other early examples, they were built by the firm of Martin & Chamberlain, mainly to J. H. Chamberlain's designs.

teachers, or ... the advancement of scholars ... except in the matter of religion, which, as nearly as possible, is altogether banished from the curriculum'.

Other School Boards, responsible for less heavily populated parts of the Greater Birmingham area, did not become active until considerably later. The Yardley Board, for instance, only erected its first schools in the 1890s. Even the Aston School Board was not formed until 1875, though it then built 7 schools in as many years. Nevertheless, by 1880 Birmingham's educational climate had been totally transformed; and from then onwards the vast majority of local children would at least grow up literate.

Despite Chamberlain's determined approach, the housing problems of the town could not be so easily ameliorated. Nevertheless, once the 1876 building bye laws had come into force, the 1,000 or more working class houses that were built every year had to conform to certain minimum standards. Most of the early bye-law housing went up in two broad swathes of territory which were about a mile out from the town centre. The swathe to the south-east stretched from Highgate, through Sparkbrook, to Small Heath, some of it being intermixed with earlier back-to-back housing. The swathe to the north-west ran from the Rotton Park area, through Winson Green, the All Saints district of Hockley, and then south of the Aston Manor boundary to Nechells.

The analysis of a sample of 522 plans approved by the corporation's building surveyor during the years 1878-84 showed that by then new accommodation for the working classes took the form of terraced through-houses and tunnel-backs. The majority of these had 4 or 5 internal rooms, exclusive of pantries, privies and cellars. About half could boast a bay-windowed front room, and 40% a small front garden. Internal water closets remained rare, and one in three artisan families still had to share their external toilet with neighbours. Yet leaving lavatory and washing facilities aside, in standard of construction and the number and size of rooms, such houses did not compare unfavourably with many of their modern equivalents. And certainly, the average run of new working class accommodation was now of a type and quality which a generation before had been the exclusive preserve of the 'labour aristocracy'.

Relatively few commodious houses were now being erected in Winson Green, Highgate and Sparkbrook. For by the 1870s the middle classes were moving out of town in considerable numbers. In addition to Edgbaston, the central part of Handsworth had been slowly developing as a select rural retreat since the days of Boulton and Watt. *Kelly's Directory* of 1874 describes it as 'a fashionable suburb', while the 'village' of Birchfield in the same parish is said to consist

Above and right: Frederick Terrace, Montgomery Street, erected in 1876. The housing bye laws were passed in June 1876, and it would be interesting to know whether these houses were built before or after that date. In any case, they can be regarded as epitomizing the dramatic improvement in the standard of working class housing which the bye laws fostered.

'chiefly of the residences of persons engaged in business in Birmingham'. Isolated villas must have been going up in all the other parishes of the Greater Birmingham area by this time. However, apart from Handsworth and Birchfield, the only 'village' suburbs which were really gathering momentum as yet were at Erdington, with 281 'private residents' listed in the 1874 *Kelly's*, Harborne with 220, Acock's Green with 175, and Moseley with 133. King's Heath, on the other hand, is credited with only 71 private residents, King's Norton with 45, and Perry Barr with 42. Hall Green, Quinton and Northfield mustered a mere 27, 17, and 16 respectively.

Systematic housing development apparently started at Moseley in the late 1850s, initially along Valentine Lane and School Road. By the mid-1860s Park Hill had been laid out, and from 1870 the triangle of land bounded by Greenhill Road, Cotton Lane and Oxford Road was in process of development.

The beginning of the suburbanization of Harborne is described by Tom Presterne in the following terms:

> We will continue our way along High Street towards the Green Man Inn. You will observe, on the right-hand side, three ugly little streets, South Street, Bull Street, and York Street. ... They were so named after the proprietor of the land, who made these streets. Anticipating the modern idea of small ownerships, he sold the land in freehold building plots. Each one of the new owners impressed the locality with his own ideas of architectural convenience; hence the motley inartistic character of these three streets. York Street was first made, and that was the beginning of the break-up of rural Harborne.

Since the name of 'the proprietor' was Josiah Bull York, South Street was originally called Josiah Street. 'However, the name was never favoured', Presterne tells us, 'and it was called Greenfield Street, and subsequently, South Street, as at present'.

Below: An early Moseley villa, 14 Park Hill. Right: Suburban houses in York Road, Harborne. The furthest from the camera is dated 1849.

The modest nature of many of the cottages along the 'three ugly little streets' hardly suggests that their original

builders were particularly wealthy. Among those living in Greenfield Road in 1874, Henry Heynes seems to have been a comb manufacturer of High Street, Birmingham; William Henry Wood a pawnbroker of High Street; James Stormont a brass founder of Constitution Hill; Frederick Edward Whittington an engraver of Sand Street, and Thomas Edward Spencer a New Street solicitor.

Some of these people may well have walked to work, as Tom Presterne himself 'walked to Birmingham and back daily to school for five years'. But in 1874 there were horse omnibuses 'every half hour' to and from Harborne. The same applied with Birchfield, while Handsworth and Moseley had 15 minute services. The railways had played comparatively little part in Birmingham's early suburban growth. But since Acock's Green and Erdington both lacked week-day omnibus services, they were presumably to some extent 'railway suburbs' in origin. Acock's Green station was opened on the GWR's Oxford line in 1852; Erdington, along with Gravelly Hill, was an intermediate station on the L&NWR's Sutton Coldfield Railway. Inaugurated in 1862, this was Birmingham's first specially designed suburban line, and within seven years even Sutton—8 miles from town—was reported to be rousing itself 'from rural sleepiness to bustling activity'.

Two further suburban railways were developed during the 1870s. The L&NWR's Harborne Railway opened in 1874, with four stations in little over 2 miles. This was followed in 1876 by the Midland Railway's Birmingham and South-West Suburban line, which ran from its original terminus at Granville Street to King's Norton, with intermediate stations at Church Road, Somerset Road (both in Edgbaston), and Selly Oak. These lines must have given additional impetus to suburban expansion. Yet, as their prospectuses explained, they were conceived specifically for 'business people' looking for 'favourite neighbourhoods'. For the less well-off, particularly in the absence of workmen's tickets, commuting by rail remained quite out of the question.

Within the borough itself there was a 15 minute omnibus service to Edgbaston; half-hour services to Nechells Green, Sparkbrook, Small Heath, and along the Hagley Road as far as Norfolk Road; and an hourly service to Saltley. But omnibus travel would have been no more within the reach of the average working man than rail travel. The single fare from Handsworth in the 1860s was 6d.—and 'in snowy and difficult weather' this was 'sometimes raised to eightpence or ninepence'.

The vehicle which was destined to bring mobility to the bulk of the town's inhabitants was the 'tramway car'. It is therefore fitting—if not significant—that the corporation's first tram line, which was completed in 1873, ran from Colmore Row to Hockley. A second track, serving the Bristol Road, followed in 1875, with horse-drawn trams being operated on

Miss Ryland, from a contemporary photograph.

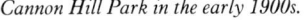

Cannon Hill Park in the early 1900s.

both routes, under lease, by the Birmingham and District Tramway Company. The plebeian possibilities of this form of transport are confirmed by a council bye law of 1873 which laid down that 'special carriages' for the 'labouring classes' were to be run from the termini at 5.30 and 6.30 a.m., and 5.30 and 6.30 p.m. daily. Yet Aston, Saltley, Small Heath, Sparkbrook, and other working class 'suburbs', all had to wait for their cheap transport until the introduction of the steam tram, and the 'tramway boom' of the 1880s.

At about the same time as Joseph Chamberlain was possessed of the idea of building Corporation Street, a spinster of the well-known Ryland family must have been experiencing what was in many ways a no less Utopian vision. Apart from the three cedar trees which Lord Calthorpe planted at its centre during the opening ceremony, the town's first major public park had been maintained for many years as little more than a railed-off expanse of open ground. But before Miss Louisa Anne Ryland presented her 57 acre Cannon Hill Park to the corporation, she decided to have what had formerly been a long stretch of Rea-side meadow land 'drained, laid out, and planted'. With not wholly inappropriate wonderment, Bunce describes the result as follows:

> . . . several acres were devoted to ornamental gardening, including shrubberies, in which were planted many choice and rare evergreens; large pools, surrounded by plantations and walks, were also constructed; and a carriage drive, nearly a mile in length, was formed round the park. A handsome refreshment room and an entrance lodge were also erected by Miss Ryland. On the margin of one of the pools, a boat-house has been provided, together with a landing stage. There is also a bathing pool, 216

by 100 feet, with a depth varying from 2 feet 6 inches to 5 feet 6 inches....
The park was opened to the public on the 1st of September, 1873. By Miss
Ryland's express desire there was no ceremony on the occasion, and
though the Corporation were most desirous that the park should bear the
name of the donor, Miss Ryland declined to assent to the request.

The corporation had been little more than a passive
recipient of parks down to this time. But the new social
conscience changed all that. One of Chamberlain's last acts as
mayor was to open the 8 acre Highgate Park in June 1876. One
of the first acts of George Baker, his successor, was to open the
12 acre Summerfield Park in the month following. Both were
purchased and laid out entirely from public funds, the total
cost exceeding £26,000. Nor was this all. Four days after
opening Highgate Park, Chamberlain had accepted the 41½
acre Small Heath Park as 'another noble gift' from Miss Ryland.
And despite 'some unfavourable comment' from ratepayers,
the council eventually decided to add over £8,000 to the £4,000
provided by Miss Ryland herself for converting this park 'to an
ornamental use'. William Middlemore gave the 4 acre Burbury
Street Recreation Ground, or 'Hockley Park', to the town in
1877. So the total area of Birmingham's park land was increased
from 91 to 215 acres in a mere four years. Thanks to Miss
Ryland, moreoever, the whole conception of this basic urban
amenity had been changed — quite literally — out of all recognition. Meanwhile, greenery had come so much into fashion
that during 1876-7 trees were being planted by the corporation
along Broad Street, Bordesley High Street, Camp Hill, the

*Small Heath Park, soon after the turn
of the century.*

Moseley and Pershore Roads.

Showell wrote in 1885, 'improvements are being carried out so rapidly now that in another generation it is likely that old Birmingham will have been improved off the face of the earth altogether'. One of the most conspicuous of these improvements, apart from Corporation Street, was the creation of an imposing administrative and cultural centre in the vicinity of what was at first called Council Square, and from 1901 onwards, Victoria Square. The Council House itself was under construction from 1874 to 1879, while the building of Mason College in Edmund Street was commenced in 1875. Among the already existing buildings in this complex were the Town Hall of 1832-61, the Birmingham and Midland Institute of 1855-7, and facing it across Paradise Street, Queen's College of 1843. The original Birmingham Reference Library had to be completely rebuilt after the disastrous fire of 1879, while new buildings of the early 1880s included the College of Arts and Crafts in Margaret Street, and the Birmingham Museum and Art Gallery. Happily, this last was a by-product of municipal gas, being built at the expense of the Gas Department, on top of its new offices.

The Chamberlain Memorial was erected in 1880 at the centre of what had previously been 'a squalid area of land between the Town Hall and Sir Josiah Mason's College', but which was thereafter to be known as Chamberlain Place. Chamberlain was only 44 at the time, and on the loss of the

The Council House, built by Yeoville Thomason, 1874-9.

Chamberlain Place, looking towards the Art Gallery.

Reference Library in the previous year, he had urged that the £3,000 which had been raised should be put towards its rebuilding. But the subscription committee would not hear of this, and went ahead with its perpetually cascading Gothic fountain that was intended to remind posterity of the municipalization of water. Very fittingly, Chamberlain's memorial was flanked on one side by a canopied statue of George Dawson; and in 1885 a seated figure of Josiah Mason was added on the other. At first Council Square was under the surveillance of Joseph Priestley, along with Sir Robert Peel, founder of the Metropolitan Police and repealer of the Corn Laws. Nor were these dignitaries upstaged by Queen Victoria until a few months before her death in 1901.

The work of the corporation in developing Corporation Street, Chamberlain Place and Council Square was paralleled by scarcely less ambitious private projects. When the leases along Ann Street began to fall in after 1866, this thoroughfare was re-aligned, widened, and re-named Colmore Row after its landlords. The Colmores then ensured that its redevelopment took the form of the magnificent business street which — in the main — can still be seen today. Apart from the banks and office blocks in various Classical styles, other architecturally distinguished buildings along its length included Thomason's Union Club of 1869, and the huge bulk of the Grand Hotel, which was completed in 1875. In that year, too, from opposite the nearby Snow Hill station, and on top of the GWR tunnel, the Great Western Arcade was under construction. The first of several such speculations, this glass-roofed and balconied shopping promenade originally came to a dead end in Temple Row. But in the early 1880s its line was continued, as the North Western Arcade, right through into Corporation Street.

Quite startlingly now, the town was beginning to take on the appearance of a flourishing provincial metropolis. New

Left: Colmore Row, looking west from St. Philip's churchyard. Above: The Grand Hotel, still with its original façade, by J. A. Chatwin. Right: An early twentieth-century photograph of the Great Western Arcade.

Street and Bull Street were largely rebuilt, giving it—with Corporation Street and Colmore Row—a fine inner circuit of principal streets. At the same time, small bow-windowed shops catering for a few hundred prestigious customers were being succeeded by well advertized emporia aiming to attract a much wider clientele. Often occupying one or two floors only of five- or six-storied 'Buildings'—with business chambers above them—boot and shoe shops, milliners, jewellers and grocers became spacious, brightly lit, and beckoning. Multi-floored outfitters, furniture stores and fancy repositories had large plate glass windows, passenger lifts and mahogany counters.

Wholesale trading—always a cinderella in Birmingham—was less well served. A capacious and desperately needed covered Vegetable Market was at last opened in Smithfield in 1884, and a major extension of the Fish Market was completed in the same year. As late as 1891, however, the Markets and

Left: Lewis's, at the junction of Corporation Street and Bull Street, c.1890. Below: Hall and Polly, Corporation Street, c.1890. Right: New Street, soon after 1900.

Fairs Committee was still lamenting the hopeless inadequacy of its facilities. A 50% decline in the live cattle and sheep trade had by then largely 'solved' the Cattle Market problem. Yet proper provision for the resulting increase in the carcass trade had to wait for the opening of the new Meat Market six years later.

Some modern historians have poured gentle scorn on 'the construction of new grand civic buildings ... which proclaimed to the world the greatness of the municipality', and the 'concern with maces and regalia, coats of arms and robes' that went with them. And indeed, there was widespread criticism along similar lines at the time—from Tory and economist politicians, for instance, and incredulous ratepayers. Yet it would probably be a mistake to see such phenomena as expressing nothing more than the megalomania of the town's

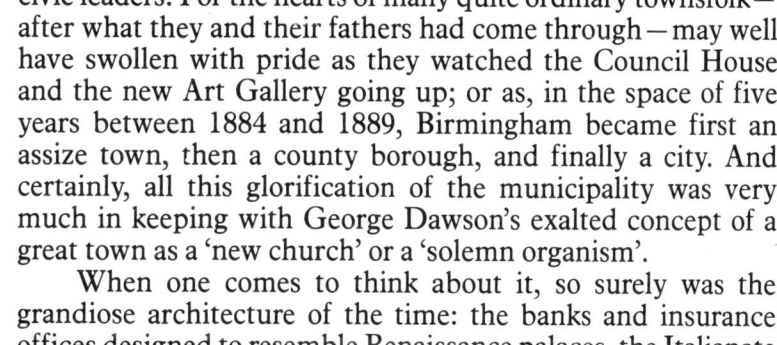

civic leaders. For the hearts of many quite ordinary townsfolk — after what they and their fathers had come through — may well have swollen with pride as they watched the Council House and the new Art Gallery going up; or as, in the space of five years between 1884 and 1889, Birmingham became first an assize town, then a county borough, and finally a city. And certainly, all this glorification of the municipality was very much in keeping with George Dawson's exalted concept of a great town as a 'new church' or a 'solemn organism'.

When one comes to think about it, so surely was the grandiose architecture of the time: the banks and insurance offices designed to resemble Renaissance palaces, the Italianate and Gothic factories, the pinnacled hotels and shops of Corporation Street, the high-towered, 'spiritually uplifting' Board schools of Martin and Chamberlain, the medievalized red-brick villas of Edgbaston, even by the late 1870s, the artisans' tunnel-backs with Romanesque doorways or 'pointed fourteenth-century' windows. It is almost as if this ornate, over-earnest architecture — along with the civic pomp and circumstance — were trying to tell us something: that at some deep subliminal level, for those who had fought to create it out of a hellish past, high Victorian Birmingham really did bear some resemblance to a promised land, a holy city.

In any event, what was happening in the Birmingham of the Chamberlain era made a most profound impression on contemporaries. So arresting was the precept and example of its civic gospel, that before long, as a late nineteenth-century student of local government put it, 'municipal reformers were looking to Birmingham as the eyes of the faithful are turned towards Mecca'. Thereafter, of course, Victorian Birmingham was also looking towards itself. Thus, in 1902, Bunce's continuator, C. A. Vince, after describing the Chamberlain period as 'the heroic age of municipal history', went on to explain that during the rest of the Queen's reign 'progress has largely followed directions already plainly indicated'.

At the same time, it is also true that by 1883, when Chamberlain retired from municipal politics in order to devote himself to the affairs of the nation and the empire, Birmingham was beginning to enter a rather different phase in its history. New market conditions, new products and new production methods were already transforming its industrial structure, while the Cadburys, having moved their chocolate factory out of town, were on the verge of setting it a new example in working class housing. With the industrial and suburban diaspora, the relative compactness of the early Victorian town was now becoming a matter for old men's recollections. By the same token, from 1877 onwards, the extension of the borough's boundaries provided a constant subject of debate; and indeed, Harborne, Balsall Heath, Saltley and Little Bromwich were brought into the city in 1891. Meanwhile, if only because of the gates which Dawson and Chamberlain had thrown open, municipal government itself was becoming ever wider in its scope, and ever more complex in its implementation. After being staunchly Liberal for half a century, even Birmingham's political complexion suddenly underwent a dramatic change. In the elections of 1886, following the split of the Liberal party and Third Reform Bill, the Birmingham caucus stayed Liberal. But Chamberlain turned Unionist, and carried the town in which he was so highly respected with him.

So by the mid-1880s, with the rebuilding of the town centre nearing completion, the electrical engineering, cycle and motor trades in prospect, and Bournville, Birmingham University, Birmingham's first bishop, and Greater Birmingham coming over the horizon, at last our theme seems to be changing. To go any further would be to turn from the making of Victorian, to the making of modern Birmingham.

In researching and writing this book I have become acutely aware of two things. The first is that none of the existing accounts of Victorian Birmingham — including that given in the standard history of Gill and Briggs — are altogether satisfactory. The main reason for this is that they were written too soon, as it were, before a generation of work on 'urban studies' had begun to make us sufficiently aware of the tremendous problems which confronted our Victorian predecessors.

Secondly, I have become no less conscious of the unsatisfactory nature of my own book. This is because, although representing upwards of eighteen months' full-time work, it has had to be based almost exclusively on printed sources — Timmins' *Birmingham and the Midland Hardware District*, Bunce's *History of the Corporation of Birmingham*, Showell's *Dictionary of Birmingham*, contemporary directories, guide books, and so on. Yet beyond these sources there exists — in the Birmingham Reference Library and elsewhere — an enormous collection of other source material, local Acts of Parliament, countless official reports on almost every aspect of Victorian life, a vast corporation archive, newspaper files, local biographies, industrial histories, etc., etc., etc. For one person to have worked through even a tithe of this material would have taken decades. However, it is hoped that by providing a new and up-dated general framework, or synoptic view, of the making of Victorian Birmingham, this book may help to stimulate others to undertake detailed research into various themes within this huge topic. Then perhaps, one day, a fully worthy account of the amazing experiences and endeavours which went into the creation of one of Britain's most influential cities may at last be written.

Select Bibliography

Allen, G. C., *The Industrial Development of Birmingham and the Black Country, 1860-1927* (1929).
Briggs, A., and Gill, C., *History of Birmingham,* Volumes I and II (1952).
Bunce, J. T., *History of the Corporation of Birmingham,* Volumes I and II (1878, 1885).
Dyos, H. J., and Wolff, M. (eds.), *The Victorian City* (1973).
Dent, R. K., *Old and New Birmingham* (1880).
Dent, R. K., *The Making of Birmingham* (1894).
Fairn, A., *A History of Moseley* (1973).
Horsfall, J., *The Iron Masters of Penns* (1981).
Langford, J. A., *A Century of Birmingham Life . . . 1741 to 1841* (1868).
Langford, J. A., *Modern Birmingham and its Institutions, 1841 to 1871* (1911).
Little, B., *Birmingham Buildings: the Architectural Story of a Midland City* (1971).
Macmorran, J. L., *Municipal Public Works and Planning in Birmingham* (1973).
Morland, O., *William White, A Brother of Men* (1903).
Muirhead, J. H., *Birmingham Institutions* (1911).
Pevsner, N., and Wedgwood, A., *The Buildings of England: Warwickshire* (1966).
Presterne, T., *Harborne Once Upon a Time* (1913).
Showell, W., *Dictionary of Birmingham* (1885).
Stephens, W. B., *Victoria County History of Warwickshire, Volume VII, The City of Birmingham* (1964).
Tangye, R., *'One and All', An Autobiography* (1889).
Timmins, S. (ed.), *Birmingham and the Midland Hardware District* (1866).
White, W., *The Story of the Severn Street and Priory First-Day Schools* (1895).
Waterhouse, R. E., *The Birmingham and Midland Institute* (1954).
Wilson, W., *The Life of George Dawson* (1905).

Research Studies

Behagg, C., 'Custom, Class and Change: The Trade Societies of Birmingham', *Social History,* Volume IV, No. 3 (1979).
Cannadine, D., *Lords and Landlords: The Aristocracy and the Towns, 1774-1967* (1980) — Part 2, 'The Calthorpes and Birmingham'.
Chapman, S. D. (ed.), *The History of Working Class Housing, A Symposium* (1971) — Chapter 4.

Chaplin, R., 'Discovering the Lost New Towns of the Nineteenth Century', *The Local Historian,* Volume 10, No. 4 (1972) — includes discussion of Aston New Town.

Duggan, E. P., 'Industrialization and the Development of Urban Business Communities', *The Local Historian,* Volume 11, No. 8 (1975) — based on Birmingham.

Flick, C., 'Muntz Metal and Ships' Bottoms: The Industrial Career of G. F. Muntz', *Transactions of the Birmingham and Warwickshire Archaeological Society,* Volume 87 (1975).

Flick, C., *The Birmingham Political Union and the Movements for Reform in Britain, 1830-1839* (1978).

Fraser, D., *Power and Authority in the Victorian City* (1979) — Chapter 4, 'Birmingham'.

Hennock, E. P., *Fit and Proper Persons: Ideal and Reality in Nineteenth-Century Urban Government* (1973) — Book I, 'Birmingham'.

Kellet, J. R., *Railways and Victorian Cities* (1979) — Chapter 5, 'Birmingham'.

Moss, D. J., 'The Bank of England and the Country Banks: Birmingham, 1827-33', *Economic History Review,* Volume XXXIV, No. 4 (1981).

Redfern, J. B., 'Élite Suburbians: Early Victorian Edgbaston', *The Local Historian,* Volume 15, No. 5 (1983).

Reid, D. A., 'The Decline of St. Monday, 1766-1876', *Past and Present,* No. 71 (1976).

Wise, M. J., 'On the Evolution of the Jewellery and Gun Quarters in Birmingham', *Transactions of the Institute of British Geographers,* Volume XV (1949).

Index

References associated with illustrations are indicated by an asterisk.

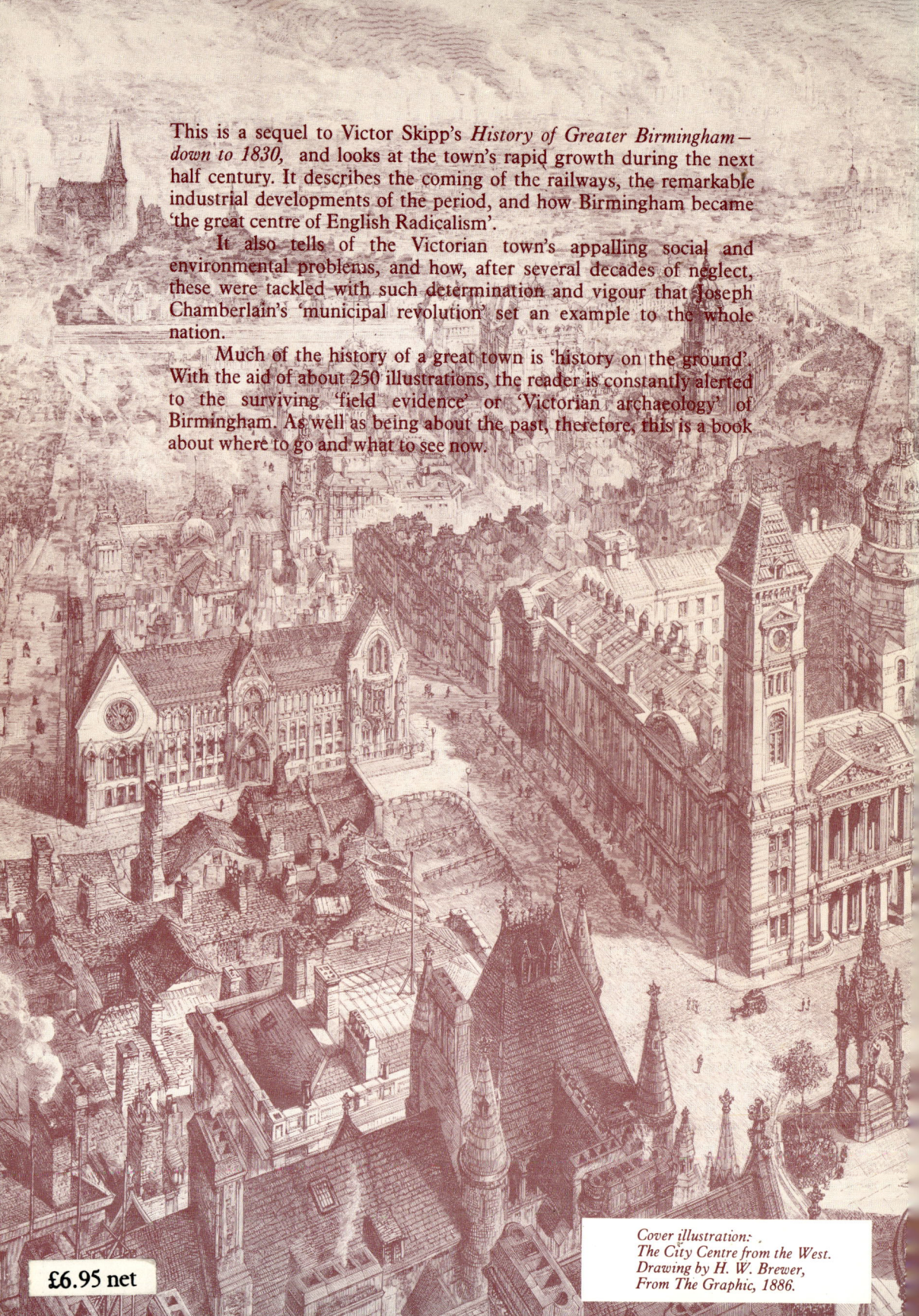

This is a sequel to Victor Skipp's *History of Greater Birmingham—down to 1830*, and looks at the town's rapid growth during the next half century. It describes the coming of the railways, the remarkable industrial developments of the period, and how Birmingham became 'the great centre of English Radicalism'.

It also tells of the Victorian town's appalling social and environmental problems, and how, after several decades of neglect, these were tackled with such determination and vigour that Joseph Chamberlain's 'municipal revolution' set an example to the whole nation.

Much of the history of a great town is 'history on the ground'. With the aid of about 250 illustrations, the reader is constantly alerted to the surviving 'field evidence' or 'Victorian archaeology' of Birmingham. As well as being about the past, therefore, this is a book about where to go and what to see now.

£6.95 net

Cover illustration:
The City Centre from the West.
Drawing by H. W. Brewer,
From The Graphic, 1886.